Going Pro with Cubase® 5

Steve Pacey

Course Technology PTR

A part of Cengage Learning

COURSE TECHNOLOGY
CENGAGE Learning™

Australia • Brazil • Japan • Korea • Mexico • Singapore • Spain • United Kingdom • United States

COURSE TECHNOLOGY
CENGAGE Learning™

Going Pro with Cubase® 5
Steve Pacey

Publisher and General Manager, Course Technology PTR: Stacy L. Hiquet

Associate Director of Marketing: Sarah Panella

Manager of Editorial Services: Heather Talbot

Marketing Manager: Mark Hughes

Acquisitions Editor: Orren Merton

Project Editor and Copy Editor: Kim Benbow

Technical Reviewer: Robert Guérin

Editorial Services Coordinator: Jen Blaney

Interior Layout: Macmillan Publishing Solutions

Cover Designer: Mike Tanamachi

Indexer: Broccoli Information Management

Proofreader: Tonya Cupp

For product information and technology assistance, contact us at
Cengage Learning Customer & Sales Support, 1-800-354-9706

For permission to use material from this text or product, submit all requests online at **www.cengage.com/permissions**
Further permissions questions can be emailed to **permissionrequest@cengage.com**

Nuendo, Cubase, VST and ASIO are registered trademarks of Steinberg Media Technologies GmbH. Microsoft, Windows, and Internet Explorer are either registered trademarks or trademarks of Microsoft Corporation in the United States and/or other countries.

All other trademarks are the property of their respective owners.

All images © Cengage Learning unless otherwise noted.

Library of Congress Control Number: 2009933298

ISBN-13: 978-1-59863-971-1

ISBN-10: 1-59863-971-4

Course Technology, a part of Cengage Learning
20 Channel Center Street
Boston, MA 02210
USA

Cengage Learning is a leading provider of customized learning solutions with office locations around the globe, including Singapore, the United Kingdom, Australia, Mexico, Brazil, and Japan. Locate your local office at: **international. cengage.com/region**

Cengage Learning products are represented in Canada by Nelson Education, Ltd.

For your lifelong learning solutions, visit **courseptr.com**

Visit our corporate website at **cengage.com**

Printed in Canada
1 2 3 4 5 6 7 11 10 09

This book is dedicated to my lifelong friend,
Houston Curtis, and Big Vision Entertainment
for providing many priceless opportunities
for me to share my music with the world.

Acknowledgments

Thanks to Course Technology, Cengage Learning for giving me the opportunity to write this book. Special thanks to Orren Merton, who put his trust in me once again. Special thanks to Kim Benbow for her sharp eye for details and extreme patience with a guy who's more of a Cubase dude than a professional writer. Special thanks to Robert Guérin for sharing his expertise as both a writer and Cubase user, and for making sure that my scattered thoughts translated into text that makes sense. Both of these editors' perspectives were very important to the overall development of the book. Thanks to my wife Amber who puts up with me working late hours and never leaving my computer. Also, thanks to Matt Piper for always lending an ear and sharing his wisdom with regard to writing and technology. Thanks to the brilliant people at Steinberg for continuing to take Cubase to levels I never dreamed possible. And last but not least, thank you (the reader) for allowing me to share my thoughts with you on working with Cubase professionally.

About the Author

Steve Pacey is a television music producer/composer who has been a devoted Cubase user since 1990. Steve began using Cubase professionally while composing background music in EPKs from MCA/Universal films in 1994. Since then, he's written for theater, commercials, a video game, video, and various television programs, including the animated series *Head Trip* on MTV and most recently *The Ultimate Blackjack Tour* on CBS. He is currently composing music for *Cheech and Chong's Smokin' Animated Movie*, which is expected to be released in theaters in 2010. Steve Pacey has also written two other Cubase books for Course Technology, Cengage Learning: *MIDI Editing in Cubase: Skill Pack* (2007) and *Your Cubase Studio* (2008).

Contents

Chapter 3
Taking Audio to the Limit in Cubase 5   105

Chapter 4
Mastering the Art of Mixing Within Cubase 5   151

Chapter 5
Interfacing Cubase 5 with the Rest of the World   175

Introduction

What does going "pro" with Cubase mean to you? To me, it means that I feel comfortable enough using Cubase in a situation where the clock is ticking and my career depends on the fact that I know what I'm doing—I'm ready for any technical obstacle that might come up in the process. As a professional Cubase user, you simply can't afford to *not* know what you're doing in Cubase.

From One Pro to Another

I use Cubase professionally to produce and compose music for TV, film, and video. My first experience with a MIDI sequencer was in 1990 using an Alesis hardware sequencer. I was excited to switch to Cubase that same year when I started on the Atari 1040ST computer. I never used the Atari computer for anything except Cubase. The Atari was my dedicated "music" computer, though I didn't own any other type of computer. I received my first paycheck using Cubase around 1994 with the same computer (along with a Roland S-330 sampler). In 1999, I stopped using tape machines and external hardware for audio and completely switched to recording digitally using Cubase. By 2000, I switched from using a hardware Akai S3000 sampler to using HALion as a virtual sampler in Cubase. Today, I have a massive sample library and tons of virtual instruments and plug-in processors, all within 2 TB of external hard drive space. In fact, the only thing that has remained the same since 1990 is that Cubase is still the heart of my studio.

It takes a lot of skill for the music professional to survive in today's demanding world. Besides knowing an instrument and the music business, if you really want a paycheck, you have to continuously relearn the technology. Over half of what I've learned regarding computers throughout my career has now become what I consider "obsolete knowledge." For instance, who cares what a SCSI terminator does these days? It doesn't matter that I know what polyphonic aftertouch means! The main goal in *Going Pro with Cubase 5* is to try to cut through as much of the technical jargon as possible—I understand that as a Cubase pro user, you just want to jump into using the software. You don't need to learn things that will most likely be forgotten two years from now when you're working in Cubase 6.0 or who knows what!

What Exactly Will This Book Cover?

If you've already worked in Cubase 5, you've probably realized it's a massive program that can take you in all sorts of directions. I have written two other books (*MIDI Editing in Cubase* and *Your Cubase Studio*) that I consider to cover the beginner-to-intermediate skill range. If you have absolutely conquered those books, then you are technically ready to "go pro." In *Going Pro with Cubase 5*, I'm targeting users who have already gone through my Cubase "bootcamp." This book focuses on techniques that people who have had some experience using Cubase will appreciate. Everyone's skill level is different in the professional world, and some people *are* technical geniuses. But it doesn't take a technical genius to make a living using Cubase.

The Cubase manual is massive and intimidating, and often seems as though it's missing a *lot* of basic information. Its approach breaks the program into sections and discusses certain tools in detail, but it often doesn't discuss how the different components function together in a practical scenario. As users, we can often overlook some very useful and practical aspects of the program. My goal is to be your Cubase "buddy" and break down the software for you in a way that's different from the manual. However, don't throw out that manual just yet. It contains a lot of valuable information, and I make some references to it throughout the book.

In *Going Pro with Cubase 5*, I will show you how to use Cubase efficiently when you're working under pressure. I will focus on what I consider to be the "meat and potatoes" of Cubase without wasting your time with things that are not as important. I also summarize certain components in ways that the manual doesn't so that you can get a quick overview without getting lost in details. This book also steps outside the manual to discuss features from Steinberg's innovative CC121 controller and MR816 CSX audio interface. It also touches on using WaveLab and HALion 3 and explains why you might want to consider adding them to your setup if you haven't already. I will show you some techniques in regard to making professional-sounding mixes without even touching a fader. You'll also get step-by-step instructions on how to interface your Cubase projects with Pro Tools, Nuendo, and other DAWs available on the market. The overall goal is to get you working quickly and utilizing the newest features in Cubase 5 at a professional level without wasting your time.

Here is a list of a few basic things you should understand up front that will make reading this book a more enjoyable experience:

1. You should already know how to record MIDI and audio in Cubase.

2. You should know how to interface your controllers and sound cards with Cubase and your computer.

3. You should know the basic functions of your computer's operating system.

4. You should know the basics of editing audio and MIDI within Cubase and understand how to access and use all the basic tools.

5. You should have the ability to think in musical terms (such as bars and beats) and understand pitch.

Let's Go Pro!

One more thing you should know is that I am currently using a Dell PC Core 2 Quad processor with Windows XP Professional. If you are using a Mac, you're probably already used to translating from PC to Mac, as most of the Cubase manual is written for PC/Mac. Since I'm not working with a Mac, you will not see screenshots for Cubase with Mac in this book. Sometimes I will refer to Windows Explorer, and so on. If for instance I say "press Ctrl-Z," you should automatically know that this means Command-Z on a Mac. If you're still unfamiliar with the differences between PCs and Macs, you can refer to the beginning of the Cubase manual for a brief explanation. Despite minor variations in the naming of keys on the keyboard and the way the mouse works, there really aren't that many differences between the Windows version of Cubase and the Mac version. If you still haven't figured out which computer type is more "pro," don't fret over it. Use the computer you feel comfortable with because both platforms are considered pro.

As a disclaimer, I'd also like you to keep in mind that "going pro" with Cubase sometimes also involves getting a paycheck. I can't promise you a paycheck, but I *can* promise that if you follow along with this book, you will have an edge on over half of the pros out there who are using Cubase today. Getting the gig is another book! Hopefully, you've already started building your career, and this is just another step along the way for you. So let's get going, pro!

Sharpening Your Cubase 5 Battle Axe

I thought for starters I'd jump into some of the custom setup features that only advanced Cubase users can truly appreciate. Whether you are under the gun with a studio full of musicians and a producer, or you're just sitting down at your computer and getting ready to begin working, there's nothing like a well-organized playing field to save you headaches and let you focus on the sound you're capturing or to help you concentrate on the creative process rather than spending all day dealing with technical issues.

You may neglect to spend time fine-tuning your machine, but (besides getting an actual paycheck) taking the time to make these little adjustments is one of those things that sets the pros apart from the amateurs.

Setting Up External MIDI Controllers

Even though you can easily work in Cubase without physically touching a slider or knob, there is a good reason why so many of these generic hardware control surfaces exist. Using a controller with Cubase can just be easier, in the same manner that's it's easier for most drummers to play a physical drum kit as opposed to tapping a pattern on a hardware drum machine. MIDI controllers allow you to manipulate several things at once instead of limiting actions to editing single events at one time when using only a mouse.

There are many controllers available on the market, but I've chosen to discuss Steinberg's CC121 (for its unique abilities when using it with Cubase) and M-Audio's Oxygen 49 (as a common all-purpose MIDI controller). This section is intended to give you an overview of these controllers so you can get an idea of which direction you'd like to go in if you haven't decided yet which is best for your needs. The walkthroughs are also intended to help if you're unfamiliar with adjusting their settings. Owning an external controller is common, but it's completely optional. If you're already familiar with controllers or are not interested in working with them, feel free to skip ahead to the next section in this chapter, which discusses organizing your creative media and using the MediaBay.

Steinberg's CC121

Even though I've used only a mouse and computer keyboard for years, I finally decided to branch out and start using Steinberg's CC121 remote control to help me work more efficiently in the studio. Even if you've never used a controller, Steinberg's new CC121 is an easy way to jump in without any setup headaches (see Figure 1.1).

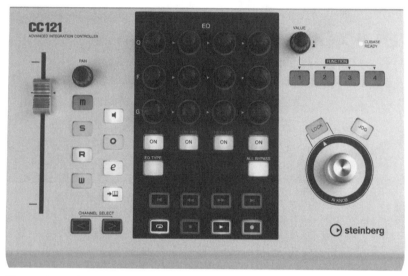

Figure 1.1 The Steinberg CC121 Advanced Integration Controller.

Don't let its simple looks fool you. The CC121 is a pro piece of gear, and while it might not appear too flashy, it shines on performance. I'm not going to go into details on a personal review of the controller, but I think the CC121 is a very simple and well thought out alternative to your basic generic MIDI controller. If you're looking to get your hands on some buttons and a fader, and you want to be able to plug-in and start working right away, then this is the controller for you.

This controller was designed specifically for use with Cubase by Yamaha and Steinberg, and if you look at the buttons on the unit itself, you'll see that they are the same as the track buttons and transport buttons you'll find on your computer screen in Cubase. The hands-on EQ section of the CC121 is an exact duplicate of the Cubase EQ controls.

The best part about the CC121 is that you don't have to waste time figuring out how to set up your knobs and buttons to control certain parameters in Cubase. It's a no-brainer. The manual itself is easy to follow and only a few pages long.

As with most MIDI controllers, the CC121 uses up another one of your USB ports. If you're like me, you've got hard drives and dongles filling up most of your ports. If you have to use a hub, make sure you use a powered hub because the CC121 requires a certain power load and will not work on basic hubs (like those that are attached to computer keyboards).

The AI (Advanced Integration) knob is a great way of simplifying your setup by utilizing your mouse. Using your mouse, just point to the virtual knob you would like to turn, and click to turn the AI knob to adjust your setting. That's great! I would like to point out though that I felt I was led to believe that I could control any parameter in Cubase this way, but the truth of the matter is that only Steinberg's plug-ins (particularly those that are VST3) are compatible with the AI knob. This means that you still have to revert to the old "virtual" knob tweaking most of the time if you use a lot of third-party plug-ins. The other thing I noticed is that if you have a basic mouse with a jog wheel, you can use it just as you use the AI knob on Steinberg's plug-ins; but do it with a single hand instead of using both hands. This means, as much as I like the shiny AI knob, I don't use it as often as I could because I revert to using my good old mouse as I always have.

Again, the CC121 is set up for those who aren't into a lot of tweaking or modifying MIDI controllers, but there are some customizable options that are quick and easy. One of my favorites (long overdue) was the ability to create a simple volume control for the metronome. Like many, for years I've had to go to the Transport menu, select Metronome Setup, and then adjust the volume of the metronome using the virtual slider. That may not sound like very much work to you, but when you have to constantly make adjustments to the click volume, all of those actions become very redundant! I have been envying Reason's virtual Metronome Level knob for about three years, and I've been a little disappointed in Steinberg for not doing the same—until now!

The CC121 manual has a brief explanation on how to set up a Metronome Level knob; but this little feature is so nice that it deserves a dedicated walkthrough from me, too.

Getting Physical with the CC121 Metronome

Under the Devices menu, open Device Setup and select the Steinberg CC121 listing under the Remote Devices folder in the Devices panel on the left (as shown in Figure 1.2). This is the main user-definable setup page for the CC121. You can do several other customizable setups using this same dialog (such as setting zoom controls, foot switch record buttons, control room monitor volume controls, and so on).

The knob that you are setting up to become the Metronome Level knob is called the Value knob and is located on the top right of the actual CC121 controller (see Figure 1.3).

The Value knob can be assigned to adjust four different volume controls: the Main Mix volume, the control room (CR) volume, the control room headphone (CR Phones) volume, and (of course my favorite) the Metronome Level volume. Click the Custom Assignment drop-down list in the CC121 Device Setup dialog box. You will find the four choices I have mentioned. Select Metronome Volume if it is not already selected. Afterward, click on OK. You have successfully set up your new Metronome Volume control.

If you're not sure why it's important to have control over your metronome's volume, you might not be used to recording at multiple levels. For instance, when you're recording a soft vocal track, you don't need a blaring metronome to overpower the recording. On the other hand, if you're recording a heavy-metal guitar, sometimes you have to crank that click level up just so

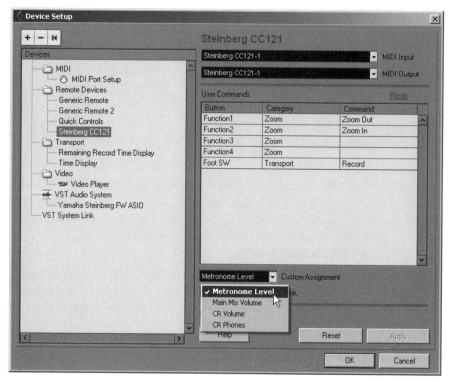

Figure 1.2 The Device Setup dialog box for the CC121.

Figure 1.3 The Value knob.

you can hear the beat. In this case, the click itself can become deafening. Having access to that click volume control comes in really handy when you're constantly changing recording levels and you don't already have a reference beat recorded.

To utilize your new toy, simply push the Value knob on the CC121 to turn the click on or off; you can adjust the volume of the click by adjusting the knob. For me, if this was all the little knob on the CC121 could do, I'd still buy it! Of course, you can always change the Value knob to control the other three volumes at any time if necessary.

As you can probably see, for those who are working and don't have time to waste, the CC121 is a great addition to your Cubase studio. For more on the CC121, please refer to Chapter 4.

Note: One thing that the CC121 manual does not mention is how your MIDI activity meter will continuously jump up and down in a pulsing fashion. Do not be alarmed by this. It is completely normal. If you're like me and you find this annoying, simply uncheck the MIDI Activity option from your transport panel's setup context menu (see Figure 1.4).

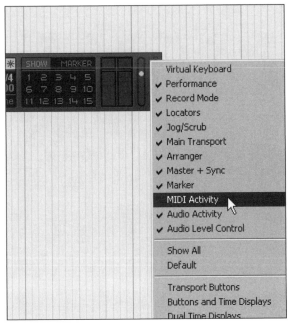

Figure 1.4   Deselecting the MIDI Activity option in the Transport menu.

Turning a Generic Controller into a Dream Controller

The CC121 is a new and innovative way to interface with Cubase, but there are plenty of other MIDI control surfaces available if for some reason the CC121 doesn't quite have what you're looking for.

I've spent years behind mixing consoles, tape recorders, keyboards, and computers, and I'm very aware that the tools you use in the studio are getting smaller, less expensive, and packed with more features. Personally, I like this trend. Since I focus primarily on MIDI and composing music for TV and film, I'm happy to say goodbye to racks worth of gear and a huge console that was cluttering up my work space. For this reason, I really like the simplicity of the CC121. I don't see the need to have a console with 100 knobs and faders around when everything can be neatly tucked away inside your computer.

I'm fully aware, however, that a studio set up to record live bands or a post-production studio might require greater demands from a control surface. Steinberg does support some other controllers that can perform well in these setups (like their older Houston controller), but most of the other controllers fall into the category described as "generic" and have to be programmed to suit Cubase in the manner that fits your needs best.

M-Audio's Oxygen 49

Years ago, my eyes lit up when I saw M-Audio introduce a tiny keyboard that had audio inputs and could be used as a MIDI control surface all in one.

Most music enthusiasts and professional composers alike know what M-Audio is by now because the company has so many useful products on the market. Because they're so common, I've chosen to demonstrate setting up the M-Audio Oxygen 49 MIDI keyboard/control surface interface with Cubase 5 (see Figure 1.5). You can apply the same principals described in this setup to set up any generic MIDI controller.

Figure 1.5   The M-Audio Oxygen 49 has 49 keys and 35 assignable MIDI controllers.

Now just because there are tons of MIDI control surfaces on the market, it doesn't mean that they're easy to set up and start using. Steinberg has a list of supported MIDI control surfaces, but it is limited. Not one M-Audio control surface made Steinberg's supported list. What this means is that you have to start with a generic remote setup in Cubase and custom design your own setup to match the interface you're using (in this case, the Oxygen 49). It's a bit of a pain because you have to do it for each and every one of your faders, buttons, and knobs. Don't worry, though, because I'm here to help.

Before you even start with the generic remote setup in Cubase, I recommend putting a little thought into how you would like to use the control surface of the Oxygen 49. In Figure 1.6, you can see that I've decided to use eight of the nine faders to control the volume on tracks 1 through 8 and use fader 9 to control the volume of the metronome. I'd also like to use buttons 1 through 8 for muting tracks 1 through 8 and use button 9 to turn the metronome on and off. I'm using the eight knobs to control the panning on tracks 1 through 8 and, of course, I'll use the transport buttons on the keyboard to control the Transport in Cubase. Of course, you can custom design your control surface however you like, but you can use my example here as a guide for this walkthrough.

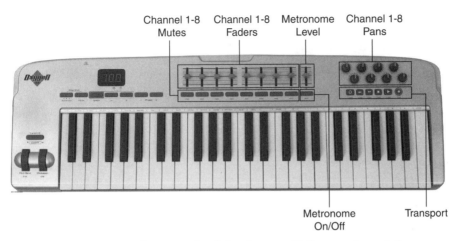

Channel 1-8   Channel 1-8   Metronome   Channel 1-8
Mutes   Faders   Level   Pans

Metronome   Transport
On/Off

Figure 1.6 Laying out the controls of the Oxygen 49 the way I want them.

Note: Remember that even though I'm using the Oxygen 49 as an example, you should be able to apply these same principles to any MIDI control surface. Always check with the control surface manufacturer to see if a pre-configured setup file already exists, making it easier to simply import these settings into Cubase. M-Audio actually has one setup for this keyboard and Cubase, but I want to show you how you can customize one yourself. Also, check to make sure that your controller is set up correctly to work with Cubase before taking the following steps.

Now that you have that all figured out, it's just a matter of telling Cubase what each slider and knob on the Oxygen 49 does. Here's how it's done. Assuming that the keyboard is connected properly and turned on, check to make sure you're sending a MIDI signal from the keyboard by hitting a few keys while connected to a MIDI track and watching the MIDI meter on the transport or track. If everything checks out, open the Devices menu, select Device Setup, and then select Remote Devices. Cubase comes with at least one premade generic remote setup (which should be located under Remote Devices), but I want to start with an even more generic remote. Select the plus (+) sign in the top-left corner of the Device Setup dialog and add another generic remote. I want to use Generic Remote 3 for this example just because I want to make sure we're starting with a fresh "canvas," so if you only have two remotes showing in the Remote Devices folder, go ahead and add another until it looks similar to what's shown in Figure 1.7; then you can select Generic Remote 3 from the Remote Devices folder.

Scroll through the list of controls for Generic Remote 3 and notice that there are 16 Fader controls, 16 Pan controls, 16 Mute controls, and 32 Send controls. These names are modifiable, but they can't be modified until you first change the settings. If you total the number of names, you'll see that there are up to 80 controls available in the Generic Remote 3 setup. If you want to build

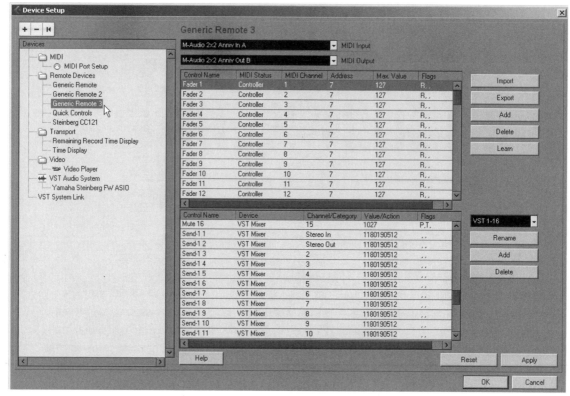

Figure 1.7 The Device Setup dialog for Generic Remote 3.

your own super controller, you can add even more controls by clicking the Add button on the right. Since for this example you only need a total of 32 controls, you can delete the extra controls. To delete, select Fader 10 and then click the Delete button on the right. Once Fader 10 has been deleted, continue this process deleting Faders 11 to 16, Pan 9 to 16, and Mute 10 to 16. Also delete all the sends except 1 to 6. This should make your setup a little cleaner.

Now your Generic Remote 3 is starting to look more and more like an Oxygen 49 remote. For the next step, you're going to define how each control functions within the remote setup. There are five fields besides the name, which will help you fine-tune each of the controls to match the Oxygen 49: MIDI Status, MIDI Channel, Address, Max Value, and Flags. Cubase has a special tool for determining what the value of the fields should be, as well as determining the physical address of each of the controls. Every MIDI controller needs its own special address so that it won't get confused with the other controllers. The Learn tool in Cubase is what determines the address. By selecting the Learn tool button while you move each Oxygen 49 fader up and down or push each Oxygen 49 button, Cubase will determine the exact address (note number) of each individual control. With fader 1 selected, move the first fader on the Oxygen 49 keyboard up and down while selecting the Learn tool button with the mouse. In the case of my Oxygen 49 keyboard, the value of fader 1 has been set to 110. Now that you have locked in that fader, you can select the Control Name field for that fader in the Device Setup dialog and name it to match the physical fader. After naming your fader, select each of the controls and continue this process until you've found every fader, pan, and button value from the Oxygen 49. When you're through, your new remote should look similar to Figure 1.8.

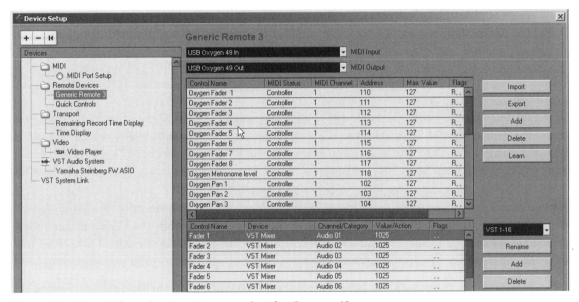

Figure 1.8   Now Cubase is set up to recognize the Oxygen 49.

Note: Prior to beginning the setup of the Oxygen 49, I read its manual and discovered that in order to properly use the Oxygen 49 with Cubase's (or any DAW's) Learn function, I had to first set the Oxygen 49 to factory preset #10. I also found that naming things in the generic remote setup was a little "glitchy." This could be a bug in Cubase, or it might be a glitch specific to my setup. If for some reason you can't name your controls appropriately, just use the generic names. The names are only there for your reference and have no real significance to the functionality of the remote.

Good news! You're halfway finished with setting up the Oxygen 49 control surface to work with Cubase. Now that you've told Cubase where each control's physical location is and how it functions, it's time to define how each of your Oxygen 49's controls communicates with Cubase when each control is activated. In the bottom half of the Devices Setup dialog, there are four fields next to each control name: Device, Channel/Category, Value/Action, and Flags. (To learn more about what each of these fields represents, select the Help button located at the bottom of the dialog box.) Each control name listed on the bottom is identical to the names listed above. Use the Device field to determine what you wish to control within Cubase for each individual controller. Set Faders 1 to 8 to VST Mixer. Set Fader 9 to Metronome. Set Mutes 1 to 8 to VST Mixer. Set Mute 9 to Command. Set Pans 1 to 8 to VST Mixer. And last but not least, set Sends 1 to 6 to Command.

Note: Sometimes there are multiple options for the same function in the Device field. You might have to play around with the different options to find the one that works best for your application. I tried a couple of different options to determine the ones that worked best with the Oxygen 49.

Now, in order to see your results as you change the settings in the Device Setup dialog, I recommend opening the Mixer window in Cubase alongside the dialog box so you can watch the virtual controls of the VST mixer move in sync with the physical faders of the Oxygen 49. Next, assign your newly created Faders 1 through 8 (in the Device Setup dialog) so that each controls its own VST Mixer audio track in the Channel/Category field. (You'll need at least eight tracks active in your project to have eight track choices.) Next select Volume from the Value/Action field. (The Flags field is not applicable to this function.) Now watch your VST mixer faders spring to life as you adjust the faders on the Oxygen 49. Your eight-channel mixer should now be working.

Next, let's get those pans working. Set each newly created pan (1–8 in the Device Setup dialog) to its own audio track (1–8) just as you did with the sliders, then assign each of their Value/Action fields to Stereo Panner (Pan L-R). Check again with the VST mixer to see that the virtual pan knobs turn as you adjust the knobs on the Oxygen 49.

Moving on, set each mute (1–8) to its own audio track (1–8). Set the Value/Action field for the all the mute buttons to Mute. Since the Mute button acts as an on/off button, you must also check Button and Toggle in the Flags field for each mute button. Now your mutes should be working for tracks 1 through 8.

Next let's make Fader 9 the Metronome volume. Change the Channel/Category field to Device, then change the Value/Action field to Click Level. After playing around with this one, I also found that checking No Automation in the Flags field seemed to help, too.

Note: Unfortunately, setting up these remotes (especially those that are "unsupported" by Cubase) usually involves a test-as-you-go and tweak-if-necessary mentality. Just make sure to do your tweaking in your downtime, and you'll save yourself a ton of headaches when the real pressure is on in the studio.

To set up the Transport buttons on the Oxygen 49, change the Channel/Category option of each button to Transport. Next, in the Value/Action field, change each controller to match its function: Rewind, Record, Start, Stop, Fast Forward, or Loop. I also found that checking Button, Toggle, and No Automation seemed to help things work a little better. Now your Oxygen 49 is set up to control Cubase (see Figure 1.9).

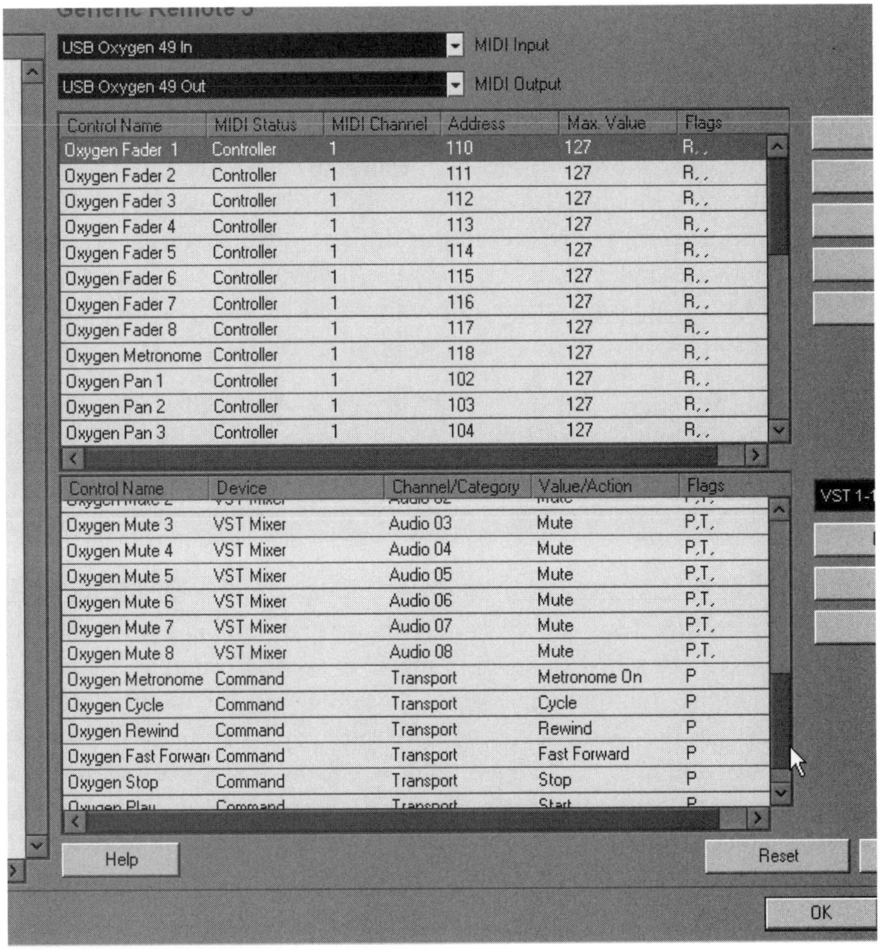

Control Name	MIDI Status	MIDI Channel	Address	Max Value	Flags
Oxygen Fader 1	Controller	1	110	127	R, ,
Oxygen Fader 2	Controller	1	111	127	R, ,
Oxygen Fader 3	Controller	1	112	127	R, ,
Oxygen Fader 4	Controller	1	113	127	R, ,
Oxygen Fader 5	Controller	1	114	127	R, ,
Oxygen Fader 6	Controller	1	115	127	R, ,
Oxygen Fader 7	Controller	1	116	127	R, ,
Oxygen Fader 8	Controller	1	117	127	R, ,
Oxygen Metronome	Controller	1	118	127	R, ,
Oxygen Pan 1	Controller	1	102	127	R, ,
Oxygen Pan 2	Controller	1	103	127	R, ,
Oxygen Pan 3	Controller	1	104	127	R, ,

Control Name	Device	Channel/Category	Value/Action	Flags
Oxygen Mute 2	VST Mixer	Audio 02	Mute	P,T,
Oxygen Mute 3	VST Mixer	Audio 03	Mute	P,T,
Oxygen Mute 4	VST Mixer	Audio 04	Mute	P,T,
Oxygen Mute 5	VST Mixer	Audio 05	Mute	P,T,
Oxygen Mute 6	VST Mixer	Audio 06	Mute	P,T,
Oxygen Mute 7	VST Mixer	Audio 07	Mute	P,T,
Oxygen Mute 8	VST Mixer	Audio 08	Mute	P,T,
Oxygen Metronome	Command	Transport	Metronome On	P
Oxygen Cycle	Command	Transport	Cycle	P
Oxygen Rewind	Command	Transport	Rewind	P
Oxygen Fast Forwar	Command	Transport	Fast Forward	P
Oxygen Stop	Command	Transport	Stop	P
Oxygen Play	Command	Transport	Start	P

Figure 1.9 The Oxygen 49 remote device setup is complete.

Of course, you might decide to control other parameters within Cubase besides your basic mixer/control functions. There are many possibilities, but keep in mind that you are still limited to the choices listed within the Device, Channel/Category, and Value/Action fields.

As you can see, setting up these control surfaces is not exactly a plug-and-play operation. Then again, if you require the real hands-on experience, taking the time to get your control surface to work its magic for you could save you bucket loads of work time in the future.

Before I wrap up this section on MIDI control surfaces, I would like to mention that even if you can't afford to blow a few extra bucks on something as nifty as the CC121, there's probably a lot more you can do by turning your computer's QWERTY keyboard into somewhat of a remote control. Not only is this option affordable, but in many ways it can be a lot more useful than any expensive control surface currently on the market. For more info on how you can do this, refer to the section entitled "Time-Saving Steps—Setting Up Key Commands and Macros" a little later in this chapter.

Organizing Creative Media and the MediaBay

As a composer, I have accumulated a huge sample library over the last 10 years. These days you need a ton of samples at your fingertips in order to stay on the cutting edge and deliver a quality product overnight. If you're like me, you sometimes get a call like this: "I need this feature scored for this much money, and I need it tomorrow." In this fast-paced world, this is becoming more and more common. Of course, you want to get paid, so you accept the job and start working right away. You know you have the perfect drum loop somewhere in your catalog, but you have a 2 TB hard drive full of samples. Where do you start looking?

Well, this problem is not by any means a new one. Since I use Windows, I've been cataloging my samples using folders and Windows Explorer. Starting with Cubase 4, Steinberg decided to take on this growing issue by adding what they call the MediaBay. The MediaBay not only offers a place to store your sample library, but is also a place to organize every possible media tool that you can use in the music creation process.

Let's talk for a moment about organization. There's no single perfect solution to this ongoing issue. If you have a hard drive full of samples and already have things organized in a way that you understand, and you feel like you can efficiently access your media as needed, using the MediaBay might appear to be a daunting and time-consuming task that isn't necessary. No matter how you have organized your files, you can use the MediaBay, but in order for you to make the most of it, you might have to rethink the way you organize. This is no different than filing paperwork in a file cabinet. If it takes you hours to find something in a file cabinet that you yourself organized, you might not have the best organization system. The MediaBay is the "shiny new filing cabinet," but if you don't know how to properly organize your files, using the MediaBay may not save you any time and could, in fact, take you longer to find what you're looking for.

Basic organization for the MediaBay doesn't have to begin in Cubase. If you already have a lot of files you're using, you should begin by using Windows Explorer (PC) or the Mac OS Finder (Mac). Using the MediaBay is like looking at the contents of your hard drive with a magnifying glass. If your hard drive is already a mess, you're only going to see a bigger mess using the Media-Bay. For this reason, I recommend first reorganizing your hard drive(s) in the following manner:

- **Samples:** If you use samples (including loops, instruments, sound effects, and so on), keep them on their own hard drive or at the very least keep them all within one folder. Once you have them separated, break them down into categories (loops, drums, bass, guitar, sound effects, vocals). Once you have put them into these basic categories, break them down even farther into subcategories (rock bass, upright bass, synth bass, fretless bass, and so on). Use labeled folders within folders to make it as organized as possible. Here's what to avoid: Don't put too many different sample types in one folder and/or put too many similar types of samples in multiple folders. For example, let's say you have 30 rock guitar samples, 1200 acoustic guitar samples, 14 metal guitar samples, and 80 funk guitar samples. You should probably group the rock and heavy metal guitar samples together and try to break down the acoustic guitar samples into more subfolders, such as jazz acoustic, country acoustic, rock acoustic. If you're creating loop folders, you can also include any REX files you might have, but I'd keep them separated in their own subfolders.

- **MIDI files:** If you use a lot of MIDI files, including those that accompany some sample libraries, they should all be organized in a location separate from your sample library, but using a similar organizational method as discussed with samples.

- **Video files:** If you compose or produce audio for video, then you should also have a folder (or separate hard drive if possible) specifically for video files. (Cubase only recognizes AVI, MOV, QT, MPG, MPEG, and WMV video formats.) For more details on video, see Chapter 5, "Interfacing Cubase with the Rest of the World."

- **Track presets:** Track presets (whether for MIDI, audio, or instrument tracks) should all be stored in a similar fashion as MIDI files and samples but in their own separate folder.

- **VST presets:** VST presets (which include settings for all VST plug-ins, including instruments and processors) should all be stored in one place and organized first by type (synth, sample player, delay). Instruments should then be classified into subcategories just as you would organize your sample library.

- **Pattern banks:** If you're creating pattern banks in Cubase 5's new Beat Designer, they should also be saved in their own folder and organized in groups.

The MediaBay is also capable of opening most audio files and Cubase project files. As far as projects are concerned, I like to keep all the audio and project files organized within a contact/project folder where I can easily access them without it getting too messy. I keep all my project files on a separate hard drive, which I back up regularly. If you need to look at individual audio tracks within a particular project, you can still use the MediaBay, but you can also use the Pool, which is located under the Media menu. The Pool is just as easy to use as the MediaBay when you're looking at one specific project. The MediaBay, however, can be very useful in transferring audio files from an old project into a new one. I'll demonstrate this a little later in this section. Figures 1.10 and 1.11 show some examples of how folders are organized on the creative media hard drive and the project drive on my own system.

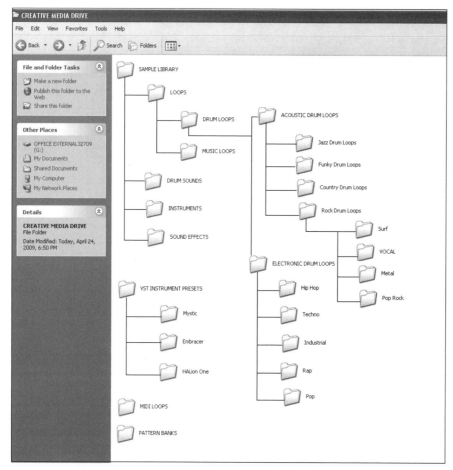

Figure 1.10   My creative media drive in Windows Explorer.

The MediaBay can also be associated with the Sound Browser and the Loop Browser. If you're new to using the MediaBay, I find that there is really no need for using either the Sound Browser or Loop Browser because the MediaBay handles everything in a more detailed and easily accessible manner. Both the Loop and Sound Browsers appear to be designed as a little more clutter free when working only with loops or sounds. The key here is to be "clutter free" from the beginning (as I mentioned before), and then you won't *need* to use the other two browsers.

Cubase often has multiple ways of approaching a task, which is good when it comes to reaching a diverse group of users; but this can also be distracting because it tends to clutter the working environment with tools you'll never need. My goal is to try to teach you the best of the tools. Once you understand the MediaBay, you can get a grasp on the Sound and Loop Browsers pretty quickly.

I think Steinberg's approach is that you should be able to use the MediaBay to find any type of file quickly and easily without the need for organizational skills. This might work well for people who

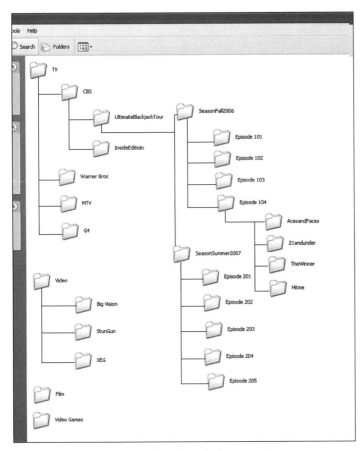

Figure 1.11 My project drive in Windows Explorer.

do two or three little projects a year; but the reality is that many of you are dealing with thousands of files, and you don't have time to search through all of the files just to find a sample when you don't even know if it's going to work with your project until you *hear* it in the project itself.

The Cubase manual spends the majority of its time focused on how you can use the MediaBay to find all your media, but it doesn't focus on the most important and incredible features of the MediaBay that *aren't* included with Windows Explorer or Mac OS Finder. *The most useful benefit to using the MediaBay is in accessing your loop library and being able to audition your loops all at the same tempo and then insert them into the project at the correct tempo!* This is a real time-saver for those who use loop libraries. It's great to have everything categorized by name and style, but auditioning and importing the audio files is the most time-consuming process when you're using Window's Explorer or Mac OS Finder. This basic function of the MediaBay is usually understated. I believe a great number of Cubase users probably skip over using the MediaBay because they simply don't want to take the time to tag their library. My point is, though tagging a library is great, there are many other ways to benefit from using the MediaBay.

Auditioning Loops in the MediaBay

Assuming that you have your loop library organized as I described earlier, here's a simple walk-through to get you auditioning and importing your organized loop library in no time.

Open the MediaBay, and in the Browser section (on the left side), locate the folder of the loops you would like to audition. Of course, the more you know what type of beat you're looking for, the easier it will be to find it. If you don't know, you can simply select the main folder, and then click the Deep Results icon (see Figure 1.12) so that all the loops in the main folder and sub-folders are revealed in the Viewer (in the center of the window). Figure 1.12 shows an example

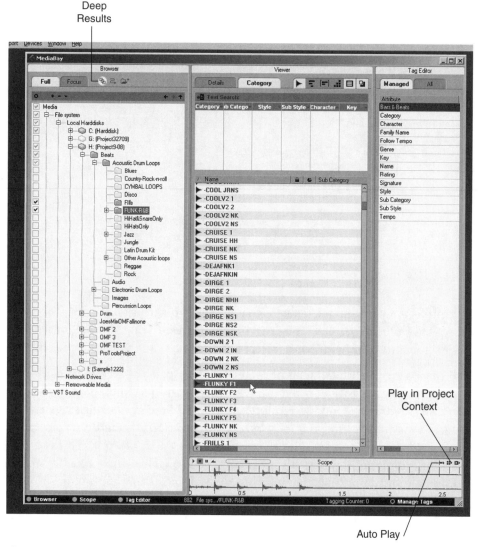

Figure 1.12 Finding the perfect funky drum loop.

of how this works. I'm looking for a funky beat on acoustic drums. I open my Beats folder, select the Funk R&B folder from the Acoustic Drum Loops folder, and then all my funky beats appear in the Viewer as shown in Figure 1.12.

All of these drum loops have been recorded at different tempos (100 bpm, 77 bpm, 127 bpm, and so on). I've already decided that my project is at 120 bpm. Instead of having to look for and convert all my beats to 120 bpm, all I have to do is select Play in Project Context (located on the Scope), and every beat in the MediaBay window will automatically be time-corrected in real time to 120 bpm, regardless of its original tempo! To speed up the audition process even more, I can select Auto Play, and then scroll through the list until I hear what I'm looking for.

Once you find that perfect beat, there are multiple ways to get it into your project. If you're able to see your project window and the MediaBay at the same time, dragging the file into the project window directly from the MediaBay's Viewer list and onto the track where you want it is probably the easiest way to go. A little blue guideline will appear to help you position the groove where you want it on the audio track. Another easy option is to right-click on the groove you want in the Viewer list and then select Import into Project from the context menu. You can either insert that groove at the cursor location, at the left locator position, or at the origin.

Note: Turn off the Auto Play on the Scope in the MediaBay before you start playing around with your project again, or else you will hear that loop continuously along with your project. Also, if at any time you would like to hear your loops at their original tempos, you can always deselect Play in Project Context on the Scope. Keep in mind, though, that in order for Cubase to import the loop at the correct tempo, Play in Project Context must be selected while importing the file.

That's about as easy as it gets for handling loops in Cubase. Keep in mind that your loops still need to actually *loop* correctly. If your loop has a little extra length to it, or if it's a little short, your groove will not fit like a glove into your project. That being said, if you're a Cubase master, it will be easy to tweak that groove to make it fit once you have it imported into a track. The other thing that I would like to mention is that Cubase is using Musical Mode to get that tempo to match your project. Musical Mode will affect the quality of the recording's playback just as your standard time-stretching will. It will also put a little extra load on your computer system to continuously process that loop in real time.

I suggest that you convert that new loop into a real audio file as soon as you decide it's working for you. There are a couple of ways to do this. The easiest (and I think the best) is to select the loop then choose Bounce Selection from the Audio menu. Once you do this, your loop is auto-matically converted to your project's beats per minute and should sound identical to the way it sounded in Musical Mode. Another way to change the sound is to "flatten" the Warp mode.

Double-click the audio part to enter the Audio Editor screen, then select Process" (if its drop-down list isn't already exposed), and then select Flatten. A pop-up window will appear giving you a couple of different time-stretch options.

There are several other benefits to using the MediaBay. Although sounds, such as a snare drum or low E on a bass guitar, can be auditioned in the MediaBay, there is no practical use for this most of the time. Most likely you'll need to trigger those from a sample player in order to get the most out of them. One of the best displays of how to use the MediaBay with a sample player is in using the Groove Agent One drum machine, which I will discuss in more detail in Chapter 2, "Maximizing MIDI in Cubase 5."

Auditioning VST Instruments in the MediaBay

Moving away from audio loops and samples, the next benefit of using the MediaBay would be to audition VST instruments. Just as with loops and samples, to really make the most out of the MediaBay, make sure that all the VST instrument presets are located in the same place. If you're already lost with this idea, look in the folder where your Steinberg software is installed and locate the two folders called Track Presets and VST3 Presets. Both of these folders will contain all the factory presets for every virtual instrument that comes with Cubase 5 (this includes Embracer, Groove Agent ONE, HALion ONE, HALion Symphonic Orchestra, Prologue, LoopMash, Monologue, Mystic, and Spector). You can access your synths from various locations using the MediaBay, but I think you will find more benefits to having them all in one place when browsing through your sound libraries. Once you have copied all of these files so that they can be accessed from one location, you should be able to open that folder (and all its subdirectories) so that it displays every preset from all nine synths and sample players (shown in Figure 1.13).

Now, instead of having to open each one to figure out which synth pad you like best, you can use the MediaBay to sort through the synth pads in the folder (using tags and/or searches) and audition all the pads without even having to load a VST instrument, create a MIDI track, or scroll through individual libraries!

Note: Of course, to hear the VST presets, you'll most likely need a MIDI keyboard. Once connected, click on the little MIDI Input button (below the Viewer), then play your keyboard after you have selected the preset you would like to hear. I noticed that this feature is a little stiff and glitchy on occasion. If you can't hear anything, try toggling the MIDI Input button on and off a couple of times and try again. Also, keep in mind that some presets do not utilize the entire keyboard, so you might want to try testing over several keys.

Once you have the sound you're looking for, simply double-click on the preset in the Viewer. A track will appear in your project, and your sound will be ready for you to start writing some MIDI! No need to load the VST instrument or create a MIDI/instrument track! Cool!

Figure 1.13 Steinberg's mega-patch bank all in one easy-access location.

MIDI files are still very popular, but I'm not going to go into a lot of detail on how you can use them with the MediaBay. All you need to do is load a VST instrument with synths or samples set up the way you need them, then you can audition multiple MIDI files (just as you would if they were tracks in the project window) without actually having to load them into the project. Since the Beat Designer is its own thing, I'm going to skip it for now and talk about it more in Chapter 2.

Note: Again, I would like to mention that the Cubase manual spends a lot of time focusing on tags and how to organize your library. This is great, but most people don't have the time to jot down every tempo, genre, family, subgenre, and so on. All in all, this organization would help (just as they help with the VST instrument presets) in the long run. I would like to say though, don't worry so much about all this tagging at first—just enjoy the MediaBay for its audition features.

Auditioning Projects Using the MediaBay

Speaking of audition features, I would like to discuss one more feature of the MediaBay. Let's say you work on a lot of music that is similar. Maybe you've produced a track that features a guitar part that you'd like to use in another project. There have been ways to do this in the past, but nothing as easy as it is with the MediaBay. While working in your new project, just open the MediaBay and select your old project from the Browser. Once you've selected your project, browse for audio files in the Viewer just as you would browse for a loop. Remember that you can audition and import the file at your current project's tempo. If you're looking for MIDI files, you might need to actually go back into your old project, which is a little more complicated. Simply select the project from the MediaBay, and when it asks if would you like to activate (so that you can hear) the project, select No. Then minimize your old project's window so that you can see the old and new projects together. Lastly, select the MIDI track you're looking for from the old project and drag it into the new project on a free MIDI track.

Note: In case you didn't know, Cubase asks if you would like to activate the project because it can only have one project "active" (where you can *hear* it) at one time. You can always activate the old project when you open it; you'll just need to reactivate your new project when you go back into it.

As a final note, I would like to add that the MediaBay was a completely new feature as of Cubase 4. I believe that there will probably be a few more tweaks in this version before Cubase 5 makes the leap to Cubase 6; and by the time that happens, it will most likely evolve into something else. For what it's worth, as a user you should be taking advantage of Cubase's current features but not getting yourself too wrapped up in the details due to the fact that the format is currently so "liquid." After all, the main purpose of having the MediaBay is so that you can make music more quickly and efficiently and waste less time with tedious issues, such as searching for samples and sounds.

Creating Templates for a Speedy Startup

The last thing I want to see when I start up Cubase is an uninspiring blank "canvas." The good news is that you don't have to start from scratch if you use a preset template. It can help you get the creative juices flowing a lot faster.

To some, the idea of working with a template sounds like working within boundaries or limits. It's not like this at all when it comes to working in Cubase. Using templates can actually get you right into the creative process and skip all the boring setup procedures that usually come with preparing for a day in the studio. Whether you're regularly recording a 72-piece MIDI or live orchestra, a 12-piece ska ensemble, a 6-piece rock group, a jazz duo, or a solo harmonica, using a customized template can take your startup time from 45 minutes to 45 seconds.

First, let's go to the very beginning. Restart Cubase. On startup (assuming you're using the default startup), a window showing recent project files should open, giving you multiple options. You can open one of the projects listed in the document window, open Other, or create a new project. Go ahead and select New Project. The New Project dialog box will appear giving you several options (see Figure 1.14). This allows you to select your template. If you want, you can just select one of the preset choices and start working on a project. But I'm going to show you how to create your own preset template as well as how to get rid of all those extra presets you never use.

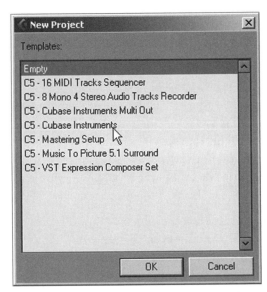

Figure 1.14   Use the New Project dialog box to select a template.

Before you get too wrapped up in this, I'll let you know that a template is pretty much identical to any project file. Many people choose to start with preexisting projects, and then erase parts and save as a new project name. That practice is fine, but working with a template can save you several steps and could also prevent you from creating a "messy" work area.

The concept is simple. Create your workspace just as you would at the start of any project. Start by adding and naming all your tracks (whether they are MIDI, audio, or something else). Take the time to color code and size your tracks the way you like them. Next, if you use VST instruments, load them up and get your presets set the way you like them. This is a must for composers like me. For example, if I need a Big Band arrangement, I can call up a Big Band template and save a ton of time going through and finding all the instruments and samples I would need to create a Big Band piece. Before the invention of VST instruments, this alone could take a composer 45 minutes to an hour to load and set up.

Note: As much as I love them, VST instruments create a major load on your system's processor and can sometimes crash or stall a system when it's booting up. As a test, I recommend saving these types of templates at different stages (i.e., fewer VST instruments, more VST instruments, most VST instruments) and under different template names so that if you have problems with the "heavy load" VST instrument template, you can always revert to a lighter load template instead.

Don't forget to set up your processors and EQ on your audio tracks. If there is a tempo that you generally record at, go ahead and set that to the correct tempo and time signature. Set your left and right locators where you would like them. Often, I like to set my left locator where the start of the song would be and the right where I *think* the end might be.

You no doubt have your own preferences when it comes to the way you need your workspace to look. Maybe you like to see the VST mixer at all times. Maybe you need to see a video screen on one monitor. I have a multiple-monitor setup, and since I compose to video, most of the time I use one of my monitors for video playback only. By setting this up in the template, I can avoid having to activate the video window, move the window to the appropriate monitor, and size the window the way I like it. The point is that anything you can do in advance to save yourself from taking those extra little steps toward getting the music into the computer should be set up and saved as a template.

Also, just because you're calling this a template doesn't mean you can't include audio tracks or MIDI tracks. Let's say, for instance, you like a certain groove, and even though you might not use it in the final mix, you like to use it as a guide for your other tracks. You can save that groove with the template, whether it's a MIDI or audio track, and it will be there at startup when you open the template. Some people actually like to have a recorded click track to play with as opposed to using the Cubase metronome. (This is especially good for clicks that need to stop and start throughout a performance). These click tracks are great to save with a template.

But let's not forget the basics. Before you save your template, go ahead and designate the settings in the Project Setup by selecting it from Cubase's Project menu (located on the menu bar). Here you can set the sample rate, bit depth, file type, and pan law, and you're good to go.

Once you're finished making all your settings so that Cubase looks the way you want it to when you boot up your system, then you are ready to save it as a template. To do so, just select Save As Template under the File menu. (This is not the normal Save As option but its own specific option.) Create a name that pertains to this particular setup (such as "Big Band setup" or "Steve's setup" or "Unplugged setup") and enter the name in the field. Once you have saved the template, there's no need to actually save the *project* unless you would also like to save it as a project file. Close the project and then select New Project from the File menu. This time when the New Project dialog appears, you'll find your new template right there waiting for you in the list. Select it and reload what you've just created.

Now that you've created one template, you can create multiple templates. Since I might go from working on a heavy metal piece of music to an orchestral piece and then over to a hip hop piece, a variety of templates is nice to have in my arsenal. Even if you have little changes, such as more audio/MIDI tracks, saving the template with a new template name will just give you another possible option when making your selection at startup.

Diving In and Taking Control of Your Templates

To take template creation one step farther, let's say you'd like to bypass the template menu option and go straight into your new template as soon as you start up Cubase. You can only do this with one template at a time, but if you always want the same thing at startup, why not skip those few extra clicks when booting up and get straight into your project? Here's how it works. First, load the template that you would like to boot up to into Cubase by creating a new project and selecting that template from the New Project dialog. Once your template is up and Cubase appears the way you want it to, go back to the File menu and click Save As Template once more. This time, however, name your template Default. After you have done this, close the project, go back to the File menu, and select Preferences. Once inside the Preferences window, select General on the left side, and click the On Startup drop-down list (located in the middle of the window). Select Open 'Default' Template, as shown in Figure 1.15. When you're finished, click Apply at the bottom of the window, then click OK. When the Preferences window closes, close Cubase and restart. On boot-up, Cubase will open your new template!

Now that *you* are the one deciding what a template should be and you know how to skip a few steps to get right into your work on startup, there's one more thing I would like to show you— how to get rid of the useless templates that you may never use.

Removing the templates can be a little tricky for some. Steinberg stores its factory-made preset templates in a folder within the Steinberg Cubase 5 program folder. The folder is called Templates (simple enough). If you've had multiple versions of Cubase installed on your system, you might have other Cubase folders which will also contain a Templates folder. Once you find that folder on your system, you can remove the actual files. But don't delete them yet. Just put those useless presets in another folder outside of the Templates folder. The files have the same name as what appeared in the New Project Templates list. So if there are particular presets that you'd like to keep in the Templates list, just keep their related Project files in the Templates folder.

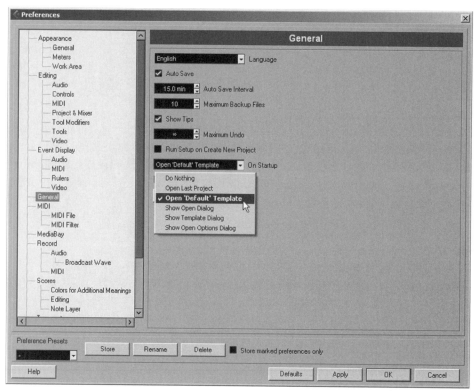

Figure 1.15 The On Startup drop-down list in the Preferences window.

In looking at that folder, you may have realized that your templates were not in the same folder along with the presets. That's because Steinberg stores user template presets in an entirely different location. On a Windows system, they are located on your C drive at Documents and Settings\<user name>\Application Data\Steinberg\Cubase 5\templates. On the Mac OS, the templates are located at Users/<user name>/Library/Preferences/Cubase 5. Once you have found the proper folder location by either using Windows Explorer or Mac OS Finder, you can also delete (or remove and store in another hard drive location) your own presets. Also, now that you know where both locations for templates are on your system, you can actually move all the files so that they are located in one folder (in whichever location you prefer—it makes no difference). *Do not move or remove the actual template folder from either location.* Whenever you create a new template, it will always go to the user folder as opposed to the folder located in Steinberg's Cubase 5 program folder. Figure 1.16 shows an example of some of my template files. Steinberg's preset templates are neatly tucked away in the user Templates folder on my hard drive.

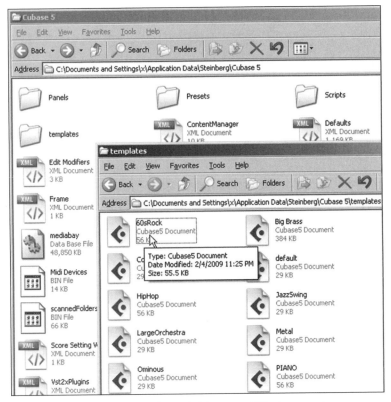

Figure 1.16   User x's Templates folder on a Windows system.

Organizing Your Plug-Ins

Since we're on the topic of organizing your template files, let's take a moment to discuss the way your plug-ins are organized. All of your plug-ins, whether they are VST instruments or effects, should be found in your Steinberg Cubase program folder. This includes any third-party plug-ins, such as Auto-Tune, Waves, Native Instruments, and so on.

Since I've been using Cubase for 19 years and I've been upgrading to every latest version, my folders and plug-ins have gotten more than a little messy over time. Not only do I have Cubase running on my system, but I also have WaveLab, and both share the same plug-ins. Because these plug-ins can be found in multiple locations, it can often make the job of finding and organizing them tricky.

On your local hard drive, in your Programs folder, you should be able to find your Steinberg folder. That folder contains almost everything currently running on your system that is related to any of Steinberg's programs. Your main Steinberg folder should contain a VSTPlugins folder. You should consider this folder to be the main folder in which all pre–VST3 plug-ins belong and are shared with all your Steinberg programs. If you take a few more steps and look into each folder within the Steinberg folder (i.e., Cubase, WaveLab, and so on), you may find other VST plug-in folders. Inside those folders are usually where the plug-ins that came with those particular programs are found. The VST3 plug-ins that come with Cubase have been bundled all together into one VST3 file and are stored in their own VST3 folder. These are kept under the same Steinberg folder as your main VSTPlugins folder.

When you're installing any new plug-ins, you should pay close attention to where they are being installed on your system. In order for the plug-in to work properly in Cubase, they must be in one of the VST plug-in folders I mentioned previously. If the new plug-in is installed in another directory, you'll most likely have to move that plug-in from its installation location to the main VSTPlugins folder within the Steinberg folder on your system in order for it to work.

Now, let's say you have a plug-in that you really like in WaveLab, but it doesn't show up in Cubase (or vice versa). It's because that plug-in isn't located in the main Steinberg VSTPlugins folder; it's in the WaveLab folder. In order for it to work in both programs, you must physically move that plug-in from the WaveLab folder to the Steinberg VSTPlugins folder. When this is done, you'll also need to restart your system. When Cubase restarts it will see the new plug-in driver and install it within its plug-in directory so that you can access it from Cubase. Check out Figure 1.17 for a close-up of a plug-in file in Cubase from my Windows system.

Figure 1.17 A DLL plug-in driver file for the Waves Gold Bundle found in my Steinberg VSTPlugins folder. This file contains all of my Waves plug-ins.

Within Cubase, you can also organize your plug-ins using the Plug-In Paths button, which is found in the Plug-In Information dialog located in the Device menu. More information is included on this in the Cubase manual, but I wanted to give you more specifics on using the "outside" approach in case you run into difficulties using this method.

Note: VST3 plug-ins are currently the latest plug-in type to work with Cubase. Older plug-in types will work as long as they're VST. VST3 plug-ins will work better and will offer a few more features than the older ones. All of Cubase 5's plug-ins will be updated to the latest version available each time you update Cubase. If you're using third-party plug-ins, you should check with their respective developers for updates in order to ensure compatibility and get the most out of them.

On a Windows XP system, most pre-VST3 plug-ins are DLL files and should appear as an icon with little gears. If you look up close, you'll see the name and file type, and below it you'll see the version number. If you find multiple DLL files sharing the same name, check the version number. If the version number is older, remove the driver file from your VSTPlugins folder. To be on the safe side, do not delete any file until you test run Cubase and make sure it is working properly. If there are problems after running Cubase, move the file back and try again. This process might sound a little scary for someone who's not used to digging into file systems, but it's really not that difficult.

Now that you know where all your plug-in drivers are, there's something you can do to clean them up. What I've done is simply organize the files in a way similar to organizing my samples. I put all the VST instruments under one folder, and then created subfolders for them. I also did the same with my effects. Now if I'm looking for a delay, at least most of my delays are in one place. If I'm looking for a synth, all my VST synths are in one location. By grouping these in folders within the VSTPlugins folder (see Figure 1.18), I now have them organized better in my Effects and Instruments windows within Cubase (see Figure 1.19). You can name your own folders, but since Steinberg's VST3 plug-ins are bundled and not modifiable, I've chosen to name the folder for my Auto-Tune plug-ins to match Steinberg's preexisting VST3 folder. Folders with the same names will be grouped together automatically. If all your plug-ins are individual and in one location, then you can name that folder whatever you want, and it will appear and work correctly in the processor list.

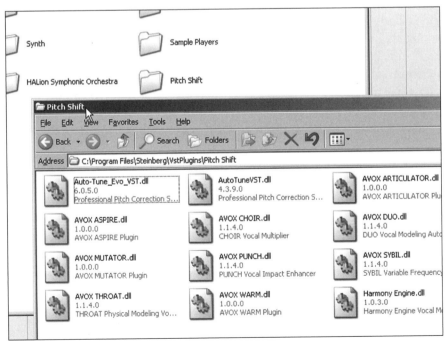

Figure 1.18 I've grouped my VST2 Auto-Tune plug-ins into a folder I named Pitch Shift.

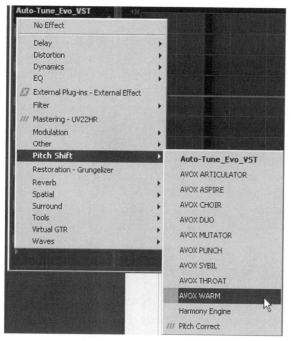

Figure 1.19 Now Steinberg's VST3 Pitch Correct processor appears with Auto-Tune's VST2 processors in Cubase.

Once you have all your VST plug-ins organized on your system the way you like, you can then optimize it by deactivating the plug-ins you don't use on a regular basis. When deactivating a plug-in, you don't actually remove it from your system or your VSTPlugins folder. By deactivating the plug-in, you're simply telling Cubase to *ignore* particular plug-ins while running. The fewer plug-ins that Cubase has to manage (especially those that are older than VST3), the better Cubase should run.

To deactivate unwanted plug-ins, select Plug-In Information from the Devices menu. Your current plug-ins will appear in a list.

Note: Notice that your plug-in list should include even more detailed information, such as its exact location, version number, name and file type, and so on. This is a great list to have, but the reason I wanted to show you first how to organize the actual files is because if Cubase can't properly locate the driver file, chances are that it won't appear in this list.

Once the list is visible, simply uncheck the plug-ins that you don't wish to use by clicking in the left column.

Note: One of the new features of VST3 technology is one that automatically disables the plug-in when it is not in use. Because of this, it's really unnecessary to deactivate any VST3 plug-ins, as doing so will not free up any extra resources for your system (which you'll be learning more about in the next section). You can easily identify which plug-ins are VST3 by the three slashes (///) symbol before their names in your processor/instrument lists.

Creating the Perfect "Battlefield"—Setting Your Preferences

As I mentioned previously, Cubase was designed to work the way you want it to work. It offers several different ways of doing the same thing to fit a wide variety of user types. Setting up preferences is one of the first places any serious Cubase user should look in order to customize the setup, but often this simple feature gets overlooked. Preferences is located under the File menu for Windows users and under the Cubase menu for Mac users (for those who still didn't know).

One of the reasons that Preferences settings are easily overlooked is that, even though there are references to the section throughout the manual, there's not really a place to read why every little feature of the Preferences is there (besides using the Help feature, and sometimes that just isn't enough).

First of all, let's start with the general appearance (refer to Figure 1.15). If you ever find yourself squinting or straining to see what you're doing in Cubase, it would probably be a good idea to try adjusting the general appearance. Under the Appearance category on the left side in the Preferences window, you can adjust the colors and tone of your entire working environment. It's not exactly designed to be "pimped-out" like some other programs, but it contains some practical tools for setting up your visual workspace.

Even though most of the ways to change the appearance are located under the Appearance category, there are other ways to change these. For instance, you can change the language used to English, German, French, Italian, Spanish, or Japanese under the General category. Options within the Event Display category can also greatly alter the appearance of your working environment. As a default, Show Event Names and Colorize Event Background are checked. By unchecking those options and checking only Transparent Events, you should see only colored waves and MIDI events as opposed to seeing completely solid-colored parts (see Figure 1.20). There's also a lot you can do with the overall appearance of Wave images under the Audio category. For more information on all of this, I recommend reading the "Zoom and View Options" section in Chapter 3 of the Cubase manual.

The look of your working environment is important, but what I'd like to concentrate on are the extra little tools that can save you a few steps or at least simplify the process of day-to-day tasks.

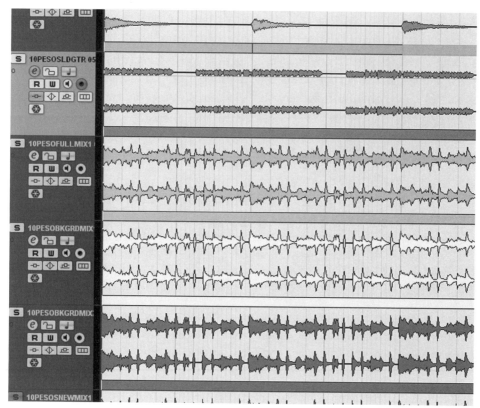

Figure 1.20 Solid-colored events without part backgrounds.

I've broken down the Preferences window into three basic categories: Preference Automation, Optimization and Warning Suppression, and Customization. These categorized references should make it easy for you to get the setup you need right away without having to skim back and forth all over the manual. The "Preference Automation" section includes things that you can set Cubase to do for you automatically. The "Optimization and Warning Suppression" section includes things that will help to lessen the load on your CPU if necessary and also eliminate automated warnings that Cubase shows when certain actions take place (this can slow you down). The "Customization" section involves defining certain attributes in Cubase to work the way you see fit.

Preference Automation

These are all quick and easy settings that will get Cubase working for you in an efficient way that meets your needs. Along with a brief explanation, I've also included a quick suggestion as to which way I think works best for "pro" users. Of course, feel free to use what works best for you.

The first set of automated preference features can be found under the Editing category. All of these preferences are related to editing in general and can help speed up your overall editing performance.

- **Auto Select Events Under Cursor:** When this option is checked, events (both MIDI and audio) are selected as the cursor (not the mouse pointer) moves across the timeline. This is helpful in determining which event to edit while playing back; but by automatically selecting events, you risk accidental altering/moving or deleting those events. My suggestion is to leave this unchecked.

- **Cycle Follows Range Selection:** When checked, using the Range tool actually moves the left locator to the left side of your created range and the right locator to the right side of your created range, thus making Cubase continuously loop your selected range while in Cycle mode. This makes it easy to quickly reposition left and right locators and audition sections. However, it's not for those who prefer to use the Range tool while cycling between the locators. You should keep this checked.

- **Delete Overlaps:** When checked, while working with multiple parts in lanes, Cubase will automatically prevent parts from overlapping so that they can easily be combined into one track. This saves you from editing, but doesn't allow you to edit. My suggestion is to leave this unchecked.

- **Link Editors:** When checked, everything you do within one editor will also reflect in the other editors. Your work stays consistent and organized, but if you screw up in one editor, you screw up in them all. My suggestion is to leave it checked.

- **Parts Get Track Names:** When checked, every time you record a part, it will be named the same as the track name (with possible numbers for multiple parts on one track). It's easy to change part names later if necessary, so my suggestion is to leave this checked.

- **Track Selection Follows Event Selection:** When checked, as you select events in the project window, the corresponding tracks are also selected. No real pros or cons to this. My suggestion is to leave it checked.

The next group of automated preference features can be found under the Editing/Audio category located just below the Editing category. Each of these preferences is more specific to editing audio and can help enhance your audio editing experience.:

- **Hitpoints Have Q-points:** When checked, Q-points are automatically generated when you create hitpoints. If you use wish to quantize audio, this is the only way to do so. My suggestion is to leave it checked.

- **On Import Audio Files:** When Use Settings is selected, you have the following options—Copy Files to Working Directory, Convert and Copy to Project if necessary, and Split

Multi-Channel Files. If Use Settings is not selected, Cubase will show a dialog box with options each and every time you import audio. Nine times out of 10, you'll need to select Copy Files to Working Directory and Convert and Copy to Project. My suggestion is to keep those two options checked. Unless you always separate stereo files into two separate mono files, I recommend leaving Split Multi-Channel Files unchecked.

- **On Processing Shared Clips:** You have three automatic options for this process. The default is to be prompted with a message that asks something to the effect of, "Would you like to create a new file version or write over existing files?" The other options are to create the new file versions or skip the message (which essentially would write over your existing files). The safe and easy solution would be to always create a new file when processing shared clips; that way you can always go back to your original clips if necessary. My suggestion is to leave Assume New Versions selected.

- **Snap to Zero Crossing:** When you're editing audio, you want a smooth transition from one cut to the next. This feature makes it easier for you to piece one audio clip to another at a location where you're less likely to hear a disturbing pop or glitch in the audio at the edit point. My suggestion is to always leave this on, and if you have difficulty making a proper edit, uncheck this temporarily to try your edit without the snap feature. (Nine times out of 10 it will have no negative effect on your editing if it is left checked and will only make your life easier.)

- **Remove Regions/Markers on All Offline Processes:** If you're using regions and markers while processing offline effects, only the selected regions are affected. In some cases this is the desired result, but in others it's not. I believe it's best to leave this box checked because it can be more beneficial to process only selected regions as opposed to the entire part when processing offline.

This next group focuses on MIDI editing preference automation and can be found under the Editing/MIDI category in the Preferences dialog. This brief list works specifically with enhancing your MIDI editing experience.

- **Split MIDI Events:** When checked, the MIDI note will automatically be turned into two individual notes when editing in the middle of a MIDI note. Even though this might not be the desired result in a lot of cases, at least a Note Off has been created for the first note, and the second note is easy to delete if necessary. This is sort of like cutting a loaf of bread into two halves and keeping both, as opposed to cutting the bread and discarding the second half in the process. Considering that the alternative is more "messy," I suggest leaving this preference checked.

- **Split MIDI Controllers** This is very similar to Split MIDI Events (except it specifies controller events), and for this reason, I recommend leaving this option checked as well.

The next batch of automated preference settings is located under the Editing/Project & Mixer category in the Preferences dialog. These automated features were designed to streamline your work when dealing with issues pertaining to the Project Window or Mixer.

- **Select Channel/Track on Solo:** When checked, the track/channel you solo will automatically be selected. Usually, when you solo a track(s) you'll want the same tracks selected, as you are most likely going to be working with the soloed tracks, and you will not be able to hear the other tracks to make proper edits anyway. I recommend leaving this option checked, and if you ever run into difficulties regarding soloing (unlikely), you can uncheck this box and try again. I can only foresee possible difficulties when you're soloing several tracks at once, yet you only want to focus on editing in one track.

- **Scroll to Selected Channel and/or Track:** When checked, your view will automatically be adjusted so that what is selected will be the center of your attention. This is nice, but you'll probably need to get into the habit of changing your selection more frequently in order to change your view. You can customize this automatic feature to work with the mixer only, the project window only, both the project window and mixer, or neither. This is purely a matter of visual preference, and I have no real recommendation as to which to choose.

- **Auto Track Color Mode:** If you're more into creating tracks than making a pretty color scheme in your project window, then this is a very handy feature. Although, using different colors makes it easier to keep your work organized, it's often an afterthought in the creation process. There are several options to choose from here. I recommend using Choose Random Color for a more diverse viewing screen. You can, of course, always change your color manually if you don't like the one that Cubase picks for you.

- **Sync Project & Mixer Selection:** When checked, when you select a track in the project window, the corresponding mixer channel will automatically be selected (and vice versa). Again, this is one of those nine-times-out-of-10 scenarios. I suggest checking this one to try it out, and in the event you require a different mixer channel than the track that's currently selected, uncheck this box and try your work again. It's much more common to have the Project & Mixer selection working in sync.

- **Enable Record on Selected Track and Enable Solo on Selected Track:** I find this option often isn't used on a regular basis. By enabling Record on Selected Track, you may accidentally record on selected tracks when it's not what you intended; and it's even less likely that you'll want to solo a track every time you select it. My suggestion is to leave both of these options unchecked and stick with your good old-fashioned tried-and-true methods.

Located under the Editing/Video category, these two automated preference features can cut out a couple of steps when working with video files in Cubase.

- **Extract Audio on Import Video File:** If you're using video, it most likely has an audio track. In order to hear that audio track in Cubase, it needs to be imported separately from the video track. I recommend checking this option and always importing the audio. If necessary, you can always delete or mute the audio (as you would any audio track) without affecting the video track.

- **Generate Thumbnail Cache on Import Video File:** Thumbnails make it easy to see your video in a "filmstrip view," where you can visually see frames from the video. The only reason you wouldn't want to select this would be if your system was having trouble with video. For more on this, check out the section in Chapter 5 entitled "Working with Video Files." I think thumbnails are a necessity, so I suggest leaving this option checked.

Located under the MIDI category in the Preferences dialog, this next group of automated features is MIDI related but only in a general sense.

- **MIDI Thru Active:** This option must be checked if you need to hear what you're playing on your MIDI keyboard while you record a MIDI part. It's very rare that you will need to have MIDI Thru Active deactivated. For this reason, just leave this checked until you have to cross that bridge.

- **Reset on Stop:** This is a handy feature to use if you have a "sticky" MIDI loop player or synth that likes to keep on going after you've stopped playback. The only thing this feature does is send a MIDI Note Off command to everything in your system when you hit Stop. This command will not affect your recording in any way; however, it will reset continuous controllers (pan, volume, pitchbend, and so forth) back to zero. So if you're using these, it might be best to leave this unchecked if you run into problems.

- **Length Adjustment:** Cubase allows you to adjust the allotted space given after every MIDI note is played (so that notes are not connected). The default setting here is –2 ticks (which is 1/60th of 1/16 note). In most cases, this is best left as is; but depending on your recording style (e.g., if you tend to hold notes a little longer than necessary), you might want to take away a few more ticks to tighten up your performance.

- **Insert Reset Events After Record:** As with the Reset on Stop option (listed earlier), this option is aimed at stopping those sticky MIDI notes from continuing after play has been stopped. The difference here is that you might want those sticky synths to stop before the song actually stops. To do so, record as normal, then when you want the sticky synth to stop, hit Stop on the Transport. Doing so will cause a MIDI reset event to be written into the part being recorded. This tool can be very useful, but it's a little more tricky than the simple Reset on Stop option. If you use a lot of sticky synths, I would recommend checking this option; otherwise, it's probably best to leave it unchecked.

- **Audition through MIDI Inserts/Sends:** If you don't have this selected when using the acoustic feedback audition feature, you will only hear the non-effected MIDI notes. Having this unchecked could be useful if you would like to concentrate on the "raw" notes recorded. However, if you would like to concentrate on each individual note as it is heard through the inserts or sends (i.e., if you would like to edit a single note while auditioning its MIDI delay), this must be checked. Ultimately, this option is nice to have, but it is usually not crucial for editing, as you can always demo your part by playing the part as opposed to using the Audition tool.

The Record/Audio and Record/MIDI categories in the Preference dialog have been combined to form a list of automated preferences that can be used to streamline your recording experience.

- **Create Audio Images During Record (Audio):** The only reason this exists is for those who think that the image drawing process is affecting the quality of their system's performance during the critical stage of recording. The image file is what you use to edit your audio (as most choose to do), so it's pretty essential to the editing process. If you hear dropouts during your recording, try unchecking this box and re-recording. If necessary, you can always draw the waveforms after the files have been recorded to save system resources.

- **Snap MIDI Parts to Bars (MIDI):** When checked, this feature lengthens MIDI parts so that they fit at bar positions. Working with partial bars is a lot trickier than full bars when it comes to MIDI editing, and this can help simplify the workspace. I think it's safe to keep this one checked (particularly as you deal with loops and repeated parts) because you can always split your parts later if necessary.

- **Solo Record in MIDI Editors (MIDI):** This feature is not to be confused with the Solo Editor feature located in the Key Editor toolbar. This is more like an automatic record-enable when you select and open a track in a MIDI Editor. This makes it easy to record new parts within the MIDI Editor, and you won't have to worry about recording on other MIDI tracks by mistake. This feature is checked by default and in most cases should remain checked.

- **Retrospective Record and Buffer Size:** This is an interesting concept. I guess it was designed for those who thought they were recording and got the perfect take, only to realize after the fact that they forgot to push Record. If this sounds like something that might happen to you on occasion, you might want to check this feature. When you realize you forgot to record, select Retrospective Record from the Transport menu, and your recording will magically appear. In order for this to work, it means that Cubase is secretly recording everything you do (sort of like Big Brother!), and when you have your oops moment, Cubase has got your back. Because this is constantly recording, Cubase allows you to set your recording limits. The default is 10,000 events (keep in mind that if you're using controllers, events can go fast). I don't see a problem with keeping this checked unless you believe that it might cause system errors. You're only dealing with MIDI when it comes to this feature, so keep that in mind before you forget to hit the Record button while recording that awesome vocal track!

The Transport category in the Preference dialog contains the following automated features that work well when dealing with issues that pertain to the Transport.

- **Zoom While Locating in Time Scale:** When checked, this is a quick and easy way to zoom in or out on your project. Simply click on the ruler and drag down to zoom in on your target or drag upward to zoom out. I recommend that this option is checked.

- **Return to Start Position on Stop:** If selected, after stopping the Transport, the cursor will return to the exact position it was at before playback started. (This does not mean it goes back to the start of the song or left locator position). Although I see how this could be handy for some, I prefer to have my cursor stay right where it stops. I recommend leaving this one unchecked.

- **Deactivate Punch In on Stop:** When checked, it's as simple as it sounds. You hit Stop and your punch in is deactivated. It makes sense to keep this one checked. Keep in mind that you will need to re-enable Punch In when you resume playback if you wish to continue performing punch ins.

- **Stop After Automatic Punch Out:** When checked, the playback will automatically stop after a punch out is performed (after and post-roll settings). This one also makes sense to keep checked.

Located under both the VST and Plug-Ins categories, these automated preference settings strictly work with the VST interface and affect the way that plug-ins are handled within Cubase.

- **Connect Sends Automatically:** When selected, any effect sends you have created will appear in the list of available effects for any newly created track. Having this checked saves you the trouble of having to select your effects from the list of available sends when setting up a new track. I recommend having this checked because the sends are not active when the new track is created, and you still have to activate them in order to use the effect.

- **Instruments Use Automation:** When selected, VST instrument tracks become automation enabled. This is checked by default, and I see no reason to uncheck it unless you would like to disable automation on all instrument tracks. No one says you have to automate anything if you don't want to.

- **Open Effects Editors After Loading It:** When checked, your Effects Editor will automatically appear when it's loaded as an insert or send as opposed to staying hidden until needed. Most of the time, the first thing you want to do when loading an effect is to start setting that effect, so I think this should be left checked.

- **Create MIDI Track When Loading VSTi:** You have several options here. By default, Cubase asks whether or not you would like a track added for that instrument every time you load a VST instrument. This is pretty annoying if you use VST instruments a lot, so I recommend you either make a decision to have Cubase automatically create a track for you every time (select Always) or opt out of this process by selecting Do Not.

- **Plug-In Editors Always on Top:** Have you ever opened a delay and then spent two minutes trying to find it only to realize that it was minimized behind the mixer? With this option checked, your VST window will appear on top of every other window in Cubase. Because the effects are usually smaller, I recommend leaving this option checked, and then closing the VST window after you've made your settings.

Optimization and Warning Suppression

As far as optimization is concerned, if you feel like your system is "up to speed," then I recommend you leave all the optimizing features unchecked to get the most out of Cubase. As far as warning suppressions are concerned, if you are new to using Cubase 5, it might be a good idea to leave the default warnings in place, and then later deactivate them as you become more aware of the reasons why the warnings occur.

The following list contains features located within the Preferences dialog box that can enhance the performance of your system. Each listing is followed by its location in parentheses.

- **Quick Zoom (Edit category):** Activating Quick Zoom means less redrawing of your display. While this saves processing power, it also means less accuracy in your zooming in and out.

- **Stop Playback While Winding (Transport category):** With this box unchecked, you can wind forward or backward while in Play mode and continue listening as you wind. When you reach your destination through winding, your playback will resume from the cursor's location. There's no need to check this unless you prefer to have playback stop or would like to optimize your system.

- **CPU Saving Scrub Mode (Transport/Scrub category):** Just like it sounds, you can choose to limit the detail in what you hear while scrubbing. While this is fine for some basic scrubbing, it could hold back some who demand more accuracy. Leave this one unchecked when you need to scrub in great detail (precise editing). Keep in mind that simple scrubbing is usually more than sufficient, and using this mode will not cause any problems.

- **Suspend VST3 Plug-In Processing When No Audio Signal Is Received (VST/Plug-Ins category):** This new optimization feature is one I'll recommend because it can save a lot of processing power. However, I'm a little suspect (it reminds me too much of "sleeping" hard drives) because I feel as though it could cause program fluctuations that could lead to crashing while you're quickly working. I have faith that Steinberg wouldn't have released this without extensive testing, though. If you're experiencing problems with crashing and you're using a lot of VST3 plug-ins, you might want to uncheck this box. (I have a feeling that's why it's there!)

Cubase likes to warn you when you're about to do something that could have consequences, but seeing these warnings over and over again can become tedious. The following list contains preferences that will allow you to suppress these warnings. The locations for these can be found in parentheses after each listed preference.

- **Warn Before Switching Display Domain (Tools category):** This warning will come up while using the Time Warp tool. Working with the Time Warp tool can be tricky, but as long as you're careful and understand how it works, this warning is not necessary. For more info on the Time Warp tool, see Chapter 3, "Taking Audio to the Limit in Cubase 5."

- **Warn On Processing Overloads (VST/Plug-Ins category):** I can understand why you might want to keep this one checked. If your system is overloaded or your level is too hot, clipping may occur. Under normal working circumstances, it will be rare that you encounter this warning anyway.

- **Warn Before Removing Modified Effects (VST/Plug-Ins category):** Let's say you're using a delay, and then you decide you'd rather try a reverb. By default, Cubase will warn that you're changing your effect and are about to lose those settings. Bypass this obvious warning by unchecking this feature.

- **Inhibit Warning When Changing the Sample Data and Inhibit Warning When Applying Offline Processes (VariAudio category):** Both of these warnings pertain to the new VariAudio feature in Cubase 5, but they're both unnecessary if you know what you're doing when using VariAudio. Instead of unchecking these, you'll need to check them in order to suppress the warnings. For more information on VariAudio, see Chapter 5 in this book in addition to the Cubase 5 manual.

Customization

Finally, the last phase in mastering the massive Preferences options is in specifying settings that will truly make Cubase meet your needs. Once you've read this final section, you'll not only be running Cubase with 100% of its potential, you'll also know where and how to make necessary adjustments if the need should arise. Each location can is noted in parentheses.

- **Default Track Time Type (Editing category):** For most Cubase users, you'll want to work in Musical time (default). For those who work with images or timed sequences (theater cues for example), Time Linear (minutes and seconds) should be your main startup format. No matter what, you can always change your time type from the Transport or by right-clicking on the ruler. Selecting Follow Transport Main Display will result in the time type adjusting to Musical time when working in Bars and Beats, and Linear Time when using any other time format from the Transport. It is automatically set depending on the way your Transport is set up.

- **Use Up/Down Navigation Command for Selecting Tracks Only (Edit category):** By selecting this feature, you limit the arrow keys to the task of scrolling up and down through the track list, selecting the track and nothing else. When this box is not checked, the arrow keys will not only move up and down through the track list selecting the track, but they will also reselect the part on the newly selected track if a part has already been selected. I personally find it much less confusing simply to use the arrows to only select the track, so I'd leave this box checked.

- **Drag Delay (Edit category):** Cubase offers a slight delay to differentiate between selecting an event and clicking and dragging. If you find yourself moving notes by accident when your intention was to simply select the note, you might want to try a higher Drag Delay setting.

- **Use Mouse Wheel for Event Volume and Fades (Edit/Audio category):** This title pretty much says it all. If your mouse has a wheel, you can conveniently use it to tweak your mix from within the events.

- **Value Box/Time Control Mode (Edit/Control category):** You can define the way you would like to handle increments within value boxes (and Time Control mode) with these three diverse options.

- **Knob and Slider Modes (Edit/Control category):** Here's where you define exactly the way the virtual knobs and sliders react when you control them with the mouse.

- **Select Controllers in Note Range: Use Extended Note Content (Edit/MIDI category):** This wordy feature allows you to automatically select controller events that occur at the same time as the notes you select within the Key Editor.

- **Legato Overlap and Legato Mode Selected Only (Edit/MIDI category):** Legato Overlap allows you to define how long you would like connecting notes to overlap, and Legato Mode Selected Only means that legato settings will only be applied to the selected events when applying.

- **Enlarge Selected Track and Deep Track Folding (Edit/Project & Mixer category):** Enlarge Selected Track basically expands the selected tracks so that they appear vertically larger than the other tracks (thus making them easier to see and work with when using a lot of tracks). Deep Track Folding allows you to quickly open and fold multiple folders and subfolders grouped together on a folder track.

- **Select Tool Shows Extra Info (Edit/Tools category):** When selected, the selection tool (mouse pointer) shows track info and time reference while mousing over the project window.

- **Pop Up Tool Box on Right Click (Edit/Tools category):** This is selected by default, and when you right-click, a small tool box appears containing the tool buttons. To get an extended view of the tool buttons, uncheck this feature. On a Windows system, you can easily toggle between the two modes by Ctrl-right-clicking.

- **Cross Hair Cursor (Edit/Tools category):** This tool makes it even easier to find gridlines when making edits.

■ **Tool Modifiers (Edit/Tool Modifiers category):** Customize which keys act as alternative functions for the tools. This can be very handy even if you memorize the default settings. I recommend jotting these settings down and practicing with them if you don't know them already.

■ **Chase Events (MIDI category):** Customize which events you would like Cubase to "chase." This is particularly helpful when you have multiple program changes or pitch bends on one track. For more on chasing MIDI, refer to the Cubase 5 manual.

■ **MIDI Display Resolution and MIDI Max Feedback (MIDI category):** You can alter the value of a MIDI 1/16 note in actual "ticks" (affecting only the display of the MIDI event) and control the amount of allowable MIDI feedback for the acoustic feedback control when auditioning MIDI events.

■ **MIDI File (MIDI category):** These options allow you to select which attribute you would like to avoid when importing or exporting MIDI files in Cubase.

■ **MIDI Filter (MIDI category):** These options allow you to select which MIDI data you wish to block as MIDI data arrives through the MIDI input in Cubase.

■ **Audio Pre-Record Seconds (Record/Audio category):** This option allows you to determine a set time (buffer) for Cubase to capture before you actually record. This is similar to Retrospect Record (except with audio, as opposed to MIDI) and only allows you to pre-record up to one minute.

■ **Audio Cycle Record Mode (Record/Audio category):** Customizes the exact way you would like to record while working in Cycle mode. By selecting Create Events, multiple takes (parts) are created on multiple lanes within a single track. When selecting Create Regions, multiple regions are created on one continuous part. Select Create Events and Regions to include both options. All methods display the active event on top.

■ **MIDI Record Catch Range (Record/MIDI category):** This option is similar to Audio Pre-Record, except with MIDI.

■ **Replace Recording in Editors (Record/MIDI category):** If you use the Replace mode, this feature allows you to specify whether you would like to just replace the controller events (commonly practiced) as opposed to both the controller and note events while working in the Key Editor. Using this feature makes it easy to re-perform pitchbends or modulation on MIDI parts, and if you want to use Replace All, you can simply re-record the part as an alternative option because it's essentially the same thing. Replace None has no effect and is only used as a safety.

■ **Cursor Width (Transport category):** This is merely a visual modification of the cursor.

■ **Wind Speed Options (Transport category):** Fast forward not fast enough? Here's where you can fix that!

- **Show Timecode Subframes (Transport category):** This only affects the display of the time-code. Your subframes are still there even if you can't see the numbers flying by.

- **Stationary Cursors (Transport category):** When the cursor arrives at the middle of the displayed project window, it will remain centered and the project window will scroll to the left past the cursor.

- **Locate When Clicked in Empty Space (Transport category):** This handy feature moves your cursor wherever you click (as long as the space is not occupied by an event, part, or automation handle).

- **Scrub Response and Volume (Transport category):** You can customize the volume in which your scrubbing action is heard in relation to your overall mix, plus adjust the speed/sensitivity of the scrub itself.

- **Delay Compensation Threshold (VST category):** This is a feature you can use during recording with VST instruments, and it's only really required if you're experiencing latency on your system. It works hand in hand with the Constrain Delay Compensation button located on the toolbar. If you're having problems, activate Constrain Delay Compensation, then adjust this setting until the problem is resolved.

- **Use Cubase 3 EQ Settings as Default (VST category):** This option is for those who preferred the "ol' skool" EQ setup found in Cubase 3, which consisted of a Hi and Lo shelving EQ and two parametric EQs in the middle. This classic style is still commonly used and can be critical when migrating older Cubase projects into Cubase 5.

- **Default Stereo Panner Mode (VST category):** You have the choice of Stereo Dual Panner (two separate controls for left and right), Stereo Combined Panner (one control for two separate linked panners), and the default Stereo Balance Panner (which is one control and most similar to the sort of standard panner you see on most common mixing consoles).

- **Sort VST Plug-In Menu by Vendor (VST/Plug-In category):** This is just another way of organizing your list of plug-ins. This option categorizes your effects by vendor name and puts everything else in alphabetical order within the submenus.

- **Map Input Bus Metering to Audio Track (VST/Metering category):** When activated, the input bus can also be metered on the track you're recording to while using Direct Monitoring.

- **Meter's Peak Hold, Fast Fallback, and Slow Fallback (VST/Metering category):** These three settings allow you to customize the way your meters react to the audio signal.

- **Zoom Tool – Horizontal Zooming Only (Edit/Tools category)** Zooming that cuts out the vertical direction. This offers a slightly more restricted zoom type when using the Zoom tool.

Saving Your Work Could Save Your Career

I've used both Macs and PCs, and the one thing they have in common is that both crash when you're working on complex programs like Cubase. But this probably isn't news to you. I regularly practice saving files and backing up my computer now. I have multiple hard drives, and I copy each drive to a completely clean backup drive every month. I have battery backups so I will have time to save and shut down my system to avoid a devastating crash in case the power suddenly goes out. But even with all this, I still lost one month's worth of work last year during a power failure, and I'm still working to rebuild that lost time. There's no insurance for this kind of loss; and when it comes to tax write-offs, this sort of thing doesn't even make the list. That work and time are gone, and the only things that can replace them are more work and time, whether that time is paid or unpaid. Always expect and be prepared for the worst.

I'm not going to preach anymore about backup hard drives and battery backups. I would like to focus on the simple task of saving your work and discuss saving methods that will hopefully (if you practice) help you avoid some of the pain I've gone through in my career.

First let's talk about the Auto Save features that come in Cubase. When I first started using Cubase and learned about the Auto Save feature, I thought, "Perfect! I hate having to save often. This thing will do it for me, and I'll be safe!" Then I learned that Auto Save was saving over my old files and preventing me from going back and correcting things if I ran into problems down the road. It was a nightmare. Well, Auto Save has gotten better, but it's still far from perfect. Now, Cubase saves the file under a new file type (BAK) under the same name, creates new backup files for the interval you set, and then only saves when changes have been made. I have tested this operation, and it works. But the true test will be when the system actually crashes. What I noticed was that for some reason, the backup files are only saved if you save your project when finished. If you select Don't Save when exiting, your backup files are removed! This process leaves me slightly paranoid (to say the least). The point is that if you plan on using Auto Save, it should only be as a last resort backup. You should still regularly back up your projects using Save or Save As throughout the recording process.

When you're working away on a project (recording and editing), you should save at least once every hour. When you save, I never recommend just selecting Save from the File menu, but instead selecting Save As, and then creating a new name for your file. For instance, I'm recording my latest hit "Stevesong." I will be working on this over the next few days, so today I will name it "Stevesong5-15-09" (including the date) as soon as I get my project setup taken care of. In one hour, I've already done a lot of MIDI work and now I will save it as "Stevesong5-15-09a" in the same project folder. Tomorrow, I'll end the day saving as "Stevesong5-16-09g" (after working for 7 hours on the project), and the next day I'll end with a final mix and save the song as "StevesongFINALMIX5-17-09" when I'm through. By the time I get to my final mix, I have about 20 different project names for "Stevesong," and I can go back into the song at any of those stages of production in case something goes wrong or I decide to make some major changes later on. Don't worry if you miss saving after one or two hours during the process of working. Just do yourself a favor and try to save as often as possible.

There's another easier way to do this, although it isn't quite as thorough. This function is called Save New Version, and it creates a new version of your current project name. But instead of getting into so much detail (as I did in my "Stevesong" example), it simply uses the same name and puts a new number at the end (such as Stevesong-17). It doesn't take a brain surgeon to figure out that Stevesong-04 was one of the early stages of my work and Stevesong-16 was one of the latter, but the more info you can put in the name, (hopefully) the less time you'll waste when you actually want to find the version you need. To try the Save New Version method, simply hit Ctrl-Alt-S on your Windows keyboard (or Command-Option-S for Macs) when you reach a good save point. This file will be created in the same project folder as your original file.

Project files don't require a lot of hard drive space. The actual audio files are the real space hogs. If you are working on a project where you've recorded a lot of audio and you're paranoid about a hard drive crash that could wipe out all of your irreplaceable recordings, then I recommend at the end of each day (before you power down the system) you do a project backup. This process takes a little longer than a basic save because every audio file becomes duplicated in the process. This process isn't much different than just dragging your project folder (using Windows Explorer or Mac OS Finder) to another hard drive. What's better about using the backup feature in Cubase is that you can exclude certain things and sort of "clean up" your project by only copying what's really important during the backup process.

Note: A lot of people don't seem to understand that if you're going to back up your project, it does you absolutely no good to back up to the same hard drive. The whole purpose of backing up is to protect you from hard drive failure. If you don't have another hard drive, back up to a DVD or CD. Once you've done your backup, load your new backup into Cubase to make sure that it is working correctly. This only takes a moment, and it's better to do at that time than to discover later there was a problem when you were really counting on that backup to work.

To utilize Cubase's project backup feature, select Back Up Project from the File menu. (Remember to select a different drive location than the one where your original project already exists!) Enter a new project name. (I suggest including the date because you'll probably have multiple backups.) Only check the option boxes if you feel it's necessary or if you want to clean up your project, and always remember to test your backup before calling it a day.

One more thing—if your system does crash while you're in the middle of a recording, Steinberg claims (along with a little disclaimer) that your audio file will still be saved. The file would be in the Audio subfolder of your project folder. I personally wouldn't bet my life or my career on it. (For more information on this, see the Cubase 5 manual.)

I'll end this section with one more tip (from a guy who thought all his bases were covered). *Always shut down your system before you step away from it.* This includes external hard drives. The reason I lost one month's worth of work was because I left my office for 20 minutes, and I came back to find that the power had gone out, as well as the power on my battery backup. This resulted in a hard drive failure on a drive I had not had a chance yet to back up. Ouch! Lesson learned.

Time-Saving Steps—Setting Up Key Commands and Macros

Cubase has offered key commands and macros in their software for quite some time, but a majority of users don't even know what they are let alone utilize them.

Key commands can involve just about *any* single function in Cubase. You can custom-assign this function to any key on your QWERTY keyboard, and then use that key to save yourself time. Setting up these key commands is much easier than setting up any other sort of MIDI controller, and it can save you loads of time in the studio. For less than $20, you can even find somebody out there to sell you stickers to make your computer keyboard look like an extension of Cubase (try Googling "Cubase sticker").

Note: For those who aren't into customizing key commands, the pre-configured commands can also come in handy. To learn the pre-configured commands, you can reference the handy list in Chapter 38 of the Cubase manual.

To jump in and start setting up your own personal key commands, select Key Commands from the File menu. When you open the Key Commands window, you should see folders upon folders of commands appearing as they would in Windows Explorer or Mac OS Finder. You can browse through these folders and open them by selecting the plus (+) sign next to them to locate the command you would like to utilize. Obviously, there are more commands in this list than you can fit on one keyboard. The idea is not to put every command on your keyboard, but only the commands you use on a regular basis and are time-consuming to access. If you don't feel like browsing through the folders, you can use the Search function to find the command you're looking for. Just enter the name of the command (usually provided somewhere in the program), then select Search, and it will most likely appear. If there is more than one command with a similar name, just keep selecting Search until the desired result appears. (They appear one at a time.) Once you've found the command you want, it's time to assign a key. In the Type in Key field, type the single keystroke or combination of keys that you would like to utilize for the selected command. In this example, I have decided to create an Add Audio Track command. I want to use the letter A, so I type the letter in the field and select Assign. When I do this, a warning comes up telling me that the A has been used for another command (see Figure 1.21).

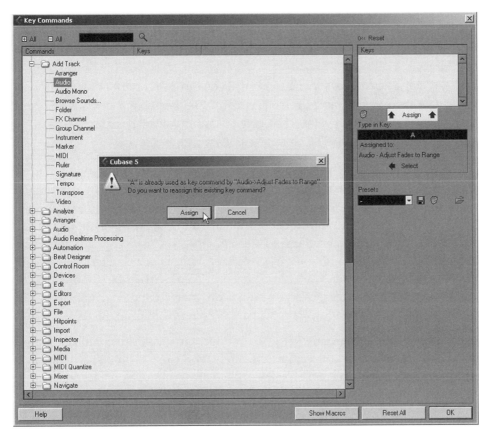

Figure 1.21 The A has already been used.

Note: You shouldn't let this warning stop you from using the keys you want to use. Most likely, all the keys have been pre-assigned to other commands. What's important is that you choose the commands that will make your life easier, and choose keys that will make it easy for you to remember. The best plan is to make a list of all the commands that you want to use, then lay them out on the computer keyboard the same as you would design a layout for a MIDI controller. Once you have the "map" put together, you're ready to turn your QWERTY keyboard into your dream controller.

If you don't get a warning, your key selection will automatically be assigned to the command. If you do get a warning, simply select Assign and your key will be assigned as you wish. While you're browsing through the list of commands, you'll probably notice that some of them already have a letter value in the Keys column. That is because they have already been assigned by default. When you're finished making your assignments, the keys you have assigned will also be located next to their proper commands. You can use this list to refresh your memory of which key is what command at any time. The default commands are also listed in the Cubase 5 manual.

Note: Besides using single keystrokes for one command, you can also combine keys (such as Shift-A) to create more command placement options. The key commands are not stored within individual projects, but within the Cubase program folder. Once you create a command, it will work with any and all projects you work with in Cubase.

You can save key commands setups into different presets. That way, you can create a particular key command setup based around recording, another based around editing audio, and another based around editing MIDI (and so on) if you desire. When you need to use a specific setup, simply load it from the menu with the key command display. Once you save your key command setup preset, it becomes an XML file, and you can save it to use in later versions of Cubase or install it in another Cubase studio that you're working in. Your XML file is stored in the same general location that your own templates are stored on your computer (Documents and Settings/<user name>/Application Data/Steinberg/Cubase 5/Presets/Key Commands).

Macro commands take key commands to another level. With macros, you can combine multiple commands on one key to get to the end result. Unfortunately, you can't get too specific in your commands (such as pitch shift up one octave) because you can't enter in specific values (such as the one octave). If you include a process that requires a value, your processor will appear and allow you to enter the required value, and then when you complete the process the next process will appear. While this can still save time, it isn't nearly as practical as setting up macros commands so the entire process is completed in one simple keystroke. An example of this might be creating a duplicate event that is reversed to follow a selected event (to sort of get a quick "push/pull" audio effect).

To make a macro command such as the one stated in my example, select the Show Macros button to open the Macros section of the Key Commands window. Next create a name for the macro by selecting New Macro and entering a name that describes your command (in this example, Duplicate and Reverse). Next, with the new macro selected, find each of the commands in the list above that is necessary to complete the new macro command. When you find each command, click Add Command while it is highlighted, and it will appear below your new macro name. Once you have all of the necessary commands under your macro, click Okay. Your new macro is now ready for you to assign a key stroke to it. Locate the Macro folder in the list of command folders. Your new macro command should be in that folder. Assign a keystroke to the macro using the same method you used to assign any key command, then click OK. Your new macro should be ready to go. This is one of those things that you have to double-check in Cubase and possibly make alterations if necessary. If you do need to make alterations, just click the Show Macros button again. You can delete commands (by clicking Delete) that don't work and/or add new commands to the existing macros. Just remember to click OK to exit. Figure 1.22 shows my new macro in its creation stage.

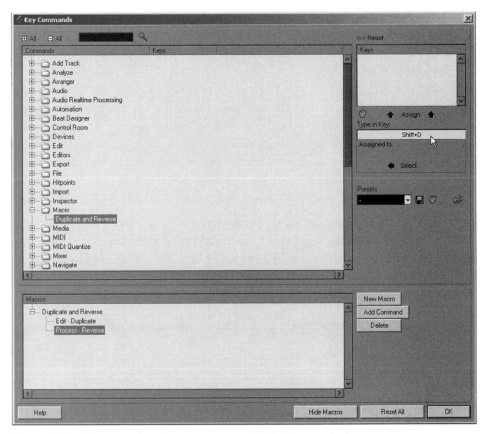

Figure 1.22 An example of a macro command being created.

Juggling Windows When the Pressure Is On

When I started using Cubase in 1990, there was one window allowed on the screen at a time. Back then, it was all my poor little Atari computer could handle. Now, there can be so many things happening at once in Cubase that you need 20 different windows open at once just to figure out what you're doing. The growing number of windows you need to use is spreading like a disease, and I doubt it's going to get any better since our demands are getting higher and higher. The only problem with having too many windows open at once is that it makes for a ridiculously messy workspace. The last thing you need in the middle of a session (when the musicians are ready and psyched up to perform) is to stop the show and make everyone wait because you can't find your Transport. The key to proper window juggling is (like everything else I've gone over so far) proper organization. Sure, it definitely helps to have a multi-monitor display, but even if you're using multiple monitors, you need an organized workspace at all times. (Cubase refers to the arrangement of your windows as a *workspace*.) You might laugh about the example I used regarding the missing Transport window, but I bet you've all been there before.

To properly organize your windows, you need to have a generalized idea of editors or controls you'll need to have at your fingertips in order to perform a certain task (whether it's working with your virtual synths, mixing, recording vocals, and so on). Then you need to arrange those in your workspace in the way that works best for you when performing those tasks. Your workspace appears the moment you start up Cubase. Even though the display might look like a blank canvas, it's still considered a workspace. When you save your project, it saves it the way you left it. If you have multiple editors spread out across the workspace when you save a project, that will be what you will see when you load that project the next time around. Workspaces only affect the appearance of Cubase. If you were to close a few open windows and resave your project, it would only make a *visual* difference in your project. (For instance, if you closed a window for a delay plug-in, you'd still have that delay in your project.)

Cubase allows you to save workspaces and recall them when needed. This is sort of like taking a snapshot of your setup, then rearranging your setup, and then recalling that original snapshot again. Just to show you what this workspace might look like, Figure 1.23 shows a workspace that I have set up for recording vocals.

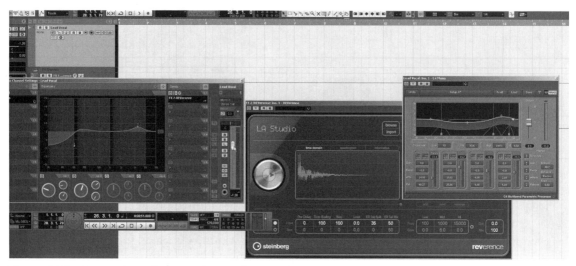

Figure 1.23 A snapshot of my vocal recording workspace.

Now that I've arranged all of my controls the way I like them, saving the workspace is easy. From the Window menu, select New Workspace, enter a name (such as "vocal recording"), and click OK. Once you've created the new workspace, you can view it by selecting Organize from the Workspace menu (located in the Windows menu). Once the Organize Workspace dialog appears, select the square under the Locked column that corresponds to your new workspace. By locking this workspace, every time you select it, it will appear just as you have set it up.

There are two types of workspaces you can set up. The default is the workspace that is saved with your project and is unique to the particular project you are working on. A *global* workspace is one that you can open in any project, and it will work. A global workspace will not remember your actual settings, but it will remember the layout of the windows and their customized size (if applicable). Keep in mind this means that if your processors aren't loaded or you don't have your tracks created, you won't see anything when using a global preset workspace.

To turn your project workspace into a global workspace, select Organize from the Workspace menu located under the Window menu. The Organize Workspaces dialog box will appear (see Figure 1.24). From the Workspaces list on the left, select the project workspace that you would like to make into a global workspace and then select the right arrow button (located between the two lists). Your project workspace has now become a global workspace preset. Now it exists as both a project workspace and global workspace. At this point the project workspace can be deleted (if you would like to clean up your existing project workspaces) by selecting it and clicking Remove. The global preset will remain intact during this process. The global presets are saved in your system and in the project (in case you open your project on another system). You can copy global presets back into the project by selecting the global workspace from the right side of the dialog and moving it to the left side using the left arrow button in the center. At this point, you are able to unlock and store them with that particular project with the settings still intact (i.e., effects settings, presets, levels, and so on). To automatically copy the global presets into the project from the beginning, check the Auto Instantiate Presets box.

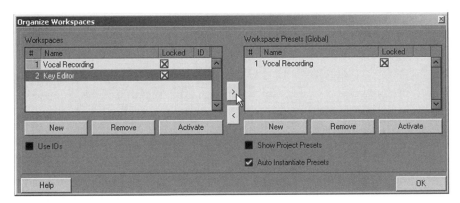

Figure 1.24 Organizing the workspace presets.

Note: Another handy feature is that you can assign key commands to each global workspace preset in order to quickly adjust your views in Cubase. Just reference the corresponding preset number and the workspace presets commands located in the Workspace folder in the Key Commands window.

Besides using workspaces, if for some reason you run into problems, you can find all currently active windows listed at the bottom of the Window menu. In regard to the Transport (as in the earlier example), if you can't find it under the Window menu, it probably got closed by accident. You can always re-open it from the Devices menu. Most windows have an Always on Top feature, which can also prevent windows from getting buried in the heap (see Figure 1.25). Just right-click on the upper-left corner of the window to open the context menu. Even though it says "always on top," keep in mind that there can only be one "king of the hill" window at one time!

Note: Just for the record, by default Cubase is set up so that you can hide and display the Transport by using the F2 key command.

Figure 1.25 The Always on Top option.

More Steps to Save Yourself a Few Headaches

I've covered quite a lot in this chapter in regard to streamlining Cubase so that it fits your needs like a glove, but there are still quite a few things you can do to take it even further. First of all, there are even more ways to customize Cubase:

- **Customizing the toolbar:** This one's super easy to do, but is often overlooked. Are there items on the toolbar that you never use and have no intention of using? Or maybe you can't even see all the tools that exist for you. If you right-click on the toolbar (above the ruler), a list of tools will appear with check marks. If you're still using the default settings, guess what—you're not seeing all the tools. Take this opportunity to place a check next to tools that you could be using and uncheck tools that will just get in your way. Also, if you run into tools you don't understand, take the time to read up on them in the manual. Did you know that each editor has its own set of tools on the toolbar? Cubase is a deep program, and it's easy to miss things if you're not using it to its full potential every day.

- **Customizing the track display:** You can also add and remove buttons from each track. Cubase comes with a factory default setup, but there's a lot more you can do with it.

(For example, if you're not into using lanes or drum maps, why clutter your tracks with them?) Also, have you ever run out of space when typing in a track name and just abbreviated it? You can lengthen the name field in the same place. Right-click on any track and select Track Control Settings to make your adjustments. Keep in mind that each track type has its own display settings.

- **Customizing the Transport:** Are you using the Transport to its full potential? Right-click on the Transport and select Show All. The Transport has become massive, as it now also contains a mini keyboard. There are so many useful features right at your fingertips, and you might not even know they exist if you just started using Cubase right out of the box.

- **Customizing the Inspector:** If you right-click at the top of the Inspector when it's open, you'll get a list of everything in the Inspector. You can check or uncheck anything that you want to appear or disappear from view. Some people don't even use the Inspector because it's hidden almost too well. If you don't know what the Inspector is, you should check it out in the Cubase manual.

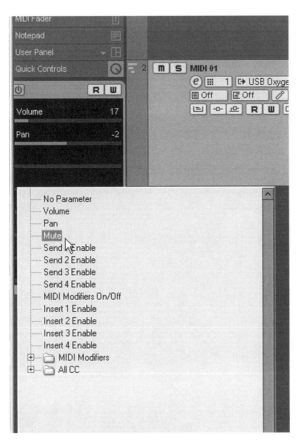

Figure 1.26 The Quick Controls.

- **Customizing the mixer:** The mixer can be full of detail. Are you getting what you need out of it? Take the time to explore the mixer to its fullest and customize the views to fit your needs.

- **Customizing the Edit Audio/MIDI Channel Setting display:** That handy little "e" button located on each channel brings up one of the most useful tools in Cubase, the Edit Channel Settings display. This display offers more features than most are aware of, and you can expose them by right-clicking almost anywhere in the display.

At the beginning of the chapter, I demonstrated how to set up the M-Audio Oxygen 49 control surface. A custom installation takes some time. If you don't have a controller with a lot of knobs and you just want a quick-and-easy setup, you can try using the Quick Controls (see Figure 1.26). The Quick Controls offer eight controllable parameters for either audio, MIDI, or instrument tracks. The setup is similar to the way you set up the Oxygen 49, but these controls offer a few extra perks that the generic control surface doesn't offer. For more details on Quick Controls, I suggest you check out the Cubase manual.

For those who remember the Cubase SX days, you might recall the ability to change skins in Cubase. You can still find the Skins folder within the Cubase 5 programs folder, but alas there is only one skin to choose. I'm sure there's someone out there altering the skin of Cubase 5, but it's not easy. For those who demand a leopard print or zebra stripe background, you'll just have to wait! Cubase 5 hasn't quite caught up with MySpace.

Of course, general computer maintenance is always important when it comes to using Cubase. Keep those hard drives defragged. Keep updating your operating system. Keep checking with www.steinberg.net for updates. All of this is important. If you need more info on optimizing your computer system, please check out another one of my books called *Your Cubase Studio* (Course Technology PTR, 2008), or refer to Steinberg's website for more info.

2 Maximizing MIDI in Cubase 5

There are plenty of pros working in the world who don't use MIDI during the recording process. MIDI is what Cubase was built on, and where it truly shines as a DAW. For me, the MIDI features in Cubase are the key ingredients for how I make my living as a composer/producer. If you're one of the pros who isn't a keyboard player, don't let that stop you from exploring the world of MIDI. It's really not as difficult as some might think.

Note: I encourage those who aren't familiar with MIDI to read my book, *MIDI Editing in Cubase: Skill Pack* (Thomson Course Technology, 2007). The book was written for beginners, but it also summarizes the vast world of MIDI in Cubase, and you can use the included CD-ROM to follow along with some exercises. The CD-ROM is revolutionary for Cubase training because you can actually hear, see, touch, and alter the MIDI, unlike with most books. Even though the book and CD-ROM were written for Cubase 4, they also work well with Cubase 5.

Primarily, this chapter's main goal is to go over MIDI features that often get overlooked or are too difficult for most MIDI novices to learn. I'll also be going over the new MIDI features included in Cubase 5.

Monitoring Raw MIDI

Steinberg has been around for 25 years, and MIDI has been around even longer. Cubase was originally designed to make working with MIDI easy by making the MIDI data look visually "pretty" and having it represented by graphics instead of numbers and hex code. This was a very welcome change for all sorts of "MIDIots" out there. However, every event that was entered into the system went through this virtual filter, and if you truly wanted to know what was going into Cubase, you could only see it after it had already been recorded from within the List Editor. For many, including myself, this was fine and dandy because we didn't care to see what raw MIDI was all about. Later, I learned that if you want to take MIDI beyond what the average DAW user can do, it can really help to have a better understanding of the raw MIDI data and how it is transmitted and received.

When it comes to seeing the data coming into Cubase, most users refer to the MIDI activity indicator on the track or Transport. When you see the indicator bouncing as you hit a key on the keyboard, you know you're receiving a MIDI signal. For those who want to know more details (such as the key that was pressed, how hard it was pressed, controller info, and so on) before the signal is actually recorded, you've been out of luck and had to use other software, such as MIDI-OX (a third-party freeware MIDI utility program), to see what was truly going on with your MIDI.

After 25 years, Steinberg finally integrated a MIDI plug-in so that you can monitor the raw MIDI signal in a more detailed fashion (see Figure 2.1) without having to exit Cubase.

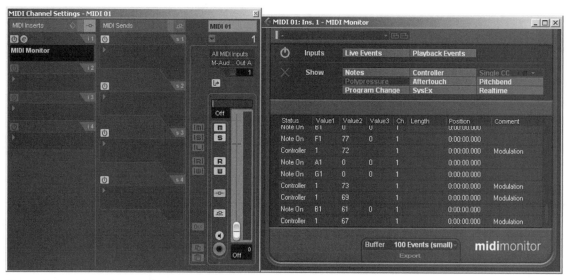

Figure 2.1   Cubase's new MIDI Monitor insert effect.

To access the new MIDI Monitor, select any MIDI track and then select MIDI Monitor from the list of insert effects. With the MIDI Monitor, you can see live events as they happen directly from the output to the input of Cubase. You can filter the view of certain data without affecting the data itself by using any of the preset filter tabs on the effect. Even though this new utility doesn't quite have the ammo that MIDI-OX has, it's simple and very effective. It's a little strange that this MIDI Monitor utility is located as a MIDI plug-in in Cubase rather than located on the Transport or in the Inspector because the primary need for the MIDI Monitor is to analyze data and it helps in troubleshooting. Nonetheless, it's a very welcome addition to Cubase 5.

Using the New Virtual Keyboard

While we're on the subject of utilities and monitoring, let's take a moment to go over the new virtual keyboard located on the Transport (see Figure 2.2). As a keyboardist, my first reaction to this new feature was, "Huh? Why would we need something silly like that when we've got a real keyboard?" It's by no means a replacement for a MIDI keyboard, especially if you're a keyboard

Figure 2.2 The virtual keyboard on the Transport in QWERTY mode.

player. What's great about the virtual keyboard is that now (if you're not a keyboard player and you want to add some MIDI notes to your recording) you can type in your notes rather than drawing them in. This is a huge timesaver for non-keyboard-player programmers who still have a basic understanding of the octave range on a piano keyboard. The best part is that you don't even need to have a MIDI keyboard connected to input real MIDI data in real time; you can use this virtual keyboard as a quick alternative MIDI tester to make sure that your VST instruments are working correctly and there's not just some other MIDI communication issue from your controller to the MIDI input in Cubase.

To view the virtual keyboard, select it from the Transport's display menu by right-clicking on the Transport and then selecting Virtual Keyboard from the top of the menu. By default, the keyboard appears in (what I call) "QWERTY mode." In this view, you see your QWERTY keyboard laid out in a pattern similar to that of a piano keyboard. The letter Q represents the pitch C, the number 2 represents C sharp, and so on through to the letter I, which represents one octave above the original C. Numbers 1, 4, and 8 are irrelevant on the QWERTY keyboard because they fall in non-piano keyboard-like places. This means when you type a Q on your QWERTY keyboard you should hear (and input) a C-pitched note. You can adjust the single octave to focus on any of the seven octaves in the keyboard's seven-octave range (C1 through C5) by using the virtual buttons located just below the virtual keyboard. You can adjust the input velocity by using the slider on the right of the keyboard. You can also switch the view to a keyboard that has more of a piano-style look. Keep in mind that with this display you can still only utilize the same keys on your QWERTY keyboard, but you can also use your mouse to play other keys (or perhaps do one of those Jerry Lee Lewis piano slides). Not that you'll be playing this virtual keyboard like Liberace—you can only play two notes at once. Unfortunately, this means that no triads or full chords are possible in real time. Of course, in order to hear anything, you'll need to have a MIDI track with its output selected to an activated VST instrument (or external synth). You can also use this virtual keyboard to audition your synths when using the MediaBay. So even though this little keyboard is limiting, it can be a handy feature to have at your disposal (especially for the ever-expanding group of laptop DAW users out there).

Advanced Quantize and Groove Features

There are plenty of Cubase users who love computer music (or dance music and the like), and this sort of music is supposed to sound quantized most of the time. There are also many other users out there who are very particular about the way a computer grooves. I've heard people say things like "this program grooves more than that one" or "that computer grooves more than the other." Personally, I don't really buy into that 100%. I think that it's the programmer (not the computer or software) who's doing the actual groovin'. Sure some programs work better for some people, and some interfaces make it particularly easy for users to program grooves—so whatever helps that person obtain that perfect groove is a good thing. But when it comes to the actual quantizing, I think it's all a numbers game.

Given that, Cubase has always been great about giving you multiple ways to calculate those numbers in order to give you your desired grooves. Even with all of these tools available, there are times when simply not quantizing your MIDI is the best way to preserve a groove. The "human" factor is extremely hard to calculate, and even though we work so hard to obtain a "tight" live performance, it's the little imperfections from each individual player that give the groove its particular "color." I don't really consider myself a keyboard player anymore; I'm a programmer. I play from two to 20 measures, and then I edit away. Because of this, I'm a quantize-a-holic. As much as I use MIDI, when it comes to drum parts that I really want to groove, most of the time I use either a real drummer or I dive into my loop library. Why? Real professional drummers usually create better grooves than keyboard player/programmers. In other words, I could paint my house myself, but a professional painter will probably do a better job.

Using real drummers is by far the best way to get exactly what you're looking for in a groove, but unfortunately there are many times when that is simply not an option in my world. I like to work with drummers who can play on MIDI kits so that I can adjust the groove (and even more importantly the sounds) hours after the drummer has packed up and gone home.

When you get a call in the afternoon from a producer who needs the mix in his iPod by 9 AM the next day, you might not even have time to set up a drum kit, let alone schedule a drummer for a track you haven't even written. For non-drummers, you can either program the groove, use virtual drummers (such as Groove Agent), or use drum loops or pre-recorded drum tracks. Once you've got that perfect drum groove loop, if you're using other MIDI instruments, you have to figure out how to get them to groove as well as possible with the audio drum loop.

Quantizing MIDI Parts to an Audio Groove

Whether you use a loop or a drum recording, if you record drums (or any instrument for that matter) without using MIDI, you are going to be working with an *audio groove*. Quantizing MIDI to an audio groove is not exactly a simple process in Cubase, and it's not quite a perfect science as it is when working only with MIDI. The first step in the process is to analyze the audio groove and create *hitpoints*.

Note: Hitpoints are virtual markers in Cubase that are used to identify where the accents of the groove (or beat) are. In a way, hitpoints are there to create a MIDI representation of the audio groove. Hitpoints can not only be used to create a MIDI "map" for your other parts, but they can also be used to quantize and alter the tempo (as you would a REX file) of your audio groove.

Before creating hitpoints, make sure that your audio groove is locked to the tempo and is edited to start at the beginning of a measure. You want to capture the main groove of the audio file (not necessarily the entire audio part), so cut your audio groove to fit between two or four measures to keep it from getting too complicated. Doing this will make your job a lot easier. Next, to create the hitpoints, you must first select and open the audio file in the Sample Editor by double-clicking on the audio track in the project window. When you open your file in the Sample Editor, you should see the two- or four-measure groove highlighted as well as any audio that happens before and after your selected groove.

Make sure the Inspector is showing within the Sample Editor window by selecting Show Inspector from the toolbar located just below the menus. Once the Inspector is showing on the left of the Sample Editor window, select the Hitpoints tab from the left of the window. Since you're going to copy an imperfect groove, click on the Use field and select All if it it's not already selected. By selecting All, you are specifying that you want to recognize all transient attacks within the groove (the transient attacks are the accents of the groove). Because all of the transient tracks will have hitpoints, you need to then specify which attacks are important and which are unimportant to your actual groove. To do this, select the empty field below Sensitivity. (It would be nice to see a real slider here.) By holding down the mouse and dragging from left to right, you'll see more and more hitpoint markers created throughout the groove (see Figure 2.3). This might take a little tweaking to get right, depending on the actual recording and groove. You can audition each section (between hitpoints) by clicking in that section using the Audition tool. This can help you determine if you are spreading enough hitpoints across your groove. If you need to make minor adjustments to the location of the hitpoint, you can do so by selecting the hitpoint event (located at the top by the ruler) and moving it left or right on the ruler timeline.

Once you have your hitpoint map set up, it's time to create your new groove quantize template from the audio groove. Simply select the button on the Make Groove field (located in the Inspector of the Sample Editor). Nothing exciting appears to happen once the button has been selected, but minimize the Sample Editor window and open your Quantize drop-down menu from the toolbar of the project window, and you'll find a new quantize type in the list named after your actual audio file (see Figure 2.4).

Now you can select your other non-quantized MIDI tracks, select the new quantize groove from the Quantize drop-down menu, and then select Over Quantize to make your MIDI track match the groove of your audio track. As I mentioned before, this is not a perfect science. In some cases, it's best if you use the Snap and manually move notes to the correct positions on the quantize groove. It all depends on how well your hitpoints are set up in the previous step and how well you performed on your un-quantized MIDI tracks. In the example in Figure 2.5, you'll see how the bass note has been quantized to match the imperfect timing of the kick drum in the audio groove. This type of quantize would not work with your standard quantize selections. If you're having problems, un-quantize your original MIDI tracks, then go back into the Sample Editor screen and adjust your hitpoints, create a new quantize groove, and try it again.

Figure 2.3   Creating hitpoints in the Sample Editor for my audio groove.

If you plan on using this quantize groove a lot, I recommend saving it as a permanent setting in your quantize setup. To do so, open Quantize Setup from the MIDI menu while your quantize groove is still selected in the Quantize drop-down menu, and then select Store. I recommend changing the name of the quantize groove to something a little easier to remember as opposed to using the default name given by Cubase (the audio file name). To rename the quantize groove, select the text within the name field (as shown in Figure 2.6) and type in something you'll remember. That new quantize groove will stay in the Cubase Quantize drop-down menu permanently (even on new projects). If you don't save your new quantize groove, Cubase will just write over it the next time you create a new quantize groove from hitpoints.

You can also copy a groove from a MIDI part and add it to your Quantize drop-down menu using the Part to Groove feature from the Advanced Quantize drop-down menu located in the MIDI menu. I will touch on this when I explain how to quantize an audio groove in Chapter 3,

Figure 2.4   Your new groove is now located in the Quantize menu.

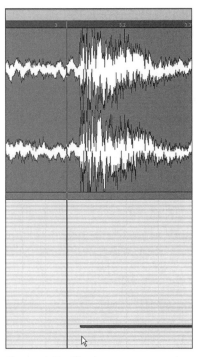

Figure 2.5   The bass now matches the slightly off kick drum from the audio groove.

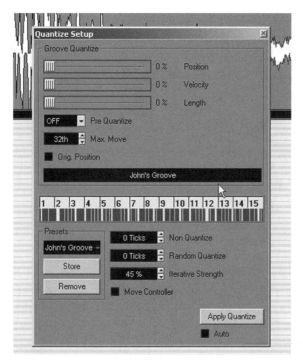

Figure 2.6   Changing the quantize groove name.

"Taking Audio to the Limit in Cubase 5." Once you learn that, you'll be able to achieve the exact opposite of what you've done in the previous exercise and instead be able to quantize your audio groove to match your MIDI parts.

Adjusting the Quantization and Feel of the Groove in Real Time

Sometimes quantizing can have annoying side effects and not only cause you to lose your groove, but also change the groove so that it just doesn't work. Going back and forth between quantizing, adjusting your quantize, and then undoing your quantize can become tedious when trying to find that magic quantize combination for complex grooves. Grooves that swing (in particular) can be a real test of your patience.

In these special cases, real-time quantization might be in order. To get real time quantization, unlike groove quantization, I recommend starting with a pre-quantized part. This means if your part is supposed to have a 1/16 note swing feel, try quantizing it to either swung or straight 1/16 notes first. This will get the quantization in the "ballpark" (even if this means losing some of the feel) using the regular automatic quantize methods. Keep in mind that you can always undo your quantization if this isn't working for you. Next, select the "e" on the MIDI track to bring up the MIDI Channel Settings window. From one of the Inserts drop-down menus, select Quantizer (as shown in Figure 2.7). As your MIDI events pass through the Quantizer effect, they will be

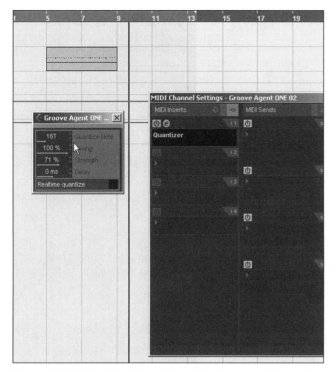

Figure 2.7   Using the Quantizer effect as a real-time Quantizer.

automatically repositioned according to the settings of the Quantizer. This means you can adjust your settings as you play back. Try to get your feel back by first setting the Quantizer to your ballpark setting, then adjusting the Swing and Strength fields while playing back. The Swing field adjusts the grid lines position, whereas the Strength field adjusts the distance between the actual note position and the grid position (the grid position being at 100% and the real position being at 0%). Both are important factors in determining the feel of your groove.

If it's still not working for you, go back and undo your original quantize and try once again with the Quantizer's Swing and Strength settings set at 0%, and then gradually adjust them while playing back. Many times you can at least get close to where you need to be with your quantization using these two methods. Once you're happy with your effects settings, I suggest duplicating your original part, and then making the setting permanent in the original file. Duplicating your original part prevents you from losing your original performance; and by "bouncing" your real time MIDI effect, you'll save your system's processor some work. Once the effected part is bounced, you'll actually be able to see the MIDI events in their new quantized positions. You can learn how to bounce these parts in this chapter a little later in the section entitled "Creating Editable MIDI Parts from MIDI Effects."

Advanced MIDI Effects and Modifiers

Since we're on the subject of MIDI effects, I'd like to mention that the actual MIDI effects in Cubase 5 have become more intuitive and user-friendly than they were in earlier versions. For those who are new to using MIDI effects and/or MIDI modifiers, let me explain by saying that these processors treat MIDI in a similar way that an audio processor treats an audio signal. Using MIDI effects can create a new sound that can always be bypassed or altered and does not affect the original MIDI data.

Even though the look and user appeal has been jazzed up a notch in Cubase 5, there's not a lot that's new in terms of added effects. The main new addition is the Beat Designer, which I will go over in a lot more detail a little later in this chapter. (More instruction can be found on these plug-ins by selecting Plug-In Reference from the Documentation option of the Help menu, as shown in Figure 2.8).

Since the list of the effects is long, I'm going to separate them into categories: MIDI Modifiers, musical and tonal altering effects, MIDI tools and controls, and programmers. Before I begin, I think it's important to understand the differences between a MIDI send and an audio send. A MIDI insert works only on the MIDI track you are activating the insert effect on (very similar to the way that an audio insert functions), but a MIDI send transfers the affected data to another MIDI channel or instrument. This means it's not designed to group or bus several instruments under the same send and share the same effect (as an audio send functions). An example of a MIDI send would be if you wanted to output a MIDI delay to another instrument so that the sound of the delay was played on an instrument other than the original MIDI track (like making the delay of a guitar a violin sound instead, and it plays the same note 1/16 note after each guitar note is played). It's not as common to work with MIDI sends, but they can be used to create some really interesting effects.

Category 1: The MIDI Modifiers

I've categorized these effects into one location because they are primarily used to make slight adjustments to the main MIDI part. These are mostly effects you could do with some simple editing; however, they automate the process and do not affect the contents of the original part. The effects that make up this category are the MIDI modifiers' effects, Compress, Context Gate, and Quantizer. I've already discussed the Quantizer, so here's a brief explanation of the others.

The first and foremost in my MIDI modifiers category is the MIDI effect that's appropriately named **MIDI Modifier**. Not only can you find this in the Insert or Send effect drop-down menu, but you can also locate the main elements from it in the Inspector. The only difference is the Insert/Send effect option of the MIDI Modifier includes a couple of extra features that the Inspector version of the MIDI Modifier doesn't (scale and delay features). Out of all of the MIDI effects, this is probably the most basic and useful real-time effect you can use, as its features act as multiple effects within it.

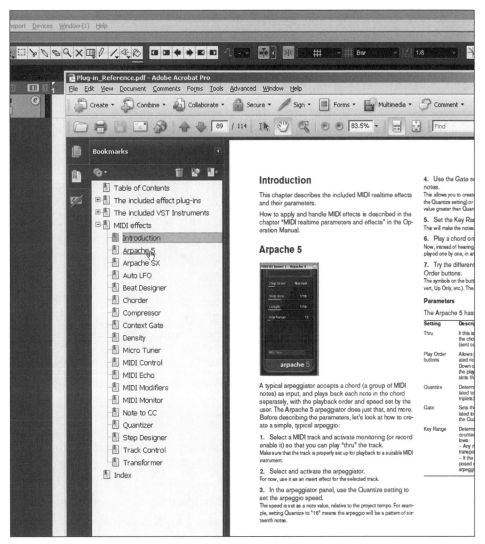

Figure 2.8 Locating the Cubase MIDI plug-in reference.

The *Transpose* feature allows you to shift the pitch of the MIDI notes (on the entire track) up or down 127 half steps. The *Velocity Shift* feature raises or lowers the velocities of the entire track without affecting each individual note's relative velocity (meaning that all velocities increase or decrease in the same increment). Keep in mind that the original notes will not be modified in any way and that you'll only be hearing the result as opposed to seeing the result. The *Velocity Compression* feature is a useful effect when it comes to limiting the range of velocity on the MIDI track. Again, the actual velocities will not be affected, and you will only be hearing the result. *Length Compression* is a quick and easy way to tighten up a performance. This is a great effect to use on instruments like bass or strings that have a tendency to overlap on occasion during a performance or recording.

The *Range* filters and limiters allow you to set a low note/velocity and high note/velocity and either limit the playing of the notes/filters within your specified range or remove any notes/ velocities that fall within a specified range. There are many ways you can utilize this effect. For instance, it can be used to remove ghost notes (low velocities) on drum parts, notes outside of an instrument's range, and so on. The *Scale* feature (located in the plug-in effect only) allows you to quantize your pitches set to a musical scale. This means that if you want all your notes to fall within a C minor scale, you can set the scale to C minor and any note that doesn't fit within that scale will be transposed to the closest note within your scale setting. This does not affect the timing of the MIDI part in any way. The *Delay* feature simply pulls the whole track forward or backward and can be very useful when it comes to tightening a mix where samples are used that have a delayed attack, and so on. This delay is not to be confused with your standard "echo" effect, although it could be used in such a manner if you're using it on a duplicated track.

Note: Even though the *Random* features are included in the MIDI Modifier plug-in, they are covered in the following section, "Category 2: Musical and Tonal Altering Effects."

The **Compressor** MIDI effect is not much different than the compressor section located within the MIDI Modifier effect or Inspector. The main difference is that it offers a slightly more "classic" representation of an audio compressor. Depending on the MIDI track or instrument you're working with, it might work a little better for you than the alternative.

The **Context Gate** MIDI effect is very similar to using the Range filter/limiter from the MIDI Modifier effect. The main differences are the snazzy look of the effect and the fact that you can filter and limit chords as well as mono parts. This is a great way to quickly restrict the polyphony of the MIDI track (for instance, change a track to a mono instrument as opposed to a polyphonic instrument).

Category 2: Musical and Tonal Altering Effects

These are the effects that the computer/dance music creators love. Most of these effects offer ways to allow the computer to randomly write the music for you. Although these effects can be a lot of fun, I thought they should be separated—if you're not into this particular type of music, then chances are you'll rarely use these effects. The components in this category include Arpache 5 and SX, Auto LFO, Chorder, Note 2 CC, Density, Random effect modifiers, and MIDI Echo.

The **Arpache 5** and **Arpache SX** are both arpeggiator effects. When using these effects, holding a sustained chord will result in each note of that chord being played individually in either an up-and-down pattern or even one that you can program yourself. You can also adjust the speed and note length as each note is played. The Arpache 5 is a slightly slimmed-down version of the SX.

This MIDI effect lets you reproduce the classic Giorgio Moroder synth effect we all have a soft spot for.

Next, the **Auto LFO** in Cubase 5 replaced the previous Autopan MIDI effect. The name changed because now the effect not only offers the possibilities of setting up an automated MIDI pan, but it also allows you to specify any MIDI controller (volume, brightness, velocity) and has the same basic effect of automatically turning a virtual knob back and forth. The effect allows you to control the range of the affected notes, waveform, density, and wavelength. This can get very complex to program due to the fact that different synths respond differently to the effect (due to parameters that aren't supported by the plug-ins). Cubase suggests you have your MIDI implementation charts on hand for your hardware synths, but even I had some difficulties using this with some of the virtual synths within Cubase.

The **Chorder** is an interesting effect that gives you the opportunity to lay out several chords across individual keys and even change chords, depending on the velocities of the individual notes. This is a great way to set up sounds like Wendy Carlos' *Tron* soundtrack and could be used as an easy way to enter chords for non-keyboard players out there.

The **Note 2 CC** effect is sort of like a very simple Auto LFO effect, but instead of having an automatic virtual knob turning back and forth, its action is more like a virtual switch flipping back and forth and that effect happens when each MIDI note occurs in sequence. This was designed to work with monophonic parts because polyphonic parts (chords, and so on) could lead to mass Cubase confusion due to the nature of this effect. Again, like the Auto LFO, different synths are going to react differently to this effect, so it might take a little tweaking to get it right. This could be a great effect for panning each individual hihat hard left and right between every hit.

The **Density** effect is also interesting and unique. You have the option of either removing MIDI notes at random, or adding MIDI notes at random from your part. Anything below 100% will have notes removed (the less density, the more notes are removed). Anything above 100% will have random notes added (the greater the density, the more notes are added).

When discussing the **Random** features (located under the MIDI Modifier effect or in the Inspector) in the "Category 1: The MIDI Modifiers" section, I mentioned that I felt they belonged more in this category. That's because they're designed to create a random effect similar to the way the Density effect works. Using this modifier, you can let Cubase decide at random how to alter a note's pitch, velocity, position, or length. Depending on the way you change these settings, Cubase could write a completely different part than what you currently have. This could be similar to having a musician play some sheet music that has been turned upside down!

MIDI Echo has to be the most commonly used MIDI effect out of all of the effects. The new MIDI Echo in Cubase is quite advanced and packed with more features than previous versions of MIDI Echo. Now the effect can be set to echo other random notes, control the velocity of the echoes, and adjust the timing, length, and decay. Keep in mind that each echo is actually a played note and all of this action can cause strange things to happen occasionally if you're pushing your system. For most simple delays, I still prefer the audio effect as opposed to the MIDI effect, but there are plenty of creative things that you can do using this effect as opposed to using an audio effect.

Category 3: MIDI Tool and Controls

I separated these MIDI "effects" into their own category because they're not really effects at all. They're tools and controls. They are only MIDI utilities or only affect MIDI like a control surface. The components of this category include the Micro Tuner, MIDI Control, Track Control, and MIDI Monitor. Since I've already discussed the MIDI Monitor, following is a brief explanation of the other three controls.

First off, I consider the **Micro Tuner** to be a utility, even though it could be used in a creative way. Its main purpose is to tune or detune instruments, and it can be used to tune or detune individual pitches within the 12 steps of a piano keyboard. This tool is almost a necessity for some types of music.

Having **MIDI Control** is like having a virtual controller to manage particular CC events without actually affecting the pre-recorded events. This is similar to playing back a MIDI track and using your pitchbend wheel from your controller keyboard without recording the track. The difference is that this is a virtual controller, and it can be automated and designed to fit your specific needs.

The **Track Control** MIDI effect is a visual interface designed to work specifically with synths that utilize the GS and XG standards (Roland, Yamaha, VST Instruments, and many others). This is a pretty self-explanatory control that is specific to these particular external synths parameters. If your synth is not affected by using this effect, it's probably not set up to GS or XG standards.

Category 4: Programmers

This category is for another group that I don't really consider to be effects. However, if anything, they resemble musical and tonal altering effects. The last of the MIDI effects are the StepDesigner, Beat Designer, and Transformer. Since the Beat Designer is brand new to Cubase 5, I wanted to go over that one in detail. See the section entitled "Step Programming Drum Beats with Beat Designer" later in this chapter.

StepDesigner and Beat Designer both have similar design concepts. The idea goes back to the ol' school way of programming in step sequence (as used with drum machines) as opposed to using a MIDI controller keyboard or similar to enter the events. StepDesigner doesn't take it quite as far as Beat Designer, though. You can use StepDesigner to create small sequences (in step time) and trigger those sequences with other MIDI notes to create a variety of patterns that will play back on command via performed or pre-recorded notes. This is similar to the Arpache 5 or SX but more specific when it comes to programming sequences.

The **Transformer** effect is similar to the Logical Editor, except it acts as a real-time effect as opposed to an editor. Even though this effect is completely different than StepDesigner and Beat Designer, it still involves a lot of programming skills to get anything to work. Since this effect is so similar to the Logical Editor, you should be able to get a basic understanding from the section entitled "Utilizing the List and Logical Editors" later on in this chapter.

Creating Editable MIDI Parts from MIDI Effects

Once you have the MIDI effect sounding exactly the way you want it to, I recommend turning the MIDI part into one that represents what's happening with the MIDI and the effect so that you can lighten the burden on your system, and you are able to edit the notes that didn't exist (before the effect was added) in more detail.

The way to do this is to "freeze" the MIDI part with the MIDI effects (modifiers). I recommend duplicating your MIDI track so that you always have the original track to go back to in case you change your mind about something down the road. You can always mute the duplicate track and keep it muted for the rest of your project. Once you're ready to "marry" the effect to MIDI (similar to bouncing audio tracks or effects), select the MIDI part and track you want to freeze, then under the MIDI menu, select Freeze MIDI Modifiers (this will "freeze" the MIDI effects, not the VST instrument track).

Keep in mind that once you have frozen your MIDI modifiers and effects, your MIDI data may look a lot different, but it might not jump out at you as a major change depending on the sort of effect you're using. For example, a frozen Arpache effect will show dramatic changes, whereas it might be hard to spot any changes in a frozen Track Control effect. For the most part, it's probably in your best interest to freeze parts that create new notes or contain a lot of velocity or CC data and to leave the other types of parts with effects unfrozen because there's not much benefit to freezing tracks that don't change. Of course, once you've frozen your tracks, you can go back to throwing more effects on the new tracks if you so desire. Figure 2.9 shows an example of a MIDI track before and after freezing a MIDI Echo effect on the part.

Advanced MIDI Functions

Cubase contains an extensive list of edit functions located under the MIDI menu. Although I went over them pretty extensively in my book *MIDI Editing in Cubase*, I think they are important enough to touch on briefly in this book for those who have skipped over them in the past. I will not provide any walkthroughs for them, but instead give a brief explanation as to what each function does. To explore the MIDI functions, select the Functions option under the MIDI menu. The options listed there are Legato, Fixed Lengths, Delete Doubles, Delete Controllers, Delete Continuous Controllers, Delete Notes, Restrict Polyphony, Pedals to Note Length, Delete Overlaps (Mono and Poly), Velocity and Fixed Velocity, Thin Out Data, Extract MIDI Automation, Reverse, and Merge Tempo from Tapping. These have not changed since Cubase version 4, so if you're already familiar with them, feel free to skip this section.

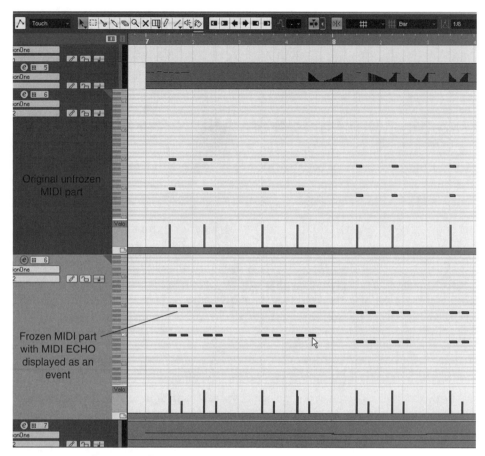

Figure 2.9 Before and after processing and freezing a MIDI Echo on a MIDI track.

- **Legato:** This function works just as you'd think it would if you're familiar with the musical terminology (played smoothly, tied together). Upon using legato, the selected note end will extend into the start of each following note. This is a great way of cleaning up a legato performance because often you'll have notes that overlap or are just a little shy of reaching the following note. Keep in mind that your samples from your instrument will only hold as long as the sample length, and there is no special MIDI magic that's going to change it.

- **Fixed Lengths:** This function is a quick way to make all your notes the same length. In many cases, there's no better way to tighten up a performance than to make those note lengths match. I find this particularly useful for MIDI bass.

- **Delete Doubles:** This function does exactly what you'd think. It gets rid of any note that may have been accidentally doubled during a captured performance or after quantizing. Doubled notes are often hard to detect because visually they look like one note. If you hear one note or drum sound that jumps out in the mix even though the velocity appears the same as the other notes, chances are it has been doubled. This function will clean up that problem.

■ **Delete Controllers** and **Delete Continuous Controllers:** These functions are pretty straight-forward as well. Using either function, you can eliminate any controller data without affecting the rest of the MIDI data and without having to open a controller lane to examine the data in the Key Editor. Once you've deleted the controller data, it's easy just to overdub new controller data over the same track. Velocity, however, is not affected by this function.

■ **Delete Notes:** This function is much more complex than it sounds. With this function, you can set up parameters that define which notes you would like to delete from a group of selected notes. The parameter options include note length and note velocity (see Figure 2.10). This is another great tool for getting rid of pesky little ghost notes that were recorded during a performance.

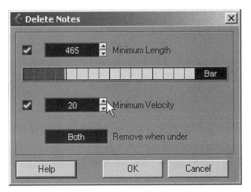

Figure 2.10   The Delete Notes dialog box.

■ **Restrict Polyphony:** This function allows you to put a limit on the notes which can occur simultaneously in the recorded MIDI part (usually as a chord). In the limiting process, it removes the notes starting from the bottom of the chord and works its way up to the top. This means that if you have a four-note chord and you want to restrict it to only two notes, only the top two notes will remain after this function has been applied.

■ **Pedals to Note Length:** This function converts sustain pedal controller events into note events by lengthening the notes that are sustained to the point where the pedal is released. This function is a little shaky because, not only does it alter the sound of the recording, but it works depending on how well your performance was with the foot pedal. However, in some cases it may be necessary to do this conversion (i.e., when you're using a synth that doesn't recognize sustain after recording with another MIDI controller and a sustain pedal).

■ **Delete Overlaps:** This function is similar to Legato, but it does not lengthen notes. Instead, it only shortens notes that extend past the start of following notes. The Mono Delete Overlaps function specifically shortens notes of the same pitch, whereas the Poly Delete Overlaps function specifically shortens notes that are on different pitches.

- **Velocity** and **Fixed Velocity:** These functions are two quick and easy ways to change the velocities of your selected notes. To correct velocities so that they are all the same (great for drum parts or bass), set the velocity that you'd like the notes to be at in the Insert Velocity box from the toolbar. Once set, use the Fixed Velocity function to bring all of the events to that particular velocity. The Velocity dialog box offers several ways to adjust the velocity (similar to the effects discussed earlier). You can add/subtract (raise or lower) the velocity, compress/expand, or limit it by setting a velocity range.

- **Thin Out Data:** This function's main purpose is to compress the data from continuous controller events. Since there are so many events that get recorded during a volume change or pitch shift (for instance) that are mostly inaudible, Thin Out Data erases a portion of the unnecessary data to save on valuable processing power, which can prevent system crashes. But this sort of a clean-up function isn't really necessary unless you are recording a lot of CC events and having system issues.

- **Extract MIDI Automation:** This function's purpose is to convert events, such as panning controllers or volume controllers, into automation lanes that work under your MIDI track in the project window. Automation lanes are usually easier to work with than controller lanes and can also save some system resources. Once the controller lanes have been converted to automation lanes, they are removed from the original MIDI part. Because of this, I recommend duplicating your part as a backup before utilizing this function.

- **Reverse:** This is sort of a fun function that takes everything selected and swaps the direction of the events (multiple events are necessary to detect the change). Unlike audio, you won't hear any backward instrument sounds. This is more like a piano player reading and playing music from the end to the beginning, as opposed to beginning to end.

- **Merge Tempo from Tapping:** This function is much different than the rest of the functions. Its main purpose is to create a tempo track for an audio recording that fluctuates in tempo. This is an advanced function, so I'll wait and go over it in Chapter 3, "Taking Audio to the Limit in Cubase 5," when I discuss creating tempo tracks and the Time Warp tool features.

Utilizing the List and Logical Editors

You can easily work through a ton of projects without ever opening the List or Logical Editors in Cubase. Both of these editors are very technical and appear to have no real musical appeal. However, if you're a dedicated programmer, they both offer possibilities that none of the other editors can match, and they are very different from each other.

List Editor

The List Editor contains a list of every single MIDI message recorded in the selected part in the order that it happens. This includes Note On and Note Off events, pitchbend or aftertouch

MIDI messages, and so on. You can edit the data within the editor, but because it's so detailed, you should limit yourself only to editing here if you're looking for very specific events.

I believe the main reason to use the List Editor is for inserting or modifying program change messages, inserting text, and for editing SysEx and SMF data. It's by far the easiest and most precise way to deal with any of these advanced MIDI events.

You can create program changes in the other editors, but I find the List Editor to be one of the best editors to perform the task. To create a program change (or in layman's terms, to change sounds during playback of a MIDI part), you simply need to find the exact location where you would like the program change (usually about a half bar before the sound starts so that you can give your synths some time to play catch-up). Then change the insert type to Program Change, and use the Pencil tool to create a program change event in the desired location (see Figure 2.11). Once you have this event in place, you need to assign the new program number.

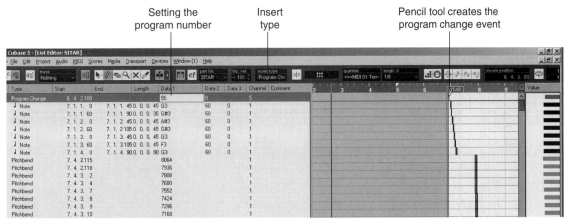

Figure 2.11   Creating a synth program change from within the List Editor.

Note: Program numbers can be confusing to work with because the numbers that are represented in your synth's patch bank usually don't match their actual program number. I find that an easy way to get around the mathematical conversions is to simply watch your synth while you scroll through the numbers in the program change Data 1 field. The programs should change on the synth as you scroll if your MIDI is set up correctly. And once you find the correct patch on your synth, you'll also have the correct MIDI program number in Cubase.

Also, keep in mind that if you create a program change event anywhere in the middle of a song, it's also a good idea to have an initial program change event at the start of the song that includes program data for the first half of your song. The reason is that once you change your sound in the second half of your song, you'll be stuck with that sound every time you replay the song if you don't have the initial program set up.

If you're using a lot of external synths, using SysEx events at the start of your project will speed up your startup time. The reason being is that you can store all of your synths' program information and other data in Cubase so that you don't have to re-program or set up each individual synth separately. Also, depending on which external synth you're using, you may be able to record the parameter controls of your synth (such as adjusting the LFO knob) during a performance. Recording SysEx events is not much different than capturing a performance (which can be accomplished on any MIDI track in the project window), but actually viewing or tweaking the SysEx data is easiest in the List Editor or SysEx Editor.

The process of recording SysEx messages usually involves recording in Cubase on the synth's MIDI track while manually sending a bulk SysEx dump from the synth. When recording any SysEx dump, it's always a good idea to leave ample room (several measures) before starting the song after the SysEx event; once your setup has been loaded, you should try to avoid constantly replaying the song over the SysEx event. The reason for all of this is that when a synth gets a SysEx message, it can be sort of like giving birth to a MIDI baby and could disrupt your system. If you want to go "super MIDI nerd" with SysEx, the MIDI SysEx Editor is the place to shine when using your MIDI Hex conversions. Of course, in order to do this properly you're going to need to get your hands on your synth's MIDI implementation charts. To open the SysEx Editor, select it from the Comments column on the SysEx message from within the List Editor (see Figure 2.12). Again, the SysEx Editor is not necessary for most programmers, but if you're having trouble getting things to work properly with regard to SysEx, it allows you the option of working with the raw data.

Adding text (lyrics, notes, and so on) along with the MIDI tracks is not something I personally do a lot of, but if you don't use the Score Editor and you just want to get some lyrics or other phrases placed along with the music, the List Editor allows you to add text in a similar fashion as adding any other event (using the Pencil tool). It's a very basic text editor. Don't expect Microsoft Word. You can, however, copy and paste words from another document type (such as Word) into the text input box. Even though you can add text here, I think it's easiest to work with text from within the Score Editor if that is an option for you.

SMF (Standard MIDI File) data is important when creating SMFs that are going to be shared universally. In the List Editor, you can specify up to 128 specific types of data, including sequence number, copyright information, track name, instrument name, lyric, marker info, cue points, key signature, and MIDI channel. If you're working with video game developers, websites, cell phone companies, or toy manufacturers, SMF data could be a very important piece to the final MIDI file you create, and this is the only place you can work with that particular data from within Cubase.

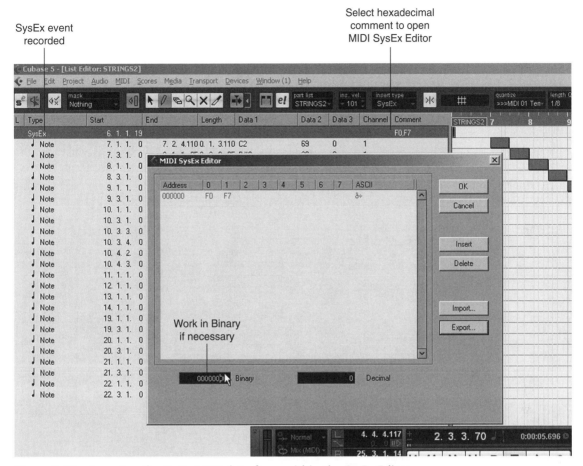

Figure 2.12   Accessing the SysEx MIDI data from within the SysEx Editor.

Logical Editor

Working with the Logical Editor is only slightly easier than working with MIDI Hexadecimal from within the SysEx Editor in the List Editor. First, you should understand that the Logical Editor, Transformer (MIDI effect), and MIDI Input Transformer are all very similar, to the point that if you know one of them, you can know and understand them all. The main difference is that the Transformer and MIDI Input Transformer operate in real time. Anyway, if you like math, algebra, calculators, and that sort of thing, the Logical Editor is for you. Working in the Logical Editor is similar to working with a basic computer language. It's a way to program very particular automatic edits that aren't included in your standard Cubase list of functions and editors tools. The Logical Editor in Cubase 5 has received a facelift from its original look. This editor is much different from any other editor in Cubase, and it is located toward the bottom of the MIDI menu.

You might be wondering, "Why on earth would I ever need to edit beyond using the many ready and available tools in Cubase?" The simple answer is that you don't have to even bother using the Logical Editor. It's designed for people who want to take editing to the max. Most likely, it would be less common for someone to start programming the Logical Editor in the middle of a recording/editing session. Using the Logical Editor is similar to setting up macros. If you're always taking the same steps when editing to get to one result, it might be easier for you to turn those multiple steps into one function in the Logical Editor. Whereas using macros can help in this matter, the Logical Editor takes it several steps beyond the limitations within macros.

By examining the presets from within the Logical Editor (see Figure 2.13) you'll see new and interesting functions that you won't see in any other editor. For instance, Delete Black Keys is found under the Experimental menu option. When using this preset function, all the notes found on black keys on the piano keyboard will be removed from the selected part.

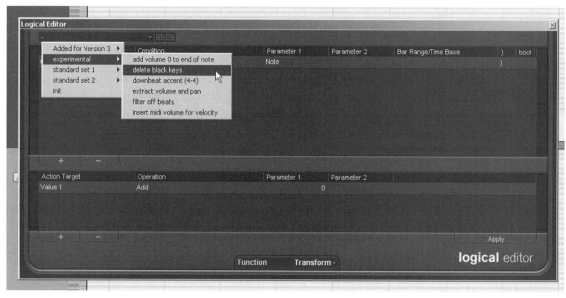

Figure 2.13 The presets found in the Logical Editor.

You can look at the Logical Editor as another completely different program within Cubase. It's a program designed to create edit functions. If you just want to experiment with creating some new functions, I recommend starting with some of the presets that are already available and adjusting the variables found within them. The Cubase manual has a whole chapter dedicated to this editor, so you can find more details there if you would like to dive deeper into this powerful tool. Just as most prefer working in Windows as opposed to working in DOS, any edit you can perform in the Logical Editor can be performed by using the other editors. It's just that it might be faster and easier to achieve results (including real-time results) by using the Logical Editor (or Transformer) if you have a preset function created to do the monotonous work for you. All that being said, if you get a headache even thinking about the Logical Editor (don't worry, you're not alone), then maybe you're better off sticking to editing without the shortcuts that the Logical Editor can provide. There is no right or wrong way to work in Cubase. As mentioned before, there are just different ways to get to the same result.

Automating MIDI in the Project Window

Since you're probably already familiar with mixing in Cubase, you are most likely also familiar with the automation lanes in the project window. If you're not, you will learn a little more about them in Chapter 4, "Mastering the Art of Mixing in Cubase 5." What you might not have known is that these same lanes are available for automating changes in your MIDI tracks as well. I mentioned earlier how you can use the Extract MIDI automation function to convert your MIDI data into automation tracks. Now, you're going to get a closer look at how to utilize those MIDI automation tracks and create more as you need them.

I'm sure you've probably figured out by now that the project window is where you'll be spending the most time while working on your project. Since this is the case, why not utilize all the features you possibly can without having to open other editors? The automation lanes for MIDI tracks replace almost everything you need to do in a standard controller lane within the Key Editor and make it easier to compare alongside your audio tracks all from within the project window. Once you've mastered the automation lanes, you'll probably spend a lot less time looking at controller lanes.

By default, after selecting Show Automation Lane under a MIDI track in the project window, you should see the MIDI volume automation lane (see Figure 2.14). To see more MIDI automation lanes, simply add more lanes by selecting the plus sign (+) located on each additional lane (see Figure 2.15).

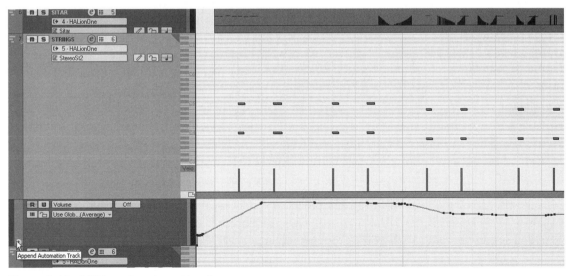

Figure 2.14 MIDI track automation lane.

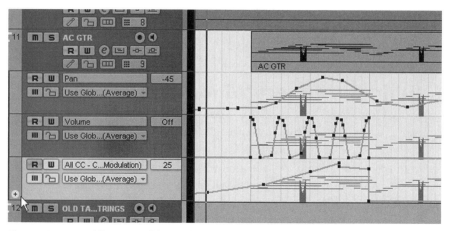

Figure 2.15 Adding an additional MIDI track automation lane.

MIDI parts can have controller events (such as pitchbend, volume changes, or panning) recorded along with them. This makes working with automation in the project window a little confusing because you can have a combination of parts that already contain controller events mixed with newly created track automation from within the project window. This can confuse the program when it comes to calculating accurate results. Because of this, you need to define how you would like Cubase to handle the automation. You have five options. You can preset particular controllers to always default to a certain setup in the MIDI Controller Automation Setup dialog box (see Figure 2.16), which is found by selecting MIDI Controller Automation Setup from the MIDI menu. You can choose to have Cubase respond to the part automation (in two separate ways) as a priority, and then switch to track automation when parts end. You can choose a hybrid method that calculates an average combination between the part and track automation. Or you can choose to combine the two so that the automation track lane accentuates the part automation if it's adjusted.

Unfortunately, there's no simple answer as to which mode you should always use because it really depends on what you've already recorded and the type of controller events that you've used. Some methods simply work better than others for certain controller types, and if you have automation on the track as well as the part, there can be conflicts if your settings aren't adjusted. All five options should work to some degree no matter which you choose. If you're not too picky, you could probably get by just using the Average setting most of the time. Select one of these five options from the Automation Merge Mode drop-down menu that's located below the Controller Selection drop-down menu (see Figure 2.17).

Using the Controller Selection drop-down menu, you'll be able to automate any standard controller as well as the MIDI Modifier, and even the parameters of the MIDI effects. Unfortunately, you're still stuck with editing pitchbend in a controller lane in the Key Editor or In-Place Editor because it's not yet available in the automation lane, as are most of the other controllers. It's also still easier to adjust individual note velocities from within a controller lane in

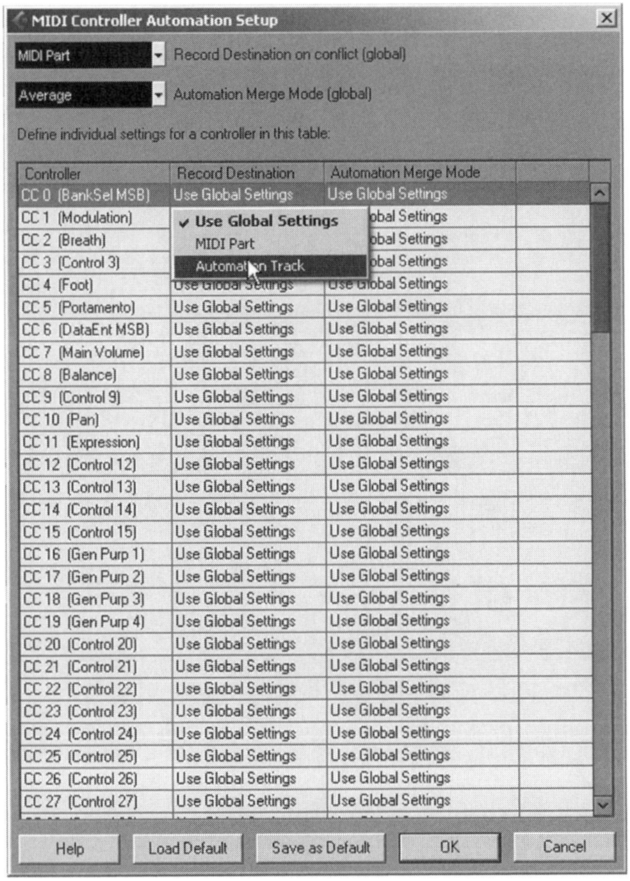

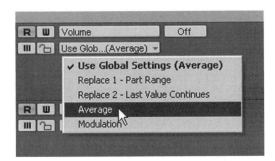

Figure 2.16 The MIDI Controller Automation Setup dialog box.

Figure 2.17 The Automation Merge Mode drop-down menu.

the Key Editor or In-Place Editor if the need arises. Figure 2.18 displays an example of using MIDI track automation to control the step size of the Arpache 5. Figure 2.19 shows an example of automating some panning alongside the other automated effect.

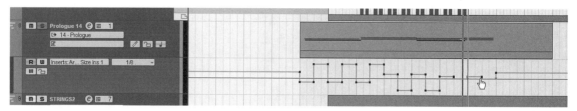

Figure 2.18 Automating a MIDI effect in an automation lane.

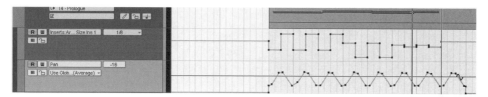

Figure 2.19 Automating a pan on another automation lane for the same MIDI track.

Using LoopMash to Take Your Old Loops to New and Interesting Places

Cubase 5 introduced its users to a new toy, particularly for those who can't get enough out of their loop library. LoopMash is similar to a multitrack REX player. It's like taking your old loops and throwing them into a blender to make a new weird beat cocktail.

If you're already familiar with REX players (or ReCycle files), the LoopMash will probably look pretty familiar to you. If you're not familiar with REX files, the concept is very similar to the way you created your own quantize groove out of an imperfect drum loop earlier in this chapter. Basically, a REX file divides an audio file by its transient attacks, therefore defining the tempo and beat of a groove whether it's in perfect time or not. This technology was brought to us by Propellerhead (for those of you familiar with their Reason software) and Steinberg way back around 1991 in a program called ReCycle. Anyway, this technology works wonders with loops, and it's also the first format that allowed us to use loops recorded at one tempo and play them back at just about any tempo. REX is sort of an audio/MIDI hybrid format.

Note: To clear things up, Cubase doesn't really create REX (or REX2) files. It just creates something a lot like a REX file but that only works within Cubase. If you really want to create REX files, you need to purchase and use ReCycle. Actual REX files that are loaded into Cubase are converted to Cubase's own REX-like format.

LoopMash not only has the ability to instantly convert any audio file into a sliced file, but it also analyzes the beat and sound of the file. When dropping in multiple audio loops, it considers one loop to be the master loop, and then uses elements from the other loops to change the color of the sound of the original loop. It actually tries to replace snare drums with other snare drums or sounds in the same general timbre, and it also tries to find similar grooves from other files to replace the original grooves. Even though it appears to be a pretty simple toy, a lot of thought went into its design. There's no other VST plug-in in Cubase that can be compared to LoopMash.

Now keep in mind that throwing an old shoe, a can of spinach, and a frog into a blender might not make a delicious piña colada in the end. The art of using LoopMash is similar to the art of cooking—it's all about using the right ingredients and how you mix them up. If you want to read more about LoopMash from the Cubase manual before you start my walkthrough, you can find a couple pages of info in the Help menu: select Documentation > Plug-In Reference > The Included VST Instruments > LoopMash.

Editing Loops Within LoopMash

Since I've gone over the MediaBay and organizing your loops, you should be able to load some loops on your system. After opening the MediaBay, locate LoopMash in your VST instruments and create a MIDI track for it as well. When LoopMash appears, select the Edit button. Search for three drum loops in your library that you know are different enough from each other and you would be able to tell them apart if you heard them separately, but maybe nothing too drastically different (although anything will work). Now, drag each of those three files to separate "tracks" in LoopMash (as shown in Figure 2.20).

Now, as fast as you have transferred the files from the Media Bay to LoopMash, LoopMash has already turned those loops into sliced loops and analyzed their rhythms and sounds. Now you have to decide which of these loops is going to be your *master* groove. Unfortunately, if you don't already know which groove you would like to set up as your master groove, there's not an easy way to solo each loop in the LoopMash. If you need to audition each groove, you should start with the loop at the top, turn the slider on the left all the way to the right, and push the button just to the right of the slider. Next, turn the lower two sliders all the way to the left. At this point, you should only see the top sliced file, which should be white colored.

If you want to hear the loop at the project's tempo, select Sync and push Play on the LoopMash Transport; also push Play on your main Transport. If you would like to hear the loop at its original tempo, simply uncheck Sync, and its original tempo will appear on the LoopMash Transport; then push Play on the LoopMash Transport. At this point you will only be hearing the first loop by itself. To hear the other loops individually, move the slider of the one you want to hear all the way to the right and push the button next to it; move the other sliders all the way to the left, and make sure their buttons are inactive. Once you have determined which of these grooves you want to be your foundation master groove, leave the button active on it. Check out the bracket located at the top of the LoopMash (over the sliced loops). That bracket can be adjusted similar to the left and right locators in Cubase so that you mark where you want the

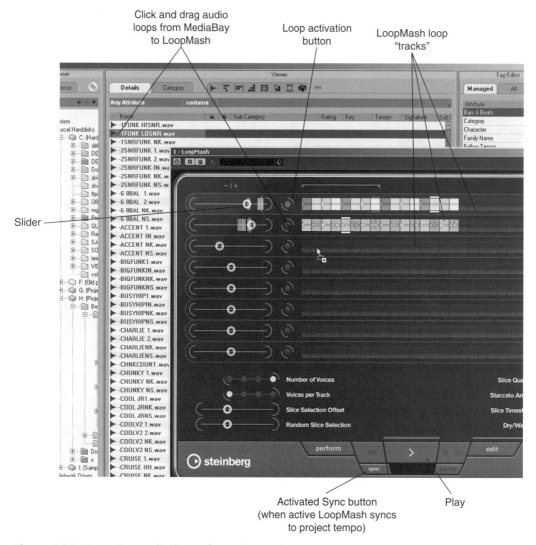

Click and drag audio
loops from MediaBay
to LoopMash

Loop activation
button

LoopMash loop
"tracks"

Slider

Activated Sync button
(when active LoopMash syncs
to project tempo)

Play

Figure 2.20 Dragging audio loops from the Media Bay into LoopMash.

start and end of your loop to be. Go ahead and set it so that your groove is as defined as it can possibly be. At this point, your LoopMash should look similar to Figure 2.21.

Now the sliders that you have been adjusting are probably the most important elements for mixing the loops within LoopMash. They work in a way similar to faders on a console mixer. However, instead of working in volume increments, the sliders work so that the higher the setting, the more elements you'll hear from the loop located on that track. The not-so-scientific way to reach the desired groove at this point is to adjust the faders until it sounds pretty darn cool during playback.

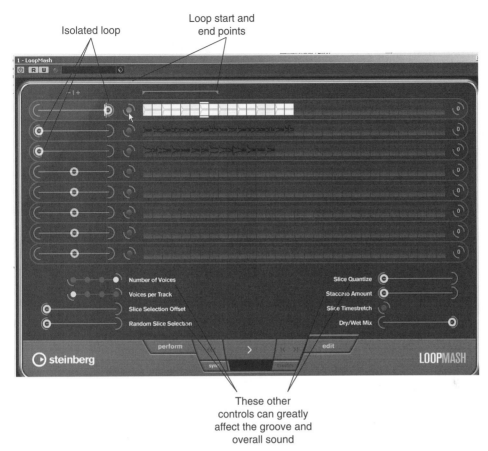

Figure 2.21   The LoopMash is set up to solo one sliced loop, and the bracket is set up for one measure.

But wait! The tweaking doesn't stop there. First listen to your beat combination. Do certain elements sound out of tune with each other? If so, you can adjust the tuning of each loop by selecting the (0) to the right of the track, then clicking and dragging to adjust the pitch up or down (see Figure 2.22). This can make a huge difference to the way the loops blend together.

Next, since you activated the Edit button at the beginning, you have access to several more controls located at the bottom of the LoopMash (refer to Figure 2.21). All of these controls can make a big difference to the sound. Following is a list of the controls along with my notes on each one.

- **Number of Voices:** This determines the number of slices that can be heard simultaneously during playback. There are four levels, but for the most part, you should keep this at level three or four to get the most out of your *slave* loops. Keep in mind that the higher you go, the harder your system has to work.

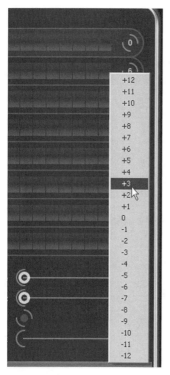

Figure 2.22 Adjusting the pitch of each loop so that they better match each other.

- **Voices per Track:** This limits the number of slices that will play from each track. To get more variety out of your loops, you should try a low number of voices per track. Remember that you can always adjust loops with their individual faders. It's normal to tweak between the individual sliders and the edit knobs simultaneously while molding your perfect LoopMash beat.

- **Slice Selection Offset:** This controls the way that LoopMash thinks and calculates the groove based on the slice tonality. The farther the slider is to the left, the closer the groove will match the original. If you move it to the right, the groove can get a little out of control (which could be exactly what you're looking for)! Even if you don't like the way it grooves when you move it to the right, you can save that particular groove as a sort of "fill" for your other groove. (I'll demonstrate more on this later when I discuss creating scenes in the next section.)

- **Random Slice Selection:** This control is similar to Slice Selection Offset, but instead of adjusting the groove on purpose, it adjusts the slices on purpose, which in turn, also affects the groove. This usually results in the groove becoming even more bizarre the more it you slide it to the right.

- **Slice Quantize:** The farther you move this slider to the right, the less human factor there is in the loops. The elements (slices) within the loops are all pulled closer to the actual grid. So stay to the left if you want to keep it funky.

- **Staccato Amount:** The farther you move the slider to the right, the shorter the lengths of the individual slices will be. This gives the groove somewhat of a gated or glitch feel.

- **Slice Timestretch:** This is a very important feature (especially when using the LoopMash at project tempos). In most cases, you'll be better off with this activated. It keeps the loops sounding closer to the original and not shortened due to drastic changes in tempo.

- **Dry/Wet Mix:** You'll probably want to keep this set mostly to wet. The closer the mix is to dry, the more it sounds like you're only listening to the master groove.

You can tweak this groove all day and night, but let's pretend that you have the perfect groove; I'll show you how you can turn it into a performance and then finally into a real drum track.

Performing and Recording LoopMash Grooves

Programming LoopMash is similar to programming an old drum machine. You set up patterns (as you did in the previous exercise) as a "scene," and then store those patterns as a preset. You can store 12 patterns per instance of LoopMash (meaning you can have 12 preset rhythm changes, but if you want more, you'll need to load another LoopMash as another VST Instrument). Since 12 just also happens to be the magic number for one octave, you can also trigger these patterns from any MIDI keyboard (or even easier, the new virtual keyboard). If you haven't already, switch to the Performance view of the LoopMash by selecting the Perform button.

The concept in programming these preset patterns is simple. You simply edit until the pattern sounds the way you want it, select the Record button (as shown in Figure 2.23), then select one of the 12 pads where you'd like to store the patterns. Continue doing this until you have all the patterns you want. If you need to delete a pattern from one of the buttons, select the X button, then select the pad you would like to delete.

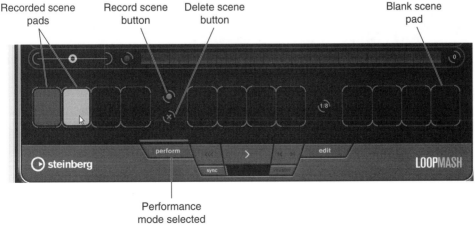

Figure 2.23 The performance view in LoopMash.

Once you have all your patterns set up, you should save your new program as a preset using the Save/Load Preset icon located at the top of the LoopMash window. You're now ready to record your new groove track.

There are multiple ways to record a groove track. I've decided to show you three completely different ways because none of them are exactly a piece of cake, and they all have their pros and cons. I figure if I show you all three ways, then maybe you'll learn something new from at least one of them! Also, you can apply all three of these methods toward using any VST instrument in Cubase.

Recording via Automation

If you would like to use the virtual pads on LoopMash to perform your groove (by selecting patterns via the Scene buttons manually during playback), you can use the W (or Write Automation) button (the W turns red when it's active) at the top of the LoopMash. Simply select the W button, push Play on the Transport, and play the Scene buttons along with the song. When you're finished, deselect the W button and select the R button next to it (it turns green when selected). Now you should be able to hear and see your performance as LoopMash plays back through your sequenced scene changes.

You can edit your performance by bringing up the automation lane of the LoopMash. To find the automation lane, open the folder called VST Instruments on the track display, then open the LoopMash folder to add automation lanes. From the list of controls, select Recall Scene. The events should be viewable on the lane, as shown in Figure 2.24. Here you can modify or erase the events if necessary, and you can re-record or add events also. You can automate every feature in the LoopMash and edit its lane using a similar method. The benefits of recording via automation are that you don't need to use MIDI; and it's also very easy. On the flip side, it's a little trickier to work with and edit in an automation lane as opposed to using the Key Editor.

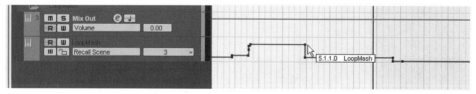

Figure 2.24 Editing from within the LoopMash automation lanes.

Recording via MIDI

If you want to record via MIDI, you can't use the fancy pads on the LoopMash. Instead, you must use your MIDI controller keyboard (or the virtual keyboard) if you want to record the pattern changes on the fly. In order to do this, set up your keyboard so that it's triggering the pads from the LoopMash, then record your MIDI as you would any MIDI track. Once you're finished, simply treat the scene (pattern) changes as notes and edit them as you would any note in the MIDI Editor. There are many advantages to recording with MIDI, and for the LoopMash in particular, having the ability to quantize your changes and move your notes on the grid in the Key Editor is really handy (see Figure 2.25). If you don't need to record your changes on the fly, then you can just create a blank part on the LoopMash track (using the Pencil tool), then open that part in the Key Editor and pencil in where you want your changes. Recording via MIDI may seem a little awkward to some, but because of its editing features, it's definitely the most exact and detailed form of recording.

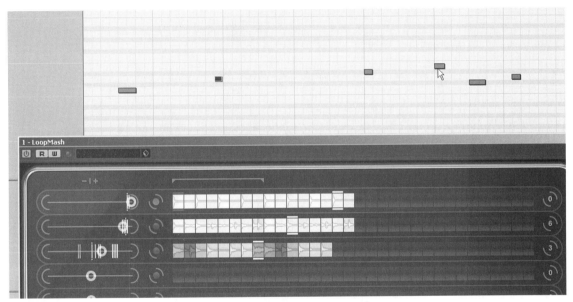

Figure 2.25   Editing LoopMash patterns in the Key Editor.

Recording Live to an Audio Track

For those of you who get very frustrated with MIDI, it's still possible to just record the LoopMash like you would if you were to plug an old drum machine into an old tape recorder and manually hit the buttons on the fly during playback.

Forget the MIDI keyboard. If you just want to hit Record in Cubase on an audio track and start playing the patterns using the virtual LoopMash pads using the mouse, you can! You just need to re-route the mix out of the LoopMash to your stereo VST inputs and then select a track and start recording. To re-route the signal, you'll need to go into your VST connections setup and create a new group channel (bus) by selecting the Group/FX tab and adding one stereo group (see Figure 2.26).

Once you have your group channel, open the mixer so that you can see the sends on your LoopMash Mix Out channel. From send one, locate Group 1, activate the send, and adjust the slider at about 3/4 (for volume). Your Loop Mash Mix Out and Group 1 Send Out should look similar to Figure 2.27 when the LoopMash is playing back. When you're ready, create a new stereo audio track, set your input from Group 1, hit Record, and get your groove on.

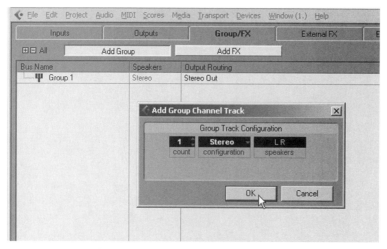

Figure 2.26 Adding a group channel under VST connections.

Figure 2.27 Adjusting the Loop Mash Mix Out and Group send from within the VST mixer.

Note: Starting and stopping LoopMash (or any other drum machine–type plug-in) during the recording process can be a little tricky because as soon as you hit Play on your Transport, the LoopMash will start playing. To work around this, you can program it to start at a certain place by selecting Play manually on the LoopMash after playback has been activated on the Transport, preprogram a play start point with automation or MIDI, or create a blank scene pad (with no beat) that can be added in LoopMash as the start of the sequence.

When you're finished, I recommend bouncing your track (exporting) to an audio track (unless you've recorded to an audio track to start with). To do so, solo the LoopMash track, and then select Export Audio. Once you have LoopMash in audio form, you can edit and take the groove to places that aren't possible from working only within the VST Instrument channel. You can also freeze LoopMash, as you can any effect, to save processing power on your CPU or simply disable LoopMash after you've created your audio file. To learn more about the process of freezing VST instruments and effects, refer to Chapter 12 of the Cubase manual.

Using Groove Agent ONE with the MediaBay

Since we're on the topic of drums, let's take a closer look at Cubase 5's new Groove Agent ONE VST instrument. If you're familiar with the other Groove Agents, they're a lot different than Groove Agent ONE. Groove Agent ONE is simply a sample player with an emphasis on drum sounds. Unlike a drum machine, it doesn't include patterns; and you can't create patterns with it as you can when using the LoopMash. Like LoopMash and the other VST instruments, Groove Agent ONE comes with a nice assortment of presets that can come in really handy throughout the creative process. You can read quite a bit more about Groove Agent ONE in the Help menu: select Documentation > Plug-In Reference > The Included VST Instruments > Groove Agent ONE.

As I briefly mentioned in Chapter 1, you can do amazing things using the MediaBay along with Groove Agent to get the most out of any sample library. Now I'm going to show you how to transfer files to the Groove Agent from MediaBay, how to spread loops across the pads of Groove Agent ONE as individual sounds, and how to quickly create a MIDI groove out of an audio loop to take your audio loops to a new place.

Dropping Individual Drum Samples into Groove Agent ONE

With the MediaBay and Groove Agent ONE both open, locate the drum sample you would like to utilize in Groove Agent ONE from within the MediaBay (e.g., a snare drum sound, kick drum, hihat, and so on). Keep in mind that you can audition your samples from within the MediaBay if necessary. Once you've located the drum sample, simply select it in the MediaBay and drag and drop it on any pad in Groove Agent ONE. Voila! Select that pad to hear your drum sample being triggered from within Groove Agent ONE. It doesn't get any easier than that! Now you can fill in all the pads with other drum sounds, and then save it as one of the preset drum kits.

You can also drag and drop entire custom-made drum kits into the MediaBay. First, start with a new blank (empty) Groove Agent ONE. If you have a folder already set up that contains all the samples of a full drum kit, select that folder in the MediaBay and then select the samples that make up that entire kit (use the Ctrl key for multiple selection). Once you have all the samples selected, click and drag the group of samples over to the E-2 pad of Group 1 on Groove Agent ONE. While pressing the Shift key on your QWERTY keyboard, drop the entire selected batch of samples onto the pad. Your samples will automatically be assigned to individual drum pads. This is a super slick and fast way to use your custom sample library (see Figure 2.28).

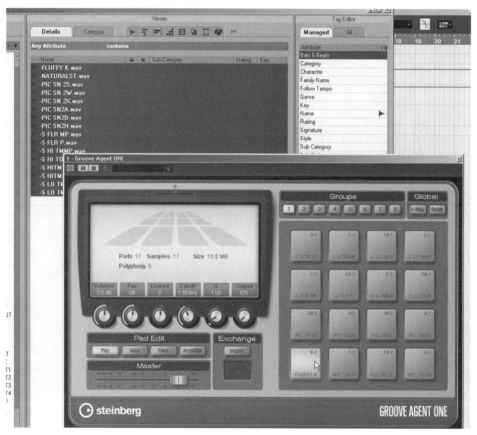

Figure 2.28   Transferring multiple samples from the MediaBay to Groove Agent ONE.

Note: I suggested the E-2 pad of Group 1 because if there are more than 16 samples in your selection, the remaining samples will spill over into the next sequential group due to the fact that there are only 16 pads per group.

Transferring an Audio Drum Loop via Slices into Groove Agent ONE

Now you can take your audio drum loops a few steps further by taking the individual sounds from within the loop and spreading them across Groove Agent ONE. By doing this, you'll have the ability to actually reprogram the original audio drum loop using MIDI.

The first step is to slice the drum loop that you want to trigger from Groove Agent ONE. Again, have both the MediaBay and Groove Agent ONE open and ready. In the MediaBay, locate the drum loop that you would like to slice from your sample library. Select and drag the desired loop to either a blank audio track or an empty spot below the tracks in the project window. (The latter choice will create a new audio track.)

Note: For this exercise, make sure that you are not using the Play in Project Context feature before dragging your loop into the project. This means you'll be working at the loop's original tempo. Once the loop is transferred into the project, you should manually adjust the tempo to match the loop. For tips on how to do this, refer to Chapter 3.

Double-click the loop when it appears in the audio track. (This should open the Sample Editor.) In the Sample Editor, create hitpoints for the loop (much like I described earlier in this chapter when quantizing MIDI to an audio groove). Once your hitpoints have been set up correctly, click the button next to Slice & Close in the Sample Editor's Inspector.

Once the part has closed, double-click it again. This time it should bring up the Part Editor. The Part Editor contains several individual sample slices (audio events), as shown in Figure 2.29. If the slices are not touching each other, it means that your project tempo is not set correctly. Try adjusting the project tempo until the slices appear as they are in Figure 2.29.

Select all of these slices of the audio loop, drag and drop them onto the bottom left pad of a fresh instance of Groove Agent ONE, as explained in the previous walkthrough. Your slices will then become individual sounds on the Groove Agent ONE pads. You can delete or mute the original drum loop that you imported into the project because you won't need it again (unless you feel you need to redo the slicing).

You can now audition each slice of your original audio loop using the Groove Agent ONE pads. While this might not seem entirely practical, from here you can substitute individual sounds from your groove if necessary. This might not make complete sense to you yet, but I will explain in the next section how you can now edit the audio groove using MIDI.

Creating a MIDI Track to Trigger a Sliced and Imported Audio Loop

For a finishing touch, you're going to take your newly converted loop in Groove Agent ONE another step further by creating a MIDI groove from it, which can be used to trigger the audio slices within Groove Agent ONE. This will allow you to work with the sliced audio file you created in the previous exercise in a way similar to using ReCycle or Dr.Rex in Reason.

Figure 2.29   Transferring slices from the Part Editor to Groove Agent ONE.

First, create a new MIDI track in the project window. Next, using Groove Agent ONE with your newly imported sliced drum loop, locate and select the arrow graphic under the Import button (it should be glowing) and drag and drop the arrow into your new MIDI track. This arrow-dragging action will create a MIDI representation of the sliced audio loops groove.

Now you can use this new MIDI groove to trigger the individual audio slices in Groove Agent ONE. To play back the slices as if the loop was still intact, assign the MIDI track to the VST instrument instance of Groove Agent ONE that contains the audio loop slices (see Figure 2.30).

Once the MIDI track has been properly assigned to Groove Agent ONE, clicking Play on the Transport should result in hearing the sound of your audio loop again. The difference is that this time your loop is actually a MIDI part triggering your audio slices in Groove Agent ONE (note the flashing pads). Now that the slices are being triggered by a MIDI part, you can easily quantize or remove any part of the groove (see Figure 2.31). If you would like, you can also replace certain drum sounds with new samples by changing the sample on the pad triggered within

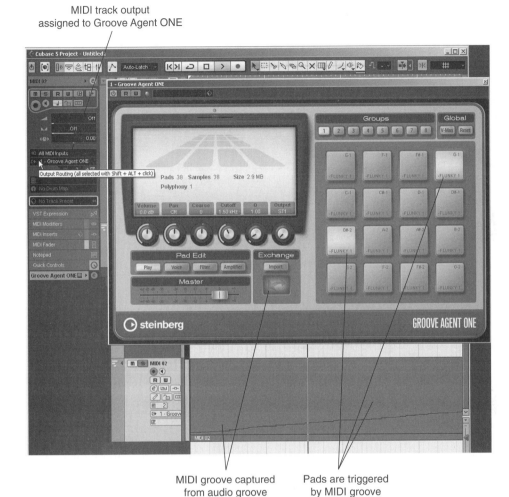

MIDI track output
assigned to Groove Agent ONE

MIDI groove captured
from audio groove

Pads are triggered
by MIDI groove

Figure 2.30   Assigning the new MIDI groove track to the new sliced loop in Groove Agent ONE.

Groove Agent ONE. The MIDI track will trigger the new samples just as it triggered the old samples. However, make sure to replace all of the correct samples because the MIDI track might be playing multiple samples of the same sound from within Groove Agent ONE.

Step Programming Drum Beats with Beat Designer

As I mentioned earlier, Beat Designer is one of the newest MIDI effect additions to Cubase, but it's not really an effect at all. It is its own program within Cubase and much more similar to a drum editor than an actual effect.

Beat Designer takes us back to the old school approach of programming beats (similar to the Roland 808 and 909 for those familiar with the good old days). As I have gone over multiple

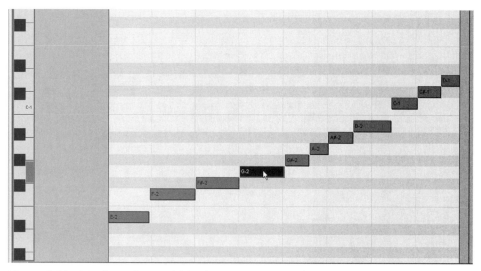

Figure 2.31   Moving a beat within the MIDI groove of the new sliced audio file.

ways to create beats already, you don't need to use Beat Designer to make your beats; it's just another option. Beat Designer handles beats differently than any other method in Cubase. It's similar to ReDrum in Reason. Obviously, this way of programming has been "reborn" because a lot of people understand its simple-to-use control surface. The Beat Designer does not actually contain any drum sounds; therefore, you need to use a source (most likely, Groove Agent ONE) to trigger sounds from. In order to do that, create a MIDI track and load in Groove Agent ONE as a VST instrument. Afterward, load one of the preset banks from Groove Agent ONE (so that you have some sounds to work with). Next, from your MIDI track, select the "e" (edit track settings) icon, and then choose Beat Designer as an insert effect. Your setup should look similar to that shown in Figure 2.32.

Pattern banks for the Beat Designer can easily be loaded from the Load/Save pop-up menu at the top of the Beat Designer window. As an alternate way of working with the pattern banks in Beat Designer, you can also locate these pattern banks in the MediaBay, and then audition them from there (see Figure 2.33). Once you have found the preset pattern you're looking for, double-click the pattern, and it will automatically create a Groove Agent ONE VST instrument track. The actual Beat Designer "effect" for this track can be found by selecting the MIDI Effects tab on the Inspector for this track (see Figure 2.34).

Keep in mind that it's very easy to load preset pattern banks from the Beat Designer, but the fact that you can audition them through the MediaBay without having to load them is a real bonus when you're searching for the perfect premade beat (or at least something close to perfect).

Since you're dealing with a pattern-based drum machine format, the concept is that you create multiple patterns and assign them to keys, which you trigger via MIDI in order to capture a performance. This sequencing method is very similar to working with LoopMash scenes.

Figure 2.32 The Beat Designer is now active on a Groove Agent ONE MIDI track.

If you follow my simple instructions from the LoopMash walkthroughs along with the extra info in the Cubase manual (located in Help > Documentation > Plug-In Reference > Midi Effects > Beat Designer), programming your sequence should be a piece of cake. The main difference is that in order to trigger and record the changes, you need to activate Jump mode, which is located in the top-right corner of the Beat Designer. Unlike the LoopMash, you only have the option of changing patterns for every bar—you can't change patterns in the middle of a measure as you can when changing scenes within LoopMash. Also, you can have up to 48 patterns per instance in Beat Designer because it uses four banks of 12 pads (four octaves) as opposed to only having access to 12 pads total when using the LoopMash.

When it comes to actually programming the beat in Beat Designer, it doesn't really get much easier. The default is set to one measure of 1/16 notes per pattern; if you want to change that, you can do so by changing the settings at the top left. To select the sounds in your pattern, click each sound in the list on the left to open a list of sounds available.

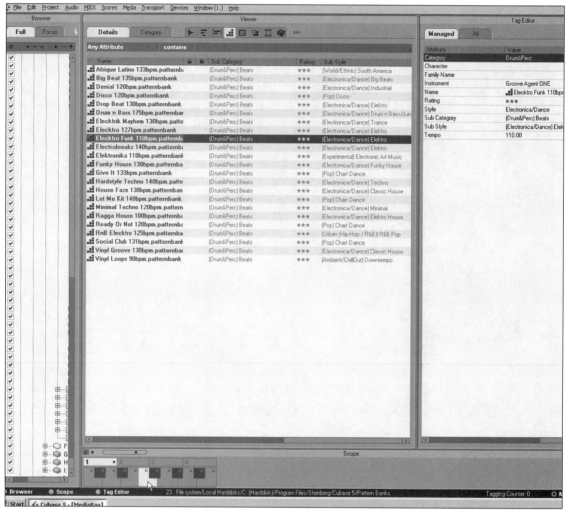

Figure 2.33 Searching through Beat Designer beat patterns in the MediaBay.

Drawing in patterns is easy. Just click in the space where you want a beat. To create an accented beat (louder), click toward the top half of the sound's track; or to create a beat with the normal input velocity, select toward the bottom of the sound's track. If you change your mind, click on the note again, and it'll be gone. You can solo each sound's track while playing the pattern in order to focus on the particular sound you're working with. You can insert up to three flams within each beat to give certain beats that extra little punch by clicking in the lower left portion of each beat. The flam's position and level are both adjustable by using the sliders located at the bottom left. One super cool feature is the ability to have two different swing settings; and then on top of that, you have the ability to adjust each individual sound in the pattern's swing. This can really add some character to the overall groove (see Figure 2.35).

Figure 2.34   Working with the Beat Designer on a VST instrument track created through the MediaBay.

Figure 2.35   Adding some swing to the hihats in a preset groove.

Figure 2.36 Inserting Beat Designer patterns into a VST instrument track using Insert Subbank at Cursor.

You have more options available in the top-left menu (the arrow pointing down) in the Beat Designer (see Figure 2.36). Most of these are fairly straightforward, but here's a quick breakdown as to what each function does:

- **Shift Left:** Simply moves the entire groove to the left one increment. The first beat moves to the last position. This is great for repositioning the start and end of the pattern loop.

- **Shift Right:** This is the exact opposite of Shift Left.

- **Reverse:** Similar to the MIDI function, this just flips the events around and starts with the events at the end. It does not create backward-sounding samples.

- **Copy Pattern:** Exactly as it sounds. This makes a duplicate of the entire pattern to the Clipboard for pasting.

- **Paste Pattern:** Allows you to put your duplicate in a new location.

- **Clear Pattern:** Wipes the pattern you're viewing clean so you can start fresh.

- **Insert Pattern at Cursor:** This handy little feature takes the pattern that is currently visible and creates either a MIDI part representation on the MIDI track (if you're working on a

MIDI track) or an audio part representation on the VST instrument track (if you used the VST instrument method). This allows you to easily edit the loop like any MIDI part. Using this method, the one bar pattern is placed at the cursor location on the track you're using.

- **Insert Subbank at Cursor:** This is even more useful than Insert Pattern at Cursor because it inserts every pattern that is within the currently selected bank (up to 12 patterns total) into the MIDI or VST instrument track at the cursor location. Once all your patterns are located on a MIDI track, you can edit their arrangement however you like without the need for programming changes.

- **Insert Pattern at Left Locator:** Exactly the same as Insert Pattern at Cursor, except it puts the pattern start at the left locator.

- **Insert Subbank at Left Locator:** Exactly the same as Insert Subbank at Cursor, except it puts the pattern start at the left locator.

- **Fill Loop with Pattern:** Fills the MIDI or VST instrument track with the currently selected Beat Designer pattern from the left locator to the right locator.

VST Instruments in Cubase 5

So far, as VST instruments are concerned, you've familiarized yourself with Groove Agent ONE and LoopMash. You've learned a lot about drum instruments. Cubase also has a great arsenal of included synths, which I could write a whole book on. If you're into synths, Prologue provides excellent classic subtractive synthesis. Spector uses a spectrum filter to create some very rich sound pads and textures. Mystic also makes some rich-sounding textures using comb filters. Embracer also works very nicely for synth pads; and when it comes to mono leads and bass lines, Monologue is usually the way to go. Whenever I need a synth sound, I'm confident that I can find or create what I need with this collection alone. If for some reason I can't find or create what I need, I use a sample of a synth in HALion ONE or its big brother, HALion 3.

I've been using HALion for years, and I'm eagerly waiting for HALion 4 to hit the scene. I've fooled around with other VST samplers, such as Kontakt and GigaSampler, and though they are all great, I personally find that HALion 3 works and sounds best with Cubase. When all my other VST instruments fail me, I'm always able to get something useable out of my sample library with HALion 3.

Even though the included VST synths are a luxury to have in Cubase, I want to spend a little more time discussing HALion ONE and HALion 3 and the differences between them. The reason these are a little more important to go over in detail than the synths is that I find them to be a little more practical to learn. A sampler can sample anything (whether it's a drum, guitar, vocal, organ, piano, or synth), and most samplers have a little synthesis added as well. Because they can sound like any instrument, they are simply more practical for most users to have in their arsenal.

All that being said, HALion ONE is not a sampler. It is a sample player and only plays sounds that have been created for it. It is currently not possible for a user to create completely new sounds with HALion ONE. For those who are new to sampling, don't let HALion ONE give you the wrong impression of samplers or HALion 3. HALion ONE is a very useful but simple sample player. With HALion 3, you can take any audio sample and layer it with other samples, lay the sounds out across a keyboard, and assign multiple sounds to several MIDI channels. You can also import libraries from Kontact, GigaSampler, Roland, Akai, Kurzweil, and so on. One setup could have 128 patches (see Figure 2.37). With 88 keys on a keyboard and using only one single layer of samples on each key (though you could use multiple), that's already over 11,000

Figure 2.37 A view of the massive HALion 3 VST sampler.

samples per HALion 3 instance. (You can also use multiple instances of HALion 3 just as you can with HALion ONE.) Imagine the full potential of this VST instrument.

> **Note:** I've mentioned the term "instances" a few times in this book. As this pertains to VST instruments, it means having several of the same instruments loaded. For example, you can have a rack full of eight HALion ONE sample players even though there is only one HALion ONE VST plug-in. Just load another *instance* of HALion ONE.

Also, other sample players that are multi-timbral (such as the included HALion Symphonic Orchestra as shown in Figure 2.38) should not to be confused with HALion 3 (or any type of VST sampler for that matter). The HALion Symphonic Orchestra is a great library of sounds, but it is still limited to playback only, and you cannot create new samples with it. *Multi-timbral* simply means that it can play many sounds at once on multiple MIDI channels. This is like having many instruments that can play simultaneously within one instrument. There are many sample players available on the market. One of my personal favorites is the PLAY player from EastWest along with the PLAY libraries. The player sounds great, and now it can be

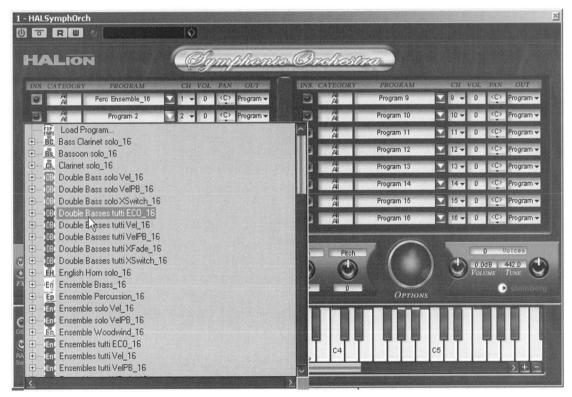

Figure 2.38 The HALion Symphonic Orchestra sample player as included with Cubase 5.

upgraded to a full-on programmable player (sampler) just like the HALion 3. Native Instruments has the Kontakt VST sampler, which is also very popular, and I've used several sample players that use their Kompakt sample player, which is very similar but without the ability to create your own library. There's nothing wrong with sample players. They're easy to use, and it's nice to have everything in one plug-and-play package. I just wanted to make sure you understood the difference between the sample players and samplers if you're just getting into them, since Cubase 5 only comes with a very limited sample player.

I've touched on the VST synths and samplers, but there are yet more types of VST instruments I haven't explored. I mentioned before that Groove Agent ONE is more of a sample player with an MPC drum machine–like interface. It actually doesn't make beats all on its own. You need Beat Designer or a Cubase MIDI track to make it really shine. Groove Agent 3 on the other hand is a virtual drummer. It's more like a drum machine and less like a sample player. Groove Agent 3 falls into a third category of VST instruments that I call *virtual musicians*. VST instruments actually have preprogrammed parts that emulate the performance of an actual musician. Cubase 5 does not come with a VST instrument of this nature. Besides Groove Agent 3, Steinberg has also come out with Virtual Bassist and Virtual Guitarist plug-ins. These plug-in types are not quite as popular for most users, but they are easy to use and get some decent results fast when you're in need.

Tips When Using VST Instruments

The VST3 platform is still pretty new at this point. Most third-party companies are still scrambling to come out with a VST3 version of their plug-ins. Steinberg sort of sets the standard for them. If you can get your hands on a VST3 version of any plug-in, you'll be better off working with it in Cubase 5. You can save system resources, automate them more easily, and overall, have better compatibility.

I've never had to use VST System Link or run my VST instruments through another computer. If you're doing some heavy-duty live recordings, I could possibly see the need to use VST System Link down the road, but I don't think most users ever need to worry about syncing two computers together in this way. Computers are getting faster, RAM and hard drives are getting cheaper, and I've had enough experience with syncing things in the past to really allow me to appreciate the fact that I can have everything in one "box." If you need to save system resources, just do what I've been doing for years when there was no such thing as system resources. Bounce your VST instruments down to audio tracks, and then disable the instrument. You can always reactivate your instrument down the road if you need to correct something in the mix. You'll save yourself a lot of headaches and never have to worry about sync issues or system resources.

VST instruments can cause major technical issues in Cubase, especially ones by third-party developers. The more instruments you pile into your system at once, the more you can expect your system to crash. Be careful when opening too many at once, and always save your work before loading instruments just to be safe.

If you ever get a stuck MIDI note on one of your VSTs (or external synths), try to first implement the MIDI reset, which is found at the bottom of the MIDI menu. This little feature can really come in handy. Using this reset won't do anything harmful to your system or project. It was designed solely to kill that stuck MIDI note.

Whenever you load a VST instrument, a VST instrument track is created for it. This is where you can find everything that has to do with the automation of the plug-in as well the audio output of the plug-in. If you want to hear your VST instrument through one of the audio plug-in effects, you can do so by activating the "e" (edit instrument channel settings) on the channel that reads Volume. (This is the output routing of the instrument.) Once you have that setting open and available, you can adjust your effects or EQ if necessary (see Figure 2.39).

Figure 2.39 Putting some audio effects and EQ on my VST sample player.

Keep in mind that this effect will be recorded to an audio track if you bounce down the instrument, but of course, it will not be recorded to any MIDI track. It can be a little tricky trying to audition the playback of the VST instrument while you're making adjustments to your instrument audio settings because both the VST instrument track and the MIDI track need to be selected, and they have a tendency to cancel each other out. It might be frustrating at times, but it is possible. Remember to use the Ctrl key while selecting multiple tracks at once.

You can also select which audio output you want to use for whatever instance of your VST instrument you're using from within the VST Instruments panel. Just click the last icon on the left side of the instrument and select the output you would like (see Figure 2.40). Using multiple outputs is great if you want to get a great mix without bouncing the instrument to an audio track first, and this is a quick and easy way to define how many outs should appear in the project window. When using multiple outputs, remember that you still have to define which sounds are routed to each individual output from within the VST instrument.

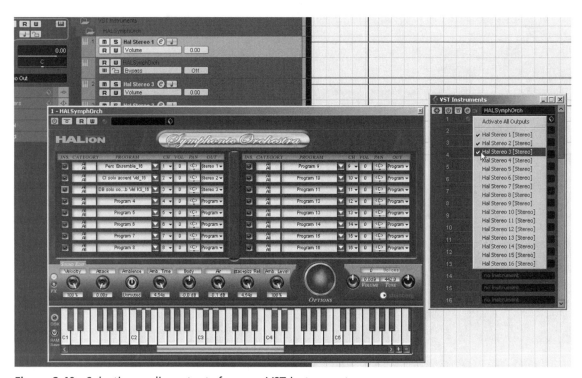

Figure 2.40 Selecting audio outputs for your VST instruments.

Managing windows can be a pain, especially if you're using a lot of VST plug-ins. In the VST Instruments panel, you can always select the second icon from the left (next to the output selection) for any instrument you wish to always see on top of the other windows in order to prevent that particular instrument from disappearing under other windows as you're working.

External synths and other MIDI devices can be controlled in similar ways as virtual instruments. The parameters of the synths can be controlled via panels from within Cubase. If you use a

Figure 2.41 Using a device panel for an external Roland MC-303 in Cubase.

particular external synth frequently, I recommend setting up a control panel for it. It's not exactly a simple process, but taking the extra time could help you get the most out of your external device. For more on external MIDI devices, refer to the Cubase 5 manual. Designing a control panel can sort of become tedious and similar to designing a website, but both the device panels and smaller user panels (within the Inspector) can make it really easy to automate those external synths (see Figure 2.41).

3

Taking Audio to the Limit in Cubase 5

MIDI is where Cubase started, but the powerful audio recording and editing tools available make it a DAW that is just as professional as Nuendo and Pro Tools in today's market.

In this chapter, I'll discuss in detail the Steinberg MR816 CSX audio interface that was specifically designed with Cubase 5 in mind in order to maximize its audio possibilities. There are a lot of choices out there for audio interfaces, but if you're a serious Cubase user, this choice can be a very attractive one (even if *only* for the fact that the MR816 CSX is the only audio interface that is fully supported by Steinberg and Cubase).

I will also be exploring time correction, pitch correction, and other audio features that are new to Cubase 5, as well as discussing the use of WaveLab as an advanced audio editor along with Cubase.

Working with the MR816 CSX

First off, there are two slightly different models of the MR816: the MR816 X and the MR816 CSX. Both are very similar, but because a few extra features come with the CSX, that's the model I'll be discussing (see Figure 3.1).

The price of the MR816 CSX is a little higher than many other audio interfaces, but since we are talking about going pro, an audio interface should be judged on how well it fits in the professional scheme as opposed to its price. I was excited by the development of this audio interface because I had previously owned a Steinberg VSL2020 and was impressed with all the sound quality and features packed into a simple PCI card. Like the CC121 discussed in Chapter 1, the MR816 CSX was built around Cubase 5; that's what makes this audio interface stand out in the oversaturated world of pro audio interfaces.

The most important aspect of any audio interface is the audio quality, and the MR816 CSX definitely delivers. When I first made the adjustment from another interface, which I liked and had gotten used to, I was disappointed in the sound at first. Then I realized that the sound from the MR816 CSX was a little less "colored" (distorted) than the other interface. After making adjustments to my mixes, the sound was not only better on my system, but my mixes sounded great on other systems as well.

Figure 3.1 The Steinberg MR816 CSX.

The MR816 CSX is a little "overkill" for me because I don't record a lot of live instruments or vocals. It's definitely designed for professional studio use, and you can interface up to eight analog XLR/TRS connectors. As with several other interfaces on the market, you can also chain up to three units together to add the possibility of recording up to 24 tracks simultaneously. The feel of the MR816 CSX is full-on professional. Steinberg didn't skimp with cheap buttons, knobs, and connectors. This audio interface is just as professional as any gear that Yamaha creates.

If you've recorded a lot of vocals with other audio interfaces without using direct monitoring, you might have noticed there's a little noticeable latency. Using direct monitoring with most interfaces will solve the latency issue, but because direct monitoring means that you're bypassing the VST engine, you will not be able to use your plug-in effects or monitor with effects. If your singer needed to monitor their vocal performance with effects (such as reverb), the process could be a little tricky. The MR816 uses direct monitoring as well, but by using its built-in reverb and compressor DSP (unlike using a plug-in effect), you can achieve zero latency; and monitoring with reverb is painless.

Keep in mind that when you monitor a performance using direct monitoring, you are not really listening to a true representation of what is being recorded. This is because when utilizing direct monitoring, you will be hearing the input bus as opposed to the output bus (which explains why you can't utilize the VST effects when using direct monitoring). If hearing a true representation of the output is a must (for instance, if there was a plug-in that you absolutely had to hear while recording), the MR816 can achieve latency as low as 1.188 ms (very low). Keep in mind that achieving this sort of latency will put a tremendous strain on your system. This means that the more you have going on in your mix (such as VST effects, EQ, several tracks, and so on) the less likely you'll be able to have extremely low latency. Although using the Constraint Delay Compensation (found on the tool bar) can help in controlling the latency when not utilizing direct monitoring, it also can impose more strain on your system as well. The MR816 and Cubase 5 are both capable of running on a 64-bit system. If you choose to go down the 64-bit road, you can utilize more RAM on your system. More RAM means that you'll be more likely to achieve lower latency without using direct monitoring.

Unless you're recording some experimental vocals, most of the time a little reverb (in the headphones) and some EQ and compression is all that you're going to need. The MR816 CSX has that covered. The included reverb is very simple, but it should cover all your bases when it comes to having a basic "recording" reverb. The Sweet Spot Morphing Channel Strip comes in handy as an alternative to using another outboard compressor/EQ on input. Another advantage to having these two effects in the MR816 CSX is that you can use them both during a mix (as opposed to using them only during recording and monitoring). You can also save their settings along with the project (just as you would an internal VST3 plug-in).

Getting back to the idea that the MR816 CSX was built around Cubase 5, the element that truly sets it apart from other audio interfaces is the Cubase 5 *link*. This link I'm referring to gives you the ability to bus your audio inputs to your audio tracks without having to continuously reset your ins and outs in the Inspector or Device Setup window. This is an indispensable tool for speeding up the process of capturing live takes in the studio. To set up your tracks, all you have to do is select the track you would like to record on in the Cubase project, then select the input button of the MR816 that you'd like to bus (see Figure 3.2).

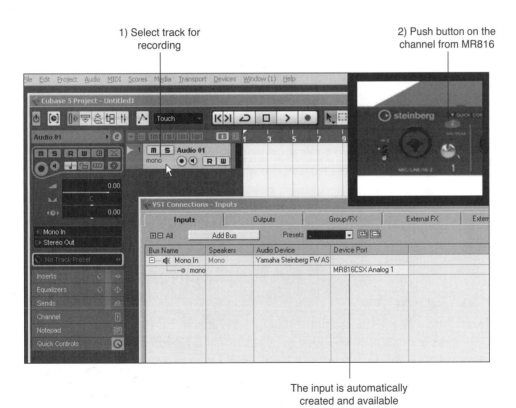

Figure 3.2 Bussing an audio input of the MR816 to an audio track.

In a case where you might want to bus multiple inputs to a stereo track (for instance, eight individual acoustic drum mics coming into the MR816 but recorded into one stereo track in Cubase), you'll need to first set up your mix in the VST mixer in Cubase in its input section, and then manually create a stereo bus (under VST connections). Afterwards, you simply send the signal from each input channel's sends to the new bus. Once the signal from the desired inputs has been routed to the appropriate bus, you can select that bus as your input under a stereo track in the project window. This method isn't quite as simple and automated, but it *is* effective and beats having to use an external submixer.

Lastly, the MR816 also allows the possibility for setting up two separate latency-free headphone mixes by using the monitoring section in Cubase 5 along with the studio sends and MR816 hardware setup window. Even though there are only two separate headphone outputs on the MR816, you can technically create four studio sends in Cubase 5 and output the other two headphone mixes through stereo outputs on the MR816 to external headphone amps. The only minor complaint about the MR816 is that there are no MIDI connections. If you're using a non-USB MIDI keyboard, you'll need some sort of MIDI interface.

Note: The MR816 can record at up to 96 KHz. It's nice to have that option, but keep in mind that although pros always strive for the highest quality possible, lower settings have been used for years. If necessary (due to hard drive capabilities), I suggest using lower settings for tracking (to save resources) and using higher settings for mix-downs. Even though the performance won't be captured at the best quality using this method, the processing in Cubase will shine through in the mix. Also, recording with compression/EQ has always been optional. There are many working pros who prefer to record using as little processing as possible as well as those who choose to utilize all sorts of processing between the recording signal and the recorder. It's all a matter of preference, and there is no real "standard" method when it comes to this sort of thing. If you don't feel comfortable using compression or EQ, you should probably avoid using it before recording it along with a performance.

Quick Audio Cleanup

Assuming you already know how to record and edit audio in Cubase, I would like to touch on a few key areas regarding file management and system performance before moving on. Keeping your projects organized and running "clean" will help you get the most out of your system and Cubase. There are a few auto cleanup features in Cubase that I will discuss briefly, but these can be a little scary to use and can sometimes lead to misplacing audio files. Nobody wants that.

As a refresher, allow me to explain how editing audio in Cubase works using my layman's terms. When you make "cuts" on an audio part, you aren't actually slicing the recording. Cubase (and every DAW that I know) utilizes what is referred to as *nondestructive editing*. Your original recording is never harmed unless you physically delete that audio file from your hard drive or your hard drive fails. Even though it appears that you are cutting audio, you are really just setting start and end location points with every edit. This means that if you like to cut and paste audio parts, you are not physically copying the audio recording (like copying a sentence using a word processor). You're simply defining that you would like that particular section of audio from your original recording to play from its "cut" start point to its "cut" end point, wherever you paste that recorded section. In other words, the original audio recording is repeating that single section of audio over and over again as it is copied throughout the song. This is a fantastic way to work with audio because you can always modify your edits later by adjusting those virtual start and end points; and you can always undo the edits if you screw up.

The big problem with this sort of editing is that it wreaks havoc on hard drives when there is a lot of start, stop, and repeat action constantly happening on every audio track. Here's an old-school example of how a DAW's audio is handled on a hard drive. Imagine your audio file is playing on a record via a turntable. The turntable is the hard drive mechanism, and the record is your audio file. Now imagine that when you get to the chorus of the song, you'd like to hear that chorus again, so you pick the needle up and replace it farther back on the record. This action is very similar to what is happening every time you cut and paste or edit out sections of any audio track. Now imagine that you have edits like this across 24 audio tracks in Cubase throughout a three-minute song. Yikes! I'm amazed at what is possible with today's external USB 2.0 and FireWire hard drives and the way they work with audio, but every hard drive reaches a point where it just can't perform the "impossible," and there's no way to accurately judge when it will reach that point. Before your hard drive crashes, my suggestion is that keeping your system running "clean" will help prevent some unnecessary crashes, protect your original recording, keep projects running smoothly, and help make the projects easier to back up and archive.

The concept behind cleaning up your audio tracks is fairly simple, and I've already touched on it in previous chapters. The key is to "bounce" edited audio parts into new, easy-to-manage audio recordings. What I will be explaining is a simple method that does not remove your original edits and again is completely nondestructive (does not affect the original recording in any way). Here's a simple walkthrough that will explain this concept:

1. Perform the edits on your audio part as you normally would.

2. When you're finished making your edits (or at least if you're finished for the time being), select the entire track and duplicate it by choosing Duplicate Tracks from the Project menu.

3. Now you should have two identical audio tracks. Mute the original track and deactivate any plug-in effects on that track. From now on, you'll be leaving the original track untouched. This has the same effect as deleting the track when it comes to your processor (meaning that it will not create any extra "work" for your system).

4. Now make sure to select all the audio edits and parts for the duplicated track (as shown in Figure 3.3). Once all parts have been selected, choose Bounce Selection from the Audio menu.

Muted original
track edit

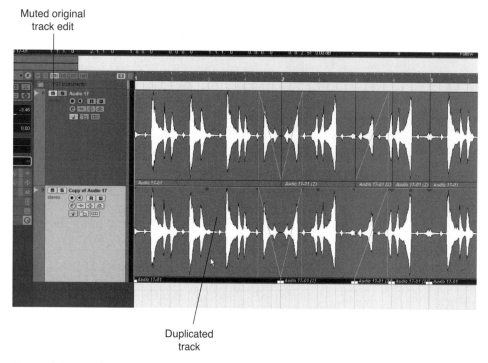

Duplicated
track

Figure 3.3 Duplicating the edited audio track and preparing to bounce the audio edits.

5.   Cubase will process the bounce and a message should appear, giving you the option to replace events. Select Replace, and all of your edits will go away; you'll then be left with a completely new replacement audio track for your original track. This track has one start and one end point (just as your original recording once had). Now when the hard drive accesses this track, it will no longer have to skip around, back and forth, across the original file (see Figure 3.4).

Keep in mind that if you need to re-edit your original part, you can always delete the newly duplicated track and un-mute the original to get back to where you were before you bounced the part. Once you've changed your edit and you're satisfied with the result, simply repeat the steps as you did before. If you would like, you can even edit the newly duplicated part and once it has been edited then create a duplicate for it as you did your original track.

If you get to the point where you're completely satisfied with your edits and you would like to remove all of the prebounced tracks, you can resave your project under a new name, then delete the original audio tracks. (Keep in mind that this will *not* remove the original audio recordings from your hard drive.) You can then resave your *project* once again under a new name. This will not affect the performance of Cubase in any way, but it should at least create a neater looking workspace.

Original edit
(untouched)

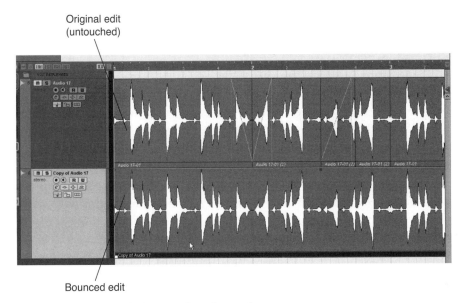

Bounced edit

Figure 3.4 The newly bounced audio track.

Note: If you have an audio recording that has several bars of "dead space," it will still save your hard drive a little work to keep that dead space within the audio track while working on your project. However, even though the unedited audio track performs better with hard drives, when it comes time to mix, you should probably edit out the dead space to minimize the chances of noise being present in the mix.

In Chapter 18 of the Cubase manual, you can learn more about cleaning up and archiving audio within the Pool window. The Pool window is where all the audio files referenced in your project can be found. If you are used to recording multiple takes, you may not be aware that even if you delete the original parts in the Project window, those original recordings are still on your hard drive and can be located in the Pool. To view the Pool for any project, select Open Pool Window from the Media menu.

When it comes to backing up projects or cleaning them up to use on another system, you'll most likely want to remove all of the unused audio recordings left in the Pool. There are many ways to do this, but the easiest is to utilize the Prepare Archive and Remove Unused Media automated features, also found under the Media menu. If you're working on multiple hard drives and multiple projects, sometimes your file management can get messy. By messy, I mean that half of your audio recordings might be in your main project folder, a few others in another project folder, and even a few others on a whole different hard drive. If you were simply to copy that project's folder and open it on another system, you would be missing half of your original audio files.

The Prepare Archive feature actually creates copies of any audio file that is *not* already located within the project folder and pastes the copies into the project's folder where they belong. Once you have all your files in one location, you should be able to easily determine which files can be removed by using the Remove Unused Media feature. After selecting Remove Unused Media, Cubase will automatically prompt you to remove the files permanently or move them to the trash. I recommend first moving the files to the trash, then playing back your project to ensure that nothing has been removed by accident (maybe I'm paranoid, but usually for good reason). Once you've determined that everything is working as it should, then right-click the Trash icon in the Pool and select Empty Trash. Once selected, you will be prompted to Remove Media from the Pool or Remove Media from Hard Drive. This is completely optional. If you decide to remove it from the hard drive, keep in mind that it will be gone forever. Since hard drive space is getting cheaper and cheaper, my thoughts are usually to just remove the media from the Pool. By doing it this way, your project will never access those files again (they will never become "missing files" either). If you need to remove the original unused audio recordings to save space (perhaps so the entire project can fit onto a DVD-R or CD-R), so be it.

Note: If you want to create a space-saving project folder (for a CD-R or DVD-R archive) by removing the unused media, I recommend first copying the archived project folder to another location before removing the unused audio recordings from disk. This is just a safety measure that will prevent you from wiping those recordings out of your system forever.

When it comes to making the final archive copy, it's simply a matter of copying the folder (as you would any folder located on your Windows or Mac computer) to the destination media or hard drive. Once copied, the project should open from its new location without any sort of hitch.

A General Overview of Audio Editing

Editing audio can be achieved in similar ways from within the project window, Audio Part Editor or Sample Editor. The project window should be utilized when you want to work with multiple tracks and parts at the same time (which is usually the norm). By adjusting your zoom level within the project window, you can easily achieve advanced cuts and splices, fade in/out, processing, and access almost every editing feature located under the Edit menu. For working on audio in context with the rest of your audio tracks, the project window can't be beat (see in Figure 3.5).

You only start to run into problems when trying to create seamless edits between two audio parts on the same track. I'm referring to a more detailed edit, such as editing a single syllable in a vocal lyric. In this case, you might want to compile two completely separate takes (or copy a single word from another section of the track) and paste it where the original recording wasn't

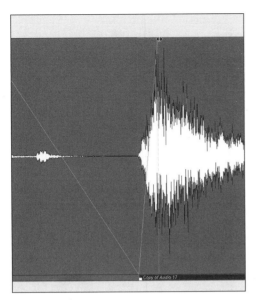

Figure 3.5 Advanced editing from within the project window.

working. In this case, you need to work on the same audio track, but with separate audio edits (at least two, but possibly several). The best place to view these edits is from within the Audio Part Editor. By default, when you double-click on any audio *event* (a part containing one audio file), the Sample Editor will open. The Audio Part Editor only opens when clicking where there are multiple audio file references (events) contained within one audio part. I find that the easiest way to get to this level of editing is to simply do a "rough edit" from within the project window (to get the edit close to where it needs to be), then utilize the Glue tool to glue these rough edits together into a single part (as shown in Figure 3.6). Once the events have been glued together into one single part, you can double-click on the part to view multiple edited audio events inside the Audio Part Editor (as shown in Figure 3.7). Within the Audio Part Editor, you can remove the Snap and change the start and end locations of the audio events and possibly create a cross-fade between the two events (if, for instance, the edit is in the middle of a held note).

Of course, crossfades can also be accomplished in the project window as well; but when you're working with such small parts in detail (such as a certain word, note, or syllable), then you'll find it much easier to make the edit from within the Audio Part Editor. To make a crossfade, simply drag one side of one event at the location where you'd like the crossfade and press the X key on the QWERTY keyboard. You can then adjust the length of the fade by adjusting the length of the event. This is a fairly simple yet effective solution when it comes to smoothing out rough patches between edits. To get an even more detailed view of your crossfades, you can utilize the Fade Editor located under the Audio menu after selecting the two events being edited together.

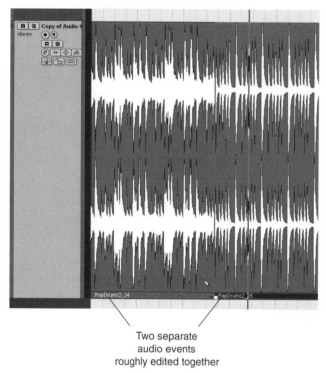

Two separate
audio events
roughly edited together

Figure 3.6   Preparing to glue two audio events together to form a single part.

Note: Here's a quick tip regarding crossfades. If you can't create a crossfade back into another section of the same event (and audio file), simply create a duplicate event and bounce it so that it creates a completely new audio file. Then use this as a way of cross-fading the event back into itself. Most of the time, Cubase will prompt a warning and offer to create a copy of the file when necessary, but sometimes you may find that manually creating another file is the only option.

You can go as far as working with multiple *lanes* of audio in the Audio Part Editor. This is similar to working with multiple lanes in an audio track. You can achieve the same results without using lanes; it's simply a matter of your personal visual working preference because you can only monitor one lane at a time.

The Sample Editor is the most detailed audio editor in Cubase. That being said, you will probably find that most of your general editing (cuts) can be achieved in the project window. I think of the Sample Editor as a zoomed-in look of what you're already working on in the project window (similar to looking through a microscope) when making precise cuts.

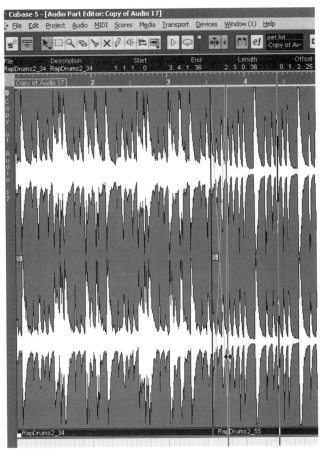

Figure 3.7 Blending multiple parts together by using crossfades in the Audio Part Editor.

Besides getting a zoomed-in view of your audio waveform, the Sample Editor is also the main access path to the AudioWarp and VariAudio features in Cubase. These features are very important to working with audio, and I will be going over them in more detail later in the chapter.

When editing in the Sample Editor, you'll be focusing on only one individual audio file at a time as opposed to multiple audio parts. I find that the Sample Editor is great for getting rid of breath noises, pops, or any other sort of noise that can happen in a short period of time in between critical parts. It's also great for getting into detail with your processing or audio analyzing tools. This editor really lets you zoom in close for a good look at what's going on. Although the Sample Editor can handle most of your detailed edits, to get even more detailed you'll have to use an external wave editor such as WaveLab, which I will be discussing a little later in this chapter.

Note: If you ever run into problems with audio pops or clicks between edits, you might want to consider using the Snap to Zero Crossing feature (located on the toolbar in the Sample Editor). This feature snaps two separate parts together at locations where there is no audio signal in danger of clipping. It's particularly useful when editing parts that have some dead space to play with.

Besides your basic cutting, pasting, and crossfade edits, the last main ingredient is the actual audio processing. You can access all the processing tools from the Audio menu. Even though processing is something you don't need to do for every edit, there are some very useful tools in this menu. Here's a quick breakdown of the audio processing features and their descriptions.

- **Gain:** Simply put, you can use this process to boost or reduce the overall volume level of your audio event. Keep in mind that boosting a signal past 0 dB will result in clipping and possible audible distortion.

- **Merge Clipboard:** This is a quick way to bounce events together, but it also allows you to mix the level between the two audio files. (One file is determined by copying it to the virtual clipboard from the Sample Editor and the other is the selected file.) While this is a quick way to mix, you can also do a quick export of multiple audio tracks (mixed the normal way), and then import the bounced audio file back into Cubase. This method might take a couple more steps, but I believe it to be more accurate in the long run.

- **Noise Gate:** This process works similarly to any noise gate effect, but it's not a real-time effect. Instead, it physically changes the audio event by replacing quiet sections (dead space) with complete silence. This can be a very useful cleanup tool; however, it could take a few processes to get the settings right. Keep in mind that you can always undo processes that go wrong.

- **Normalize:** This could be one of the most used and abused processes available. It's mainly utilized to raise a signal to its highest volume without peaking. Keep in mind that this does not compress the audio in the process; and if you have an audio event that has audio peaks and valleys, it will only raise the entire audio event's level to where the peak reaches zero and the "valley" will still remain at its relative lower level. You can also use the feature to lower the signal peaks any level below 0 dB.

- **Phase Reverse:** This is a quick way to flip the phase on a recording. Keep in mind that this is not the same thing as recording with the phase reversed on your mics, but it could help with phasing issues if you are using multiple tracks of audio recorded where the same signal has been recorded in separate places with separate mics.

- **Pitch Shift:** This can be a very complex tool for altering the pitch of any recording, but it can also be a great tool for simply raising the pitch up or down a matter of steps. I particularly find the envelope-based pitch shift useful for creating some very interesting pitchbend audio effects.

- **Remove DC Offset:** This is a utility process that does not really have an audible affect to the audio signal, but it can be utilized with the Snap to Zero Crossing feature. Basically, if you're running into issues with pops or glitches when using Snap to Zero Crossing, try processing the file with this feature, and then try snapping once more. It's not a guaranteed no-fail operation procedure, but it might help as it makes a slight binary adjustment.

- **Resample:** You probably won't use this process very often because it alters the tempo and pitch of the recording. My best guess would be to use this for beat breaks or similar effects where the beat slows down or speeds up momentarily. Alternatively, you can use this method to correct sample rates for files that have been imported at the wrong rate, but I recommend importing those files correctly from the start.

- **Reverse:** This is like playing your recording backward. It's a great effect to use on cymbals, drums, piano, and even vocals. Don't get any wise ideas about putting subliminal messages in your music, though.

- **Silence:** Anything that is selected during the process will be muted. This is a great tool when you need to keep the *space* within the part, but remove the actual recorded signal from the audio part.

- **Stereo Flip:** A very simple process that swaps the signal from the left channel with the signal from the right channel. I suppose you could use this to do some creative panning tricks, but it's mostly used as a utility for an entire audio recording.

- **Time Stretch:** This is another complex process. Since the introduction of Musical Mode and the MediaBay, Time Stretch has become more of a utility-like function used for adapting files recorded at a slower or faster tempo to match the current project. It's also handy for changing the length of an entire mix to fit within certain time restrictions (such as making a song that is 3:23 fit perfectly into a 3:30 time slot).

- **Spectrum Analyzer:** For those who require an alternative view of your audio waveform, this is a welcome addition. Instead of viewing your audio by volume definition, you can analyze the frequency as well. This is a great tool for helping you maximize your EQ settings in a mix-down session.

- **Statistics:** This is another audio analysis process that provides a list view of values for both the left and right channels of audio. This is a great tool for getting a quick, detailed, numerical analysis of the recorded audio.

- **Detect Silence:** This process is similar to the Silence process, but it also allows you to separate the non-silenced audio into individual regions, or parts (Figure 3.8). This can be useful if you need to make timing adjustments on individual notes, beats, words, or phrases.

You can also directly apply and instantly process any VST plug-in effect to the audio event (as opposed to using the effect as an insert through the mixer). Applying these effects might seem

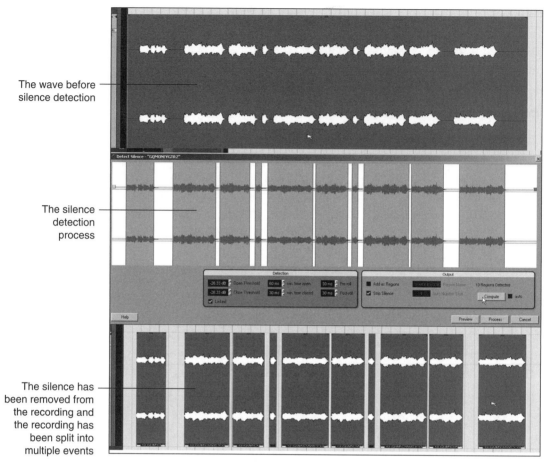

The wave before silence detection

The silence detection process

The silence has been removed from the recording and the recording has been split into multiple events

Figure 3.8 Turning one audio event into multiple individual events by silencing the dead space audio.

fully committal (as opposed to simply processing the effect in real time); however, I will discuss in the next section how you can remove effects to a certain extent. This process of "marrying" the effect with the audio part is not only a simple solution for enhancing the performance of your system, but it can also make it easier to handle the audio events if you're moving them from one system to another or archiving. To apply these effects, select them from the Audio menu once you select the audio part you wish to process.

> **Note:** The reason I suggest the possibility of applying the effects to audio parts before archiving is because three years down the road you may need to open this project again, and if your system has changed, some of your plug-ins might not be available. It's better to have the "married" effect and audio track than to not have that original effect as an option. Remember that you can always keep an un-effected copy of the original part archived as well.

Using the Offline Process History

If you haven't learned what the Offline Process History is all about, you're way overdue. As you can probably tell, I'm obsessed with saving, resaving under new names, bouncing and duplicating tracks, and archiving. Maybe it's because there's nothing more frustrating than having to shelve a project after hours of work only to come back to it later and find that it's not working right for some dumb reason. Recreating that original magic usually isn't quite as fun the second time around.

Note: The Offline Process History feature (found under the Audio menu) is not to be confused with the History feature found under the Edit menu. The History feature keeps a working list of everything you've done since last opening and saving the project, and you can undo all of your actions from various locations on that list. The irony is that saving the project actually removes its history (once you reload the project); so if you've made previous changes that you would like to undo, you're stuck with them unless you go back to an earlier version of your project (saved under another name).

Offline Process History works specifically with offline audio processing (any process that has been "bounced" along with the audio) and is more than just a simple Undo feature. Like the History feature, it keeps a list of each process but it keeps a separate list for the processing that has occurred on each individual audio event, not for the entire project. This means if there was a section of a vocal track where you reversed the audio and added a delay, only the isolated event would display the list containing the reverse and delay processes. If you process an entire part and then edit it into multiple audio event sections, each of those sections will contain the original process in its individual history list. Each individual history list can be modified without affecting the history of the other events in the project.

Note: I've previously emphasized that you should create new files as a safety measure while you're working. However, you cannot see the complete history on each individual part when you create new files because a new file has no history. So if you feel that undoing processes might be something you need to do later on, then please disregard my earlier comments about *always* creating new files.

What's particularly handy about the Offline Process History is that you can remove processes from any position in the list without affecting later processes. For instance, let's say you applied compression to a vocal track, then processed some EQ, then added a noise gate and normalized the track. After normalizing, you decided that you really should've had a little more compression on the vocal track. Instead of starting over from scratch, you can go back and modify the compression without losing the later processing. Figure 3.9 displays the Offline Process History for one audio event.

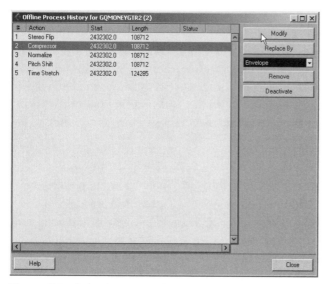

Figure 3.9 Selecting an early process in the Offline Process History.

What actually happens during a modification is this: Once you apply changes to the earlier process stage, Cubase quickly reprocesses (if necessary) the other stages in the order that they appear. Your choices for modifying each process include removing the effect completely, modifying the settings (of course the effect has to be modifiable), replacing the effect with a completely different effect, or *deactivating* (bypassing) the effect (though the effect will still be there to reactivate if needed).

Again, these processes are all associated with its respective event and played back seamlessly. Saving your project does *not* reset the Offline Process History. This means that you can go back and change processes from the project you did a "final mix" on three months earlier.

All of these features can save you loads of time in the studio, but there is a catch. There are some processes that cannot be modified due to their type and location in the Offline Process History list. Usually, it's because they alter the length of the file. An icon will appear in the Status column, and the modifier buttons will be grayed out to indicate that you're on mission impossible if you attempt the modification. The moral of this story is to do your timing processes (time-stretches) last so that they can be modified and you won't have to redo a lot of work.

Using Cubase 5 with WaveLab 6.0

I have been using Cubase with WaveLab since WaveLab was introduced to the world. WaveLab is an amazing program when it comes to working with audio in meticulous detail. There are currently three versions of WaveLab on the market, and all of them are excellent choices. I would even consider the inexpensive and "lightest" version, WaveLab Essential 6, to be good basic professional audio editing software. Assuming you already own Cubase and you're going pro, you should probably get your hands on (at least) the low-cost Essential 6 if you don't already own a version of WaveLab.

As I mentioned before, the Sample Editor provides the most detailed view when editing audio within Cubase. When it comes to editing (cutting) audio, WaveLab is sort of like working in the Sample Editor, only with even greater detail. You can work with WaveLab alongside Cubase, but you will need to use the two programs as completely separate operations so that there aren't any system conflicts. Both programs share the same audio driver, so you can't drag and drop files back and forth between the two programs (yet). For now, it's best to view WaveLab as sort of a tool for audio preparation and finalization.

Using WaveLab to Prepare Your Files for Cubase

By using the word *preparation*, I'm suggesting that before you use an audio file in Cubase (particularly one that wasn't originally recorded in Cubase), you can use WaveLab to fine-tune the audio to its most suitable format before entering it into your Cubase project. Although this isn't necessary most of the time, it does offer some benefits. Preparing audio files might involve some basic remastering (compression/EQ), time-stretching (for tempo matching), pitch correction (for transposing keys), editing loops (such as two- or four-bar phrases), removing noises (old vinyl pops or hiss, and so forth), or simply sample- bit-rate or file conversions (24 bit to 16 bit, 44.1 KHz to 96 KHz, MP3 to WAV, and so on). This act of preparing audio files for Cubase is particularly useful when working with a sampled loop library, when remixing an old track, or when using files from a preexisting song in a new song, and so on. Mostly what I'm referring to is cleaning up and converting audio files before the Cubase project import audio stage. Although Cubase offers similar tools, the tools in WaveLab offer a slightly different approach to editing.

If you're recording new files in Cubase, it's less likely that you will need to edit those audio files in WaveLab before working on them in Cubase. This is because (most likely) you're recording them as you intend for them to be recorded, as opposed to using files that weren't originally created to go within your project. When it comes to actually editing an audio track, editing audio to fit within the context of a song in a Cubase project (such as cutting and pasting parts or sections) is much easier to achieve within Cubase itself than by using WaveLab. Once all your audio is working as you'd like within Cubase, there's usually no real need to use WaveLab until you've actually achieved a final mix in Cubase. At that point, WaveLab comes in handy for some final touch-ups and basic mastering, and then it can be utilized to create even more specific audio file types (MP3, podcast, and so on) or CDs.

Besides the fine-tuning that you can achieve in WaveLab, one of my favorite tools is the batch processing. With batch processing, you can apply the same settings to multiple files at once. For instance, let's say you have 30 stereo audio tracks that were all recorded at 48 KHz, and you would like to convert them to mono tracks at 44.1 KHz. You'd also like to adjust the tempo to be 5 bpm slower than the original tempo, pitch shift the files up one whole step, and normalize everything. With batch processing, you can input a specific formula and then specify the files you would like to process as a group. When the process is complete (usually within minutes, depending on the nature of the processing), all of the files in that group will be converted. Batch processing can save you loads of time when you're working with multiple files, and it's something you can't achieve by using Cubase alone (see Figure 3.10).

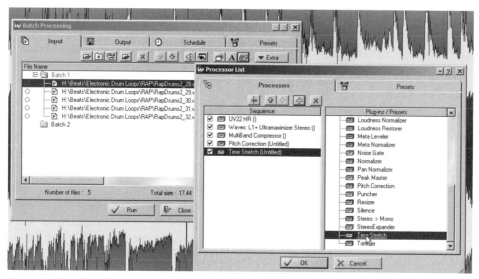

Figure 3.10   Creating a batch processing formula for multiple files in WaveLab.

Batch processing is not only a great tool for making bulk changes to files before importing them into a Cubase project, but it's also a great feature to utilize when creating your own sample library with any sampler (such as HALion 3). Another handy batch process that WaveLab provides for sample editing is the Auto Split feature. If you've ever worked with an audio CD that contains many samples of individual instruments (such as drum hits, notes, and so on), you'll often find that a single audio track might contain 10 or 15 individual samples with each sample separated by dead space (silence). The Auto Split feature (similar to Cubase's Detect Silence feature) allows you to split that audio file into segments during the silences in between the actual recording, as opposed to manually editing each sound individually (as shown in Figure 3.11). This is another priceless tool when you're crunched for time and working with samples.

Finalizing Your Mixes in WaveLab

By *finalizing* your mix-down in WaveLab from Cubase, I'm more or less referring to some basic mastering. After listening to a mix on another system, it might be necessary to make slight alterations regarding the overall EQ or compression. You might find later that the volume of the mix comes off a little low or high in relation to other audio references. WaveLab can be a quick solution to making these necessary changes. A common change would be to use a multiband compressor to adjust the overall compression in relation to a certain frequency range of the

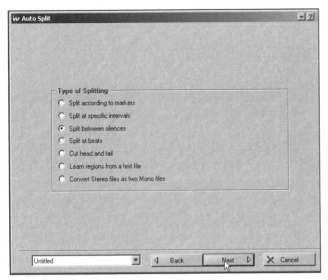

Figure 3.11 Auto split a CD track into multiple samples using WaveLab's Auto Split feature.

recording (for example, to boost the bass or reduce some mid-range volume while squashing the other frequencies). See Figure 3.12. Many pro mastering engineers would jump out of their chairs if they found out that you applied compression before handing them your mix, but if you can't afford the lofty fee of a mastering engineer and time is critical, then it's nice to have the option to make the quick fix on your own. As when working with Cubase, you can always create new audio file names and resave your work so that you have multiple options to give to a mastering engineer later on if necessary.

Like Cubase, the full version of WaveLab 6 gets deep into audio. Learning all the tools will take some time if you really want to take the leap. Currently, the program offers some of the most state-of-the-art audio analysis tools available. Again, I think that for any working pro, the program is worth owning even if you're mostly the creative music type who doesn't want to get wrapped up in the real technical side of mastering.

As I mentioned before, you'll probably end up using WaveLab and Cubase together but not simultaneously due to potential driver conflicts. If for some reason you really need to use them at the same time, you can do so by selecting Release Driver When Application Is in Background in the Device Setup dialog box within Cubase (as shown in Figure 3.13). Then go to WaveLab's Preferences section and select Release Audio Hardware When Switching to Another Application While Playback and Recording Are Not Taking Place. Though it still won't be possible to play back and record using the same driver simultaneously and the programs will not sync up in any way, but at least you can quickly switch back and forth when working in Cubase and WaveLab.

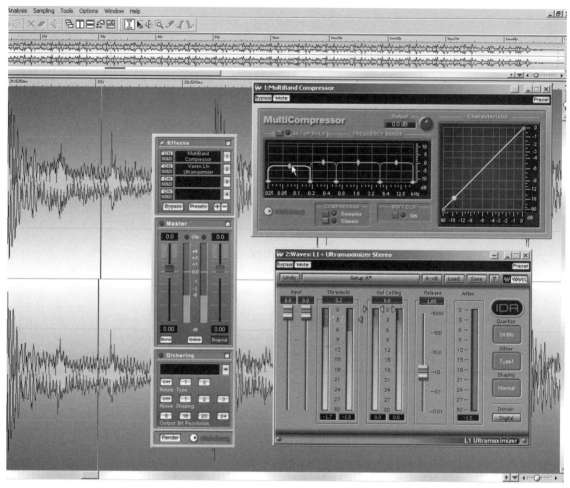

Figure 3.12 Applying some multiband compression to a finished Cubase mix-down.

Note: Another benefit to using WaveLab and Cubase on the same system is that both programs can share the same VST plug-ins. As long as the plug-ins are located within the shared plug-ins folder (in the Steinberg folder) and they are compatible with each other, they will work. Keep in mind that VST instruments plug-ins from Cubase won't work in WaveLab because it's strictly a WAV editor.

Quantizing Audio

If you've been reading this book from start to finish, you've already encountered the basic steps for quantizing audio in Chapter 2 in the section entitled "Advanced Quantize and Groove Features." Quantizing audio is really more of a MIDI/audio hybrid process. You first analyze the

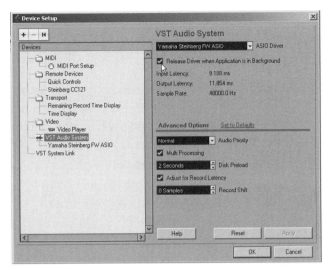

Figure 3.13 Releasing the driver when switching between WaveLab and Cubase.

audio part from within the Sample Editor and create hitpoints and slices as was previously discussed in Chapter 2.

The difference in Chapter 2 was that after analyzing the audio part, you used the hitpoint data simply as a reference to quantize other MIDI parts. This time, you're actually going to quantize the audio part to the grid. The basic idea behind quantizing audio is to get your audio part to groove "in time" with the other parts or the grid. Similar to matching a MIDI quantize to an audio track, this concept of quantizing audio is not quite as perfect and simple as quantizing a MIDI part. The process can involve some trial and error before achieving the desired result. I'm going to show you two separate ways to get your groove to play in time because, personally, I feel that quantizing audio (using the feature designed to automate the process in Cubase) can sometimes be more frustrating than just manually correcting the time myself.

The Cubase manual states that only certain types of audio files should be used when working with hitpoints based on the recording quality, production, and transient attacks of the performance. While all of this can affect the performance of the hitpoint calculations (regardless of all of those technical attributes), what's most important is the groove itself and not whether it meets the recording specs of the program. What they're really trying to say is that quantizing audio is not a perfect science and that some grooves might be extremely difficult to fix using the calculated hitpoint method. The manual also gets confusing when it discusses tempo changes in much greater detail than actual *groove* changes. The *only* reason to quantize audio is to alter the groove of a performance. If you are completely happy with the performance of an audio recording but you simply want to work on tempo changes, you should skip to the "Using Musical Mode (AudioWarp)" section later in this chapter.

To quantize an audio groove using the automated features in Cubase, you first need to create your hitpoints just as you did in Chapter 2 (from within the Sample Editor). The only difference is that when creating your hitpoints, you also need to create what are referred to as Q-points (the "Q" is obviously an abbreviation for "quantize"). The only way to create Q-points is while creating the hitpoints, but your preferences need to be set correctly beforehand if this is something you wish to do. If you've followed my suggestions with regard to setting your preferences in Cubase (see Chapter 1), then you should check the Hitpoints Have Q-points box from within the Editing/Audio section of the Preferences settings. With this box checked, your Q-points will be created along with your hitpoints (as shown in Figure 3.14).

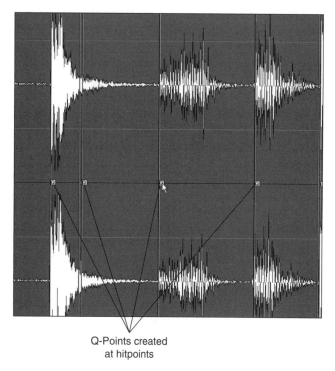

Q-Points created
at hitpoints

Figure 3.14 The Q-point is automatically created along with the hitpoint.

You should realize that even though it's a very cool process, quantizing audio is not like hitting a magic button that's going to make your groove perfect. First off, before calculating the hitpoints and Q-points in order to quantize, I recommend getting your groove to fit as closely to the grid as possible by matching the groove with the Project Tempo setting. (For more info about how to manually define the tempo of your groove, see the next section.) You should be able to compare the transient attacks of the waveform with the ruler to see where the transient attacks of the groove fall on the grid (see Figure 3.15).

Once everything is lined up as close as you can get it, create your hitpoints and Q-points (as explained in Chapter 2). However, setting up the quantize grid is not quite the same with audio as it is with MIDI. You make your quantize settings from the project window as you do when

Beats are in line with
the ruler as close as possible

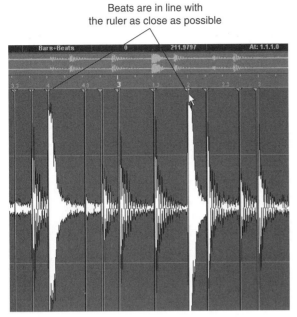

Figure 3.15 Lining up the groove to the grid as closely as possible before quantizing.

quantizing MIDI; but when quantizing audio it seems best to stick to using an 1/8 note or 1/16 note setting. Once the correct settings have been made, select the entire audio part from within the Sample Editor's hitpoint window (your hitpoints and Q-points should be showing in the window), then select Quantize Audio from the Real-Time Processing option under the Audio menu. After selecting Quantize Audio, you should see your transient attacks move to the nearest grid locations. Figure 3.16 displays a drum groove before applying the audio quantization, and Figure 3.17 displays the same groove with quantization.

The beat is not in
line with the ruler

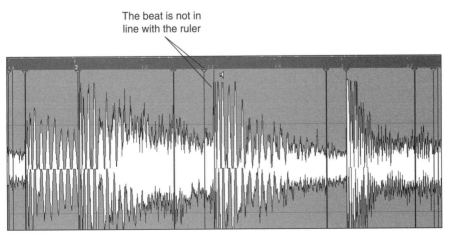

Figure 3.16 The audio groove before quantization.

Beats have been
"stretch" quantized
to match the ruler

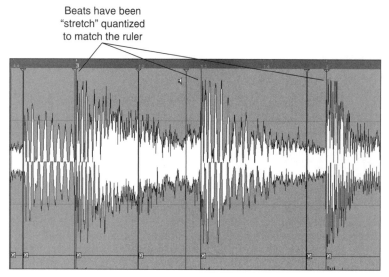

Figure 3.17 The same audio groove after quantization.

If you examine the new quantized groove closely in the Sample Editor, you'll notice some changes in the waveforms due to the fact that the individual sounds are being time-stretched in order to keep things sounding as they should in relation to the new quantized groove. You should notice that the Warping Active indicator on the AudioWarp tab in the Inspector is also lit up, displaying that the AudioWarp process is in effect. This is because what you're hearing is actually a *real-time audio process* as opposed to an edit (such as when quantizing MIDI). If you're not satisfied with the sound of the new quantized groove, I suggest undoing the process and adjusting your Q-points (in the same way you would adjust your hitpoints), and then reapply Quantize Audio in the same manner as before. If you are satisfied with the result, then I recommend "flattening" the quantization. In the *flattening* process, you're actually creating a new audio file that has been processed, and thus reducing the load on your system's processor. To flatten the audio quantize, select Flatten from the Real-Time Processing menu located under the Audio menu. (This is also available under the Process tab in the Inspector.)

Note: Quantizing audio (in general) within Cubase is a lot more limited than MIDI quantizing. For instance, by using this method, it would be very difficult to actually quantize one audio part to another audio part's original unquantized groove. In some cases, editing the audio or rerecording the audio track is the quickest and easiest solution.

There's a lot going on when using this form of audio quantizing. Even though it can come in very handy, there are times when you simply don't need to go through all of these steps or process the audio as much. If you're working with a groove where one of the beats is pushing or pulling just

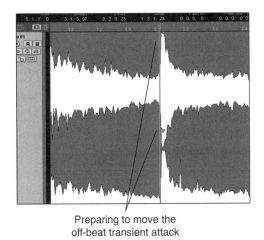

Preparing to move the
off-beat transient attack

Figure 3.18 Pinpointing and relocating a slightly off transient to create a new groove.

a little too much, there's nothing easier than simply locating the transient attack (the beat), then manually editing it and moving it to where you would like it to be. When it comes down to it, you only need to pinpoint the "problem" transient attack(s), and then relocate it to the new desired position on the grid. This simple procedure can easily be accomplished as I discussed in the previous section "A General Overview of Audio Editing." The key is in pinpointing the attack, then editing that attack from the part and moving it slightly forward or backward on the grid to the closest grid location (see Figure 3.18). In some cases, using the Snap will come in handy; but in other cases, you might need to disable the Snap feature to achieve the groove you need. Once you have the attack close to where you want it, utilize a crossfade to smooth out the transition as you would with any edit (see Figure 3.19).

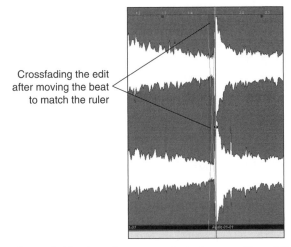

Crossfading the edit
after moving the beat
to match the ruler

Figure 3.19 Creating a crossfade to smooth out the groove.

As I mentioned before, you can also create audio slices, and then manually reposition them correctly on the grid. Working with slices might benefit someone who requires repositioning several transient attacks in a groove, as opposed to just one or two. The main purpose for working with slices is for controlling tempo changes while keeping the original groove intact. This treats grooves similarly to a REX file, which will be discussed in more detail in the following section.

Changing Audio Groove Tempos via Audio Slices

In Chapter 1, I discussed the MediaBay and the power that comes with it when auditioning and importing audio loops at the current project's tempo. This appears to be a simple process, but actually there's quite a lot going on behind the proverbial curtain of the MediaBay. The first thing is that you don't even need to know the original tempo of the audio file. The MediaBay analyzes the file and automatically determines the tempo for you. Next, it plays back the original audio through a real-time time-stretch process so that it plays back at the tempo of the current project. These might seem like basic steps for some of you; but for years it was quite a process to determine the exact tempo of your original audio track, and then have to manually time-stretch the file so that it worked and sounded correct at the new tempo. This sort of technology first made its appearance with Sony's ACID software, and it wasn't available in Cubase.

Cubase utilizes AudioWarp to make all of this possible. AudioWarp *does* affect the sound of the original file, but, it is the quickest and easiest form of creating tempo changes in Cubase; and *most* of the time it does the job with no audible side effects. For your basic tempo matching to project tempo audio file conversions, using the MediaBay is usually the best place to start.

For those who can't get the sound they're looking for from the AudioWarp time-stretch processing or simply want another solution to changing tempos, there *is* a slightly different solution that's a little more hands on. I'm referring to the REX-style groove editing features, which I've mentioned several times already (similar to the ReCycle software). By defining hitpoints in your audio file, you can then create slices. When you make tempo changes, your slices will adjust to the appropriate locations on the grid so that the groove itself is not affected; but the tempo will change along with the rest of the project, just as a MIDI part would change.

Utilizing slices is sort of an automated form of editing, as opposed to a process. When a sliced groove's tempo is increased, the slices are actually moved closer to each other. In order to smooth things out, you can also add crossfades where the slices overlap (as shown in Figure 3.20).

On playback, this sounds great. The timing of the groove remains the same, and the audio has not been processed at all (so there's no compromise in quality) when the tempo is corrected. But wait! There's a catch. If you slow down the tempo so that it's slower than the original, the slices will be spread apart from each other, leaving no room for the smooth crossfading to occur. The groove is still in time, but there's complete silence between the audio transients, which makes the groove sound choppy (see Figure 3.21).

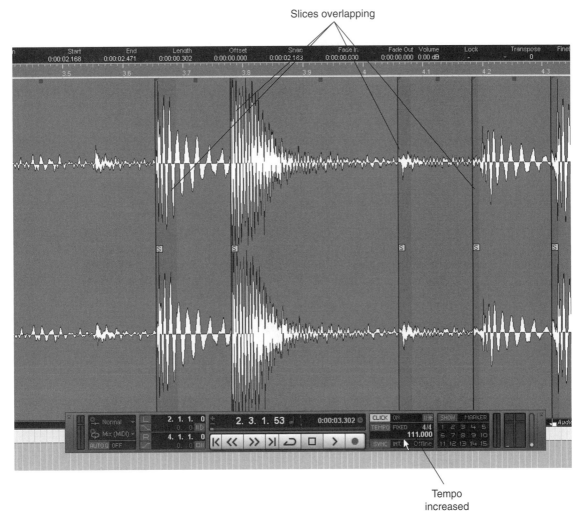

Figure 3.20 Slices are smoothed out with crossfades as the tempo of the project increases.

In some cases, the choppiness may be the desired result, but most of the time it will not sound like a "natural" effect. Because of this, the first option is to limit yourself to working with slices only when you're planning on increasing the tempo of the original file. The second option would be to go back to utilizing the time-stretch process to fill the gaps of the blank spaces.

Now to backtrack for a moment, I'd like to discuss the simple process of how I arrived at a sliced audio groove. First, I imported my audio groove (without using the MediaBay) and manually set the downbeat of the loop on the downbeat of a measure. Next, I manually determined the tempo of the groove (more info on this to come). Since this is a two-bar loop, I decided to edit it so that it was only two bars in length, and then I bounced the edit so that I would be using a completely

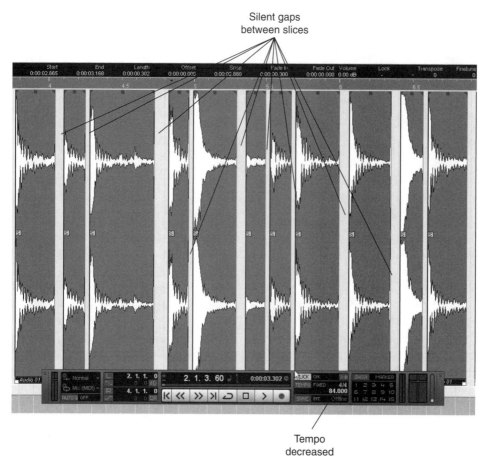

Figure 3.21 Slices are left with dead silence in between as the tempo of the project decreases.

different file than the original (because I like to work with the clean edit as opposed to having a bunch of "garbage" attached to the part, which I will never use). All of this was accomplished in the project window. After that, I opened the part in the Sample Editor and created my hitpoints (as demonstrated in Chapter 2 when creating the MIDI groove from an audio part). After placing the hitpoints where I needed them, I then selected Slice and Close from the Hitpoints tab on the Inspector. Once the Sample Editor closed, I then double-clicked on the part to open it within the Audio Part Editor to view my slices. It's using this view within the Audio Part Editor where I can see the spaces between slices increase or decrease. Not all of these steps are important in getting the same results, but I find that they help when working with loops.

When it comes to manually finding the project tempo of an audio track, there are several ways to go about it. Everyone has his own way. Tapping the tempo along with the track is a useful option. With this option you tap the space bar along with the recording (not the project tempo). The tempo will be calculated by your tapping, then you can apply that setting to the tempo of your project. This feature can be found within the Beat Calculator display located under the Project menu. Personally, I find the Beat Calculator a little clumsy to use in order to find the exact tempo. When I need to manually determine tempos, I like to use the waveform of the audio part and the tempo control on the Transport. First I edit the audio (most likely without using the Snap feature) so that it's cut just before the downbeat I'd like to use. Next, I position that downbeat (now using the Snap) so that it is locked at the start of a measure (as shown in Figure 3.22). At this point, I haven't even worried about tempo, and the only part of the file that is going to match the Project tempo is the downbeat. Now I listen to the audio track (without using the metronome) and determine where all my downbeats are. By comparing the audio that I'm hearing while watching the waveform, I can determine the exact location of the downbeats. Now it's just a matter of adjusting the tempo so that those downbeats fall

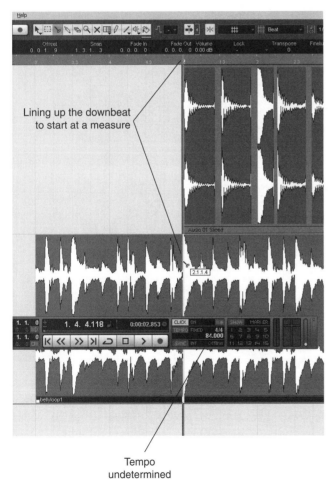

Figure 3.22 Positioning the groove's downbeat at the start of a measure when manually finding the tempo of a groove.

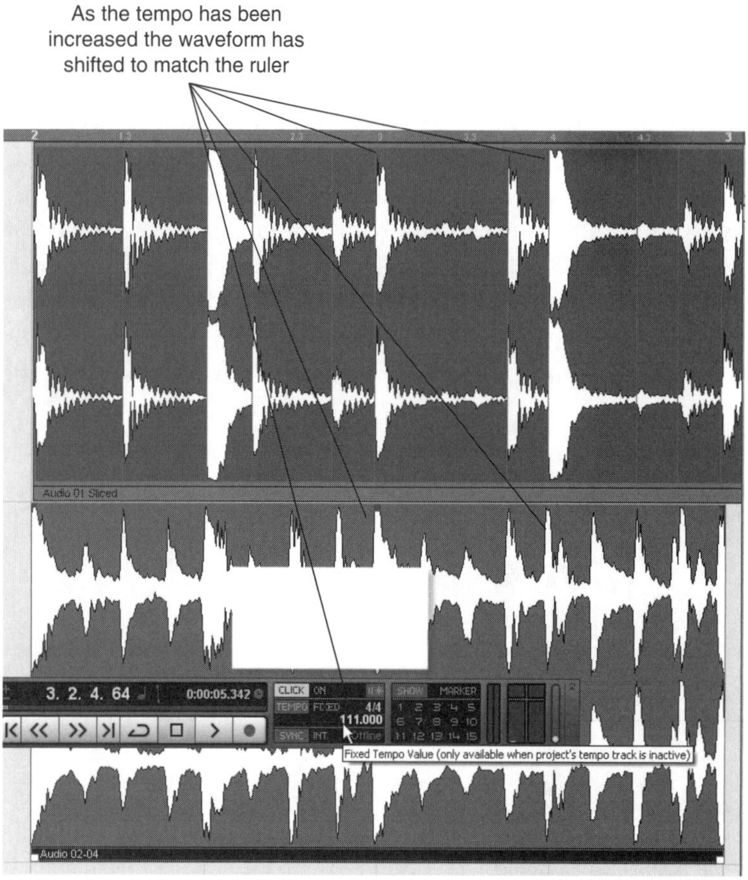

As the tempo has been
increased the waveform has
shifted to match the ruler

Figure 3.23   Adjusting the tempo on the Transport until the downbeats fall where they're supposed to.

where they're supposed to (beat one of their measures) in comparison to the ruler. I usually adjust the tempo, then play back using the metronome after the waveform is close enough to compare to the ruler, and then I make more adjustments until the tempo is locked in (as shown in Figure 3.23).

You'll most likely need to solo the track you're working with as you make adjustments because all of the other tracks will sound "off" until you reset the project to the correct project tempo. Once you've found your tempo and you have created your slices, you can reset the project tempo to where it needs to be, and your new groove will adjust with the project tempo as it's supposed to.

Now let's get back to the issue of slowing down the project tempo and having dead space between the slices of the beat. As I briefly mentioned before, the only way to remedy this situation is to use time-stretch processing (which is what I was originally avoiding). The good news is that even though this processing will affect the sound of the audio, it will (most likely) affect it less dramatically than applying time-stretch processing to the entire groove using AudioWarp. The key is to first set the tempo to match the project tempo. This will expose the dead silence between the beats. Next select all of the slices in the part, then from the Audio menu, open the Advanced menu and select Close Gaps. Cubase will time-stretch each individual slice so that there are no gaps between slices. These are newly processed audio files. This means that if you alter the tempo again, you will be adjusting the gap between these new audio slices (not the original).

If for some reason, the time-stretching effect still doesn't work for you, you can always revert to the original choppy groove by undoing the Close Gaps function; then go back to possibly adding a little reverb to the track to smooth out the gaps.

Working with Free Tempo Recordings

Who needs a click track?! For most Cubase users, the idea of working in "free tempo" (without the use any sort of metronome or meter) is absurd. But, let's face it—music doesn't have to *sound* like it was made on a computer (even if it *is*). And sometimes using the computer as you would an old analog tape machine is the only way to record a particular type of music. There might also be times you would like to remix a live recording, or sync music tracks to match video tracks. All of this can be accomplished by using both the tempo track and the Time Warp tools in Cubase.

Free tempo recordings are difficult to work with, but they aren't *impossible* to work with. After all, it's just music. Even though it was recorded freely, it's still probably in some sort of timing meter and has a somewhat predictable pattern that it follows. The difficulty in dealing with these recordings is mostly with editing and overdubbing or synchronizing with other preexisting tracks. If there is no real "grid" to follow, how can you make accurate edits, quantize parts, or sync along with the track when you don't know where beat one is? Well, just as when dealing with other audio edits, *you* have to define where beat one is; and when dealing with free tempo parts, you need to define where almost every beat is.

There are multiple ways of working with free tempo recordings. I believe the most popular way is by setting the grid to match the recording. Using this method, the Cubase project becomes a "slave" to the timing of the free tempo recording (meaning that the time base of the project is exactly the same as the free tempo recording). Once the grid matches the recording, you can then readjust the grid, which will then also adjust the recording if necessary. This method is primarily used when you are starting a project with a free tempo–based recording (or simply creating a new project with a free tempo–based recording) and you would like to edit it to a grid or add other parts later. This is usually the way I like to work with free tempo recordings because most of the time I'm trying to preserve the free timing aspect within the recording.

Re-creating the Grid Based on the Free Tempo Recording

First off, I'd like to point out that since this free tempo recording is going to be what everything else in the project is based upon, I suggest that you are absolutely pleased with the overall timing of the audio track. If there are a couple of minor adjustments that need to be made, it's not a big deal to make those changes later. If there are all sorts of issues with the timing, you're going to cause yourself a lot of headaches trying to reinvent the wheel when your best option is probably just to try to recapture a better performance instead. When working with free tempo, butchering the track with edits and processing is only going to make the track sound like garbage (garbage in, garbage out). You have to start with something that is as close to perfect as possible so you don't waste a lot of your time.

At this point, I'm going to assume that you already have an audio recording in Cubase and that you are not using a tempo setting or the metronome at all. The quickest way to set up a new "grid" based around your recording is to manually define the metronome. This means that you are going to become a human "click." Can you feel a pulse to the music track on playback? Is this something you can tap your foot along with? The harder it is to define the musical pulse, the harder it will be to set up a useful grid. First, try to define a downbeat for the actual track, and then position the track so that downbeat falls on beat one of a measure. If you can adjust the tempo in Cubase so that it's in the ballpark of the track, you'll probably be better off in the long run.

Now that your track is prepped for the grid re-creation process, you'll need to create a MIDI track to create your new "human click track" in. I suggest loading in an instance of HALion ONE (or another VST instrument), and then finding a sound to use as a click that will complement the audio recording. For an acoustic guitar, piano, or vocal track, a simple side stick sound from any drum kit will work. For a full instrumental track or drum track, you might need to use more of a pitched instrument (or tone) to help the MIDI part stand out and define the beat. Since the track I'm creating a grid around is an acoustic piano track, I've found a side stick sample on a drum kit in HALion. I've also utilized the virtual keyboard so that I can trigger that sound by pressing W on my QWERTY keyboard.

Make sure that the tempo is in Track mode on the Transport and that the click is off. The only reference you will be using while creating this human click track is the free tempo recording. Now, while playing back the audio track, record a MIDI track by simply tapping along with the free tempo performance. You can tap out 1/4 notes or whatever you feel makes sense with your recording. Once you're finished tracking a human MIDI click track, go back and edit any MIDI click that doesn't feel as though it's in time with the free tempo audio recording. The Key Editor is usually the easiest place to make your edits. You'll most likely need to deactivate the Snap while repositioning your human MIDI clicks. When you're finished editing the MIDI track, it should sound almost as though the free tempo recording was recorded using your human click (or as perfectly synced as possible). Now that the MIDI track has been recorded and edited to match the free tempo recording, set the quantize setup (on the toolbar) to 1/4 and select all the MIDI events in the new MIDI part. Under the Functions menu (located in the MIDI menu), select Fixed Length (all your notes will become 1/4 notes). This process will help to keep the click track sounding consistent. Listen back again to make sure the performance is sounding right on with the click track.

Finally, from the same Functions menu, select Merge Tempo from Tapping. A dialog box will appear asking you the value of the tapped note. (In most cases, that will be the 1/4 note unless you're tapping double time or half time). In most cases, you'll also check Begin at Bar Start. Select the appropriate setting, and then click OK. During this process, Cubase will be analyzing your MIDI reference and translating the MIDI events to events on the tempo track at the appropriate tempo. After this quick process, you should open the Tempo Track Editor (either by using Ctrl-T or selecting it from the Project menu) and view your newly created grid map (as shown in Figure 3.24). Now that you have this grid map, you should mute your original human MIDI click track and activate the metronome on the Transport. The metronome will now follow your audio track the same way you programmed your human click.

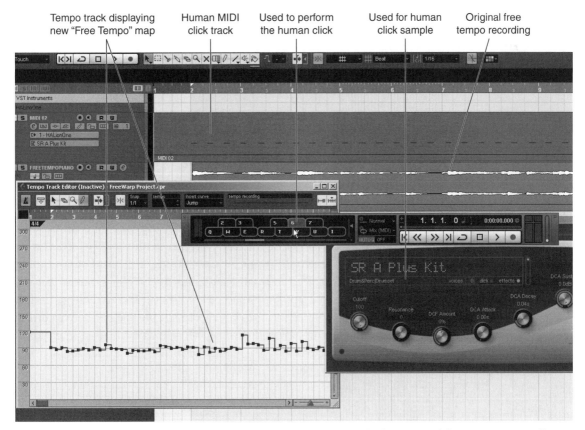

Figure 3.24   The new tempo map after being created along with the original free tempo recording.

Depending on how much the tempo fluctuates during the performance, the tempo map may vary greatly in its tempo settings. The important thing is that now you should be able to edit the audio track to a grid, just as you would edit any audio track to any standard grid. Keep in mind that replacing one section with another may still involve some slight timing differences. For these variations, you can apply some Free Warp adjustments, as I discuss in the next section. If for some reason the metronome is not currently matched up to your track at this point, you can either make slight adjustments to the tempo track using the Time Warp tool to reposition the tempo events in the Sample Editor, or you can erase all the events on the tempo track and start over by correcting the issue on the original MIDI human click track and re-creating another tempo map using Merge Tempo from Tapping.

Note: The default time signature for the tempo map is 4/4. However, just as you can change tempos, you can also change time signatures from with the Tempo Track Editor. It's best to find your tempo base before attempting to set up time signatures, and then go back and make your time corrections later if necessary. To change time signatures, use the Pencil tool to create a location for the change in the gray area just below the ruler in the Tempo Track Editor, then select Open Process Bars Dialog from the toolbar to enter the new time signature info as necessary.

Making Timing Adjustments to Free Tempo Recordings

You might find that a few notes or beats are slightly off within your free tempo recording. Now that you have a basic grid in place, you should easily be able to define where you would like these off notes to be. I find that the easiest way to make slight changes is to utilize the Free Warp tool from within the Sample Editor. The Free Warp tool is a real-time processor similar to that of Quantize Audio. The main difference is that *you* define the specific areas where you would like to reposition the notes or beats as opposed to setting up Q-points and allowing Cubase to make the adjustments automatically. Because of the nature of free tempo recording, using any sort of hitpoint calculation and automated quantize could result in other undesirable nonhuman timing issues. Speaking of which, you should also keep in mind that using AudioWarp may affect the tonal quality of the track, so be careful when applying the process. If you feel that the sound of the process detracts from the performance, you can always revert to simple cut and move editing with a little crossfading in between (as I demonstrated earlier). Most likely when editing, you'll want to avoid using the Snap feature so that you can place notes or beats where you *feel* like they should belong as opposed to where your imperfect humanized grid says they belong.

To utilize the Free Warp tool, first open the audio recording in the Sample Editor. Next, select the AudioWarp tab in the Inspector and select Free Warp so that the indicator is highlighted in blue.

Note: Even though you're using the AudioWarp tab, do not activate Musical Mode. Musical Mode is strictly reserved for audio tracks that have a fixed tempo. Using Musical Mode on a free tempo recording will result in a big mess.

The Free Warp tool gives you the freedom to create what's called a *warp tab*. A warp tab defines a location where AudioWarp should occur, and it works along with the tempo map you've created to ensure that it warps at the correct tempo. To create a warp tab, simply click in the ruler around the point at which you would like to alter the placement of the note or beat. The first warp tab that you create will actually create two warp tabs. The reason for this is because when warping, you need to define a warp "in" and a warp "out" point. Imagine the warp tabs as sort of a virtual audio "rubber band" between their in and out points on the ruler. You should reposition them somewhat close together, but far enough apart so that you have room to select the beat or note you're working with and then drag it to the desired location.

Once you've defined a section of audio as the stretch zone, you can use the Free Warp tool to locate and move (stretch) the note or beat to its proper location (shown in Figure 3.25). Use the Free Warp tool to create another warp tab right on the waveform and at the location you would like to edit. Next, drag the newly created warp tab to the left or right to get to the correct position in the track using both your ear and the ruler as a reference. Once the note is in position, release the mouse and play back the track to check your work (see Figure 3.26). Listen for the timing and processing issues. First, make sure your timing is accurate, and if not, readjust the position of the note or beat. The numbers shown by the warp tabs in the ruler (see Figure 3.27)

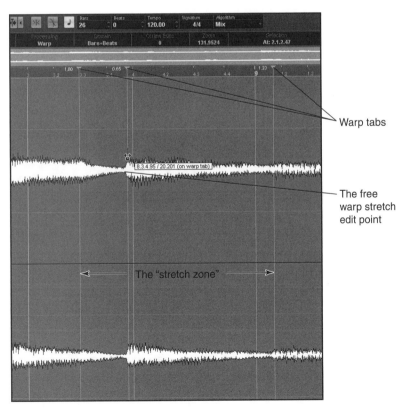

Figure 3.25 Creating a warp tab within the "stretch zone" at the edit location.

Warp point has been
stretched to a new location

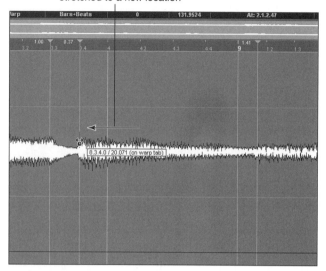

Figure 3.26   The note has been stretched to a new location. No audio has been affected before or after the "stretch zone."

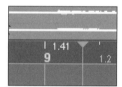

Figure 3.27   A close-up of the warp factor number next to the warp tabs.

indicate the amount of stretching that's occurring to achieve the desired result. The less stretching necessary, the better the sound quality will be. Ultimately, it's in your best interest to try to keep the number close to 1.0. This setting can get as high as 10.0 (10 times slower) and as low as 0.1 (10 times faster).

When you're satisfied with your edit, you can apply the processing just as you would when quantizing audio. Select Flatten from the Real-Time Processing menu, and the real-time processing will be converted into a new audio part.

Note: When you can, it's best to flatten using the MPEX4 technology as opposed to the real-time technology. Also, don't bother using the Preview setting (all you'll get is a poor representation of the quality). During this flatten process, it is possible that the quality of the actual process will improve over what you were hearing in real time. As always, you can undo the process if you aren't completely pleased with the result.

Using Musical Mode (AudioWarp)

There are so many "warp" words being thrown around (warp this, warp that), sometimes it feels like my brain is going to warp. To make sure we're on the same page, here's all you need to know: AudioWarp is basically a fancy name for real-time time-stretching technology. Free Warp is the ability to define time-stretch points in real time. Time Warp is the ability to switch between bars and beats and linear time (like a clock) when editing. I haven't gone into detail regarding Time Warp, but it can also be used as an alternative to creating a grid for a free tempo recording. I personally find it a little more difficult to work with, so I opted for the alternative method, but it does work well (particularly with short time free sections of songs). To learn more about Time Warp, you can refer to the Cubase 5 manual. To clear things up, though, Time Warp has more to do with making tempo changes on the Tempo Track then it has to do with the actual time-stretching of audio. In order to make the most out of Time Warp, your audio should already be set to Musical Mode (as discussed in this section).

For now, I would like to move on to another type of warp that isn't called "warp"—it's called Musical Mode. Musical Mode is the most basic form of warping, and it's partially the magic behind importing an audio track into a project at the correct tempo when using the MediaBay. As I mentioned before, Musical Mode was designed to work with audio that is set at one locked tempo. If you are using a free tempo recording, Musical Mode will just cause you more trouble than it's worth. When importing an audio file, Cubase will automatically attempt to calculate the tempo of that file. This is not always an accurate calculation. It really helps to have files that have been cut into perfect bar sections (two bars, four bars, and so on). After importing your audio file, you can view this automatic calculation in the toolbar of the Sample Editor (as shown in Figure 3.28).

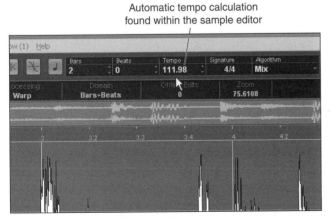

Figure 3.28 Cubase's automatic tempo calculation for an imported audio file.

> **Note:** I'm going to continue this exercise as if that automatic calculation Cubase made for you is correct. But if you find that your tempo isn't locked to the project, revert to determining the tempo of your audio manually as I discussed earlier in the section "Changing Audio Groove Tempos via Audio Slices." Once you've determined the tempo, you can manually change the auto-calculation to the real tempo by typing in the correct info.

By opening the AudioWarp tab on the Inspector, you will find "Musical Mode." The basic idea behind Musical Mode is that when any audio file has Musical Mode activated, it will follow the tempo track of the project. This means, in theory, that even if you have created your own tempo map with a free tempo recording, a prerecorded groove that has Musical Mode activated should sync along with your free tempo recording with no problems. In other words, you could almost create a free tempo sounding track out of an audio loop with a locked tempo when that audio loop is utilizing Musical Mode.

You can also adjust the quantize of an audio track that's in Musical Mode and utilize the Free Warp tool as you did when working with the free tempo recording. Another interesting item is the Swing feature, which allows you to manipulate the groove using the AudioWarp processor (as shown in Figure 3.29). This is a difficult trick to master, and it will most likely just sound like garbage if you're using an audio part that already has some sort of groove and doesn't have the audio specs that Steinberg recommends its samples have. To adjust the Swing quantize, use the Quantize settings just above it.

Figure 3.29   The Swing feature available in Musical Mode.

To wrap things up in this section, Musical Mode can be a very useful production tool, is not very difficult to master, and should not be overlooked among all the many features that are available in Cubase.

Vocal Pitch Correction Using VariAudio

The Auto-Tune effect (real-time vocal pitch correction) has been used and abused on vocal tracks for well over 10 years. Even though it's been popular, Steinberg has not offered any sort of similar plug-in to complement Cubase until now. Even though Auto-Tune is popular, the actual software is far from perfect. Anyone can tell that there's "something strange" about the way a vocal recording sounds when using it. The Auto-Tune effect can almost sound like a vocoder (the classic "robot voice") at times, especially when it's over-compensating for horrible singers! It doesn't really matter because people seem to enjoy the sound enough. When it all boils down, it's no different than hearing any other effect (such as reverb or echo) on a vocal, and often it's used on great singers just to get that "sound." More and more great singers are shunning the use of the effect because they don't want people to think they use it because they can't sing!

Because the Auto-Tune "sound" has become such a staple, it will always be around (just like the reverb and echo classics). The real question is, how do you achieve pitch correction without it becoming labeled as Auto-Tune? What about those who simply use it as an editing tool to get the most out of a captured performance? After all, pitch correction shouldn't be looked at any differently than altering the timing or cutting and pasting a chorus or verse in a project. In fact, what's the difference if a singer has to sing multiple tracks where each word is edited together to form a pitch-corrected melody. Even some producers of well-respected popular singers use pitch correction. Who wants to tell a major artist that her last "perfect" take was a little flat? That could mean you'll get a $9000 microphone thrown through the studio window, and you'll be looking for a new job the next day. The bottom line is that you need pitch correction, and you need the effect of it to be discreet.

For those who have done your homework, you've probably already heard of Melodyne by Celemony. Melodyne has been available for several years now and offers a slightly different approach to pitch correction. The key ingredient to Melodyne is that the audio is analyzed to extract pitch, length, and timing information. The notes and timing are displayed as if they are on a MIDI-like grid (like the Key Editor in Cubase). The basic principal sounds simple, but it's a very innovative technology. In fact, Melodyne has developed a new technology called Direct Note Access (DNA), which will allow users to analyze recordings of chord structures (up until now it's only been available for vocals and mono instruments), and break each individual pitch away from its chord in order to change the harmonic structure of the chord. These guys are definitely on to something, and they've won multiple industry awards to prove it.

Now Cubase introduces VariAudio (which can be found in the Sample Editor by selecting the VariAudio tab). VariAudio is Steinberg's solution to pitch correction. It bears more resemblance to Celemony's Melodyne than it does to Antares' Auto-Tune. The biggest problem with Melodyne is that it's not easily integrated into another DAW. This alone has caused users to choose Auto-Tune over Melodyne in the past. Like the original version of Melodyne, VariAudio was designed specifically for vocals and monophonic instruments (with more of a disclaimer toward monophonic instruments).

VariAudio utilizes yet another somewhat generically named "warp" effect called Pitch & Warp. When using Pitch & Warp, a single audio wave is analyzed and broken into so-called segments, which represent the various notes (pitches) within the recording. The pitches, of course, are also shown with their actual note length and in the appropriate locations on the grid. When notes are slightly out of tune, VariAudio assumes that you were aiming for a certain pitch and categorizes it with one of the 12 tones in the chromatic scales as opposed to breaking it down into detail. Intonations and voice inflections that fall within the general area of each of the 12 tones can be important and shouldn't always be raised or lowered to the exact pitch. Intonations and inflections are made up of small pitch increments, or *micro pitches*. The more the micro pitch is altered, the more of the robot voice effect you're going to hear. Micro pitches are very important to human vocal inflections, and are particularly important when a singer uses vibrato. Unfortunately, micro pitches are also the same things that cause flat or sharp sounding notes. The key to editing vocal pitch has always been a balancing act of these particular micro pitches.

In essence, pitch correction should be viewed similarly to time correction or quantization. You want it to sound "on," but you don't want it to sound like there are robots making the music. Sometimes the best choice is not to use it. After all, let's take a moment to reflect on the recordings of the greatest singers in history and remember that automated pitch correction has only been around for a short period of time. There are plenty of hit records that exist with vocal pitch problems; and if you were to take away those pitch "problems" using today's technology, the recording would most likely *lose* something that most of us didn't notice to begin with. The *performance* is always the most important element to the recording, regardless of pitch.

In the example shown in Figure 3.30, I have taken a snippet from a vocal performance in an area where the pitch was off. To keep my view simple, after snipping the audio section in the project window, I bounced the audio snippet so that it became its own file. Then I opened the part within the Sample Editor, selected the VariAudio tab from the Inspector, and selected Pitch & Warp to create the segments shown. This vocal is a quick descending melody that would be hard for even good singers to sing without slight pitch difficulty.

If you examine Figure 3.30, you'll see that there is a keyboard on the left, which represents the pitch that's been captured. The pitches have been analyzed and converted into the so-called segments, which are displayed as little boxes over the actual waveform. By using the keyboard as a reference, you'll also see that almost none of the pitches exactly falls right on the line of the piano key. That doesn't mean every note is going to sound out of tune. It's simply an analysis stating that the center of that pitch does not fall on the exact frequency of the given pitch in the chromatic scale for the entire given length of the note. Note-to-note transitions, such as those found in a melody like this, will make it difficult to calculate, so don't assume that the computer is 100% correct. If I position the mouse cursor over one of the notes (zoomed in close-up), it will reveal the general pitch as well as the + or – amount that the micro pitch varies from the exact pitch frequency for the duration of that note (see Figure 3.31).

There are several options when it comes to editing the pitch of the notes in question. The most basic option is to hone in on the problem note, then move it to the correct position with the cursor. In this particular recording, what has been calculated as a D#3 should actually be a D3. By simply selecting the note and moving it down to the D3 position, I have transposed the note. What's great about this form of editing is that the micro pitches are transposed the same. This keeps the natural

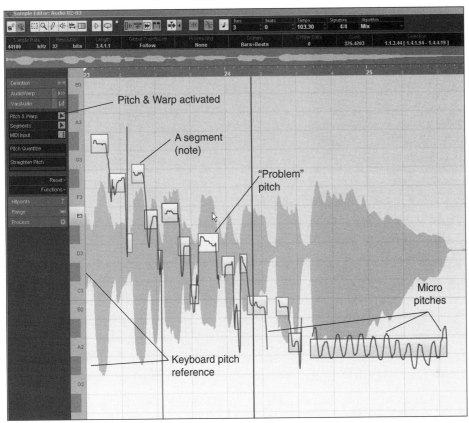

Figure 3.30 A melody slightly out of tune displayed as segments in VariAudio's Pitch & Warp Editor.

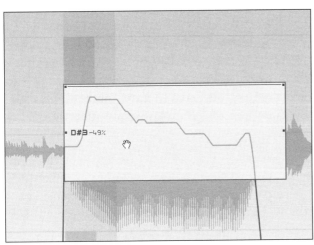

Figure 3.31 Pitch information displayed on each individual audio segment of the vocal recording.

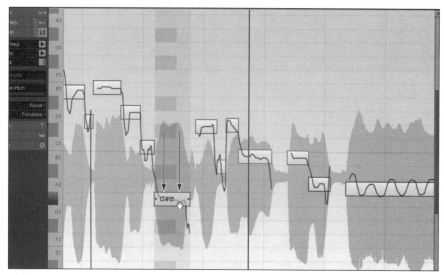

Figure 3.32 I've transposed the D#3 note to a G#2, and it still sounds natural.

vocal sound that you're looking for. As a matter of fact, the pitch shifting is so dead on, that you can completely change the melody by transposing individual notes (see Figure 3.32).

One thing I've noticed from time to time is that you might get some noises or slight pops during the transitions from the processed pitches to the unprocessed pitches. Sometimes this can be smoothed out with some of the other processing tricks within this editor; but other times, you might have to tweak it some more within the Sample Editor after processing.

The great thing about changing pitches is that you don't lose your original timing when manually moving the note up or down the scale. If you *do* need to change the position of a lyric or note, you can move either side of the segment to the left or right using the mouse. Keep in mind that this "moving" process is more of an AudioWarp process (as I demonstrated earlier when discussing Free Warp), as opposed to simple cut and move editing (with no time-stretching). When you move the note, you're actually stretching the note to the left or right as well as affecting the note just before or after the note you're working with. You can select several notes to move at once, but this is also utilizing Free Warp. Keep in mind that any process you make (moving, pitch shift, stretching, and so on) using any form of AudioWarp could affect the quality of the recording.

Just as you can quantize the audio to fall on certain beats using the Quantize Audio feature, you can also quantize the pitches to move closer to the pitches that VariAudio has automatically determined (see Figure 3.33). This is a very nice feature for some basic "tightening" of a vocal performance (regarding pitch). In order to utilize the Pitch Quantize feature, you need to first select the notes you wish to quantize, then use the virtual slider (just like the one you use to calculate hitpoints) under the Pitch Quantize control on the Inspector.

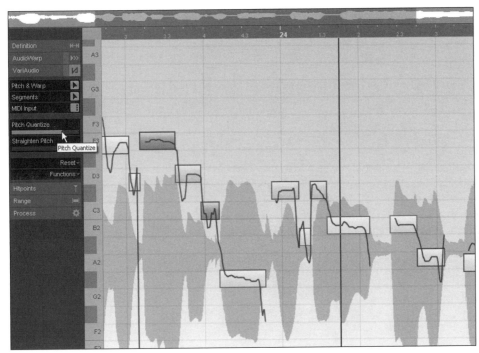

Figure 3.33 Quantizing pitches from within the VariAudio Pitch & Warp Editor.

Another pitch-correcting feature is the Straighten Pitch control, which gives you the ability to quantize or "compress" the micro pitches for each individual segment. I use the word compress, because it acts similar to pitches in the way a compressor works with dynamics. It actually limits the range of the micro pitches. The more you adjust the Straighten Pitch slider in the Inspector (just like the Pitch Quantize control), the more the micro pitch variations are reduced and brought to the center of the pitch.

In Figure 3.34, I used the Straighten Pitch feature to remove the vibrato from the last note in my example. The result was a lot more synthetic, but a majority of the vibrato disappeared. Unfortunately, what happens is that in replacing the vibrato, I now have a flat vocal with slight volume changes. The quality has also been affected due to the AudioWarp process and is more noticeable during the peaks and dips where the vibrato originally existed. If the vibrato was milder to begin with, I would probably have had less trouble flattening it. Then again, if I'm going for a somewhat more synthetic sound, I've got one!

If you would like to achieve some pitchbending to a vocal note, you can do so by adjusting your zoom for a close-up look at the segment, then creating something similar to a warp tab (the manual refers to is as an *anchor point*) within the actual segment. To create the tab, simply move the mouse pointer to the location where you would like your bend at the top of the segment. An "I" will appear. When you click while viewing the "I," a slight line will appear. This is

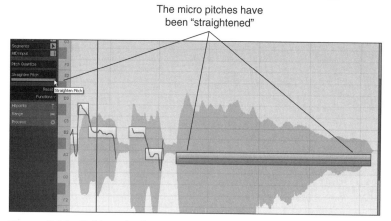

The micro pitches have been "straightened"

Figure 3.34 Taking the human micro pitches out of the performance.

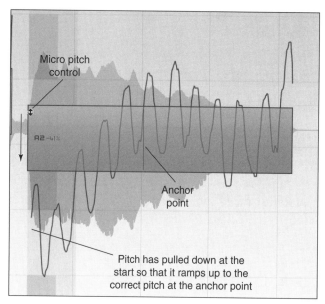

Micro pitch control

A2 -41%

Anchor point

Pitch has pulled down at the start so that it ramps up to the correct pitch at the anchor point

Figure 3.35 Using the anchor point to create a pitchbend up to the note in the segment.

the bend point. Next, position the mouse to the top left or right corner of the segment and click and drag up or down to raise or lower the pitch at a curve. (This does not alter the micro pitches' relation to each other.) This can be great for adding or removing any sort of bend up or down to the note (see Figure 3.35).

During a vocal performance recording, there can be a lot of nonpitched audio recorded. This can be anything from dead silence to breath noises and paper rustling. VariAudio is pretty good at determining what should and should not be considered a pitch, but sometimes the process of creating these pitch segments can result in an undesirable effect. If you need to, you can manually adjust the start and end locations of the segment itself, as well as cut or glue segments (in a case where two notes might have been confused as one or vice versa), or even delete the segment altogether. In order to make these types of edits, select Segments under the VariAudio tab in the Inspector. When using the Segments tab, Cubase automatically generates multiple copies of your audio track, which can increase the size or your project and the performance of your system. If you're going to use this mode, I highly recommend starting with a small section of audio that has been bounced (as I demonstrated at the start) to keep your system running "clean." Once you're in Segments mode, you'll find that working with segments is similar to working with notes from within the Key Editor.

Note: You can also use a MIDI keyboard to change the segment's pitch positions by activating the MIDI Input tab. However, I believe that this feature is mostly for keyboard players and not a real timesaver otherwise. More useful is the Export MIDI Data feature, which enables you to create a printable score with your melody line.

All in all, VariAudio is a wonderful new addition to Cubase. It's easy to work with and a must-have for anyone producing vocal tracks. Be on the lookout for more advancements in this area of pitch correction, as this is a completely new feature in Cubase 5.

4 Mastering the Art of Mixing Within Cubase 5

When most of us think of mixing, the first thing we gravitate toward is using a mixing console. In Cubase, however, you can achieve a professional mix without using a mixer. In fact, you rarely need to utilize the VST mixer from within Cubase. While it's true that certain external gear is irreplaceable in terms of its particular sound, Cubase has made it possible for you to get a similar sound with greater flexibility, and sometimes that flexibility can outweigh the irreplaceable hardware's capabilities.

Another thing many think of when mixing is *automation*. This can range from simple volume changes to panning, muting tracks, EQ, and special effects. Like digital recording, the term "automation" is relatively new to audio and mixing; however, the simple idea of achieving a perfect mix has been around since the beginning of the recording studio when automation meant an engineer sitting behind a recording console making adjustments to certain controls as the mix was being created in real time. Later on, engineers used the bouncing of audio tracks as a form of automation (by actually recording effects or volume changes on other tracks). Next came the "Cadillac years" of automation, which involved motorized controls and faders that physically moved during a mix-down session to match the engineer's maneuvers. While these mechanical faders saved engineers from the signal loss that occurs during the bouncing process (when using analog tape machines), the clunky-ness of programming the mechanical faders was tedious, not always 100% accurate, and ridiculously expensive to own and maintain.

I wanted to spend a little time on the history of automation and mixing to make sure you're aware that automation, like everything else, is a process that is still evolving. The automation features in Cubase are much more advanced than any automated features ever were in the days of analog recording. I've embraced some of the changes in music and technology, but I've tossed aside other changes that I found to be a little clunky and got in the way of achieving the perfect mix—sometimes the new ways are not always better than the old ways.

Besides discussing the automation elements in Cubase, this chapter will briefly touch on the other mixing tools and show that, even though they exist, they're not always necessary to use. There are easier and (in my opinion) better ways within the program to achieve the best results possible. I'll also discuss some of the new features in Cubase 5, interfacing Cubase 5 with other hardware outboard gear, the included plug-ins, and some basic tips and settings to use when creating the final output mix-down file. I will also include a special section on mixing using the new Steinberg CC121 controller for those who would like to physically get their hands on the mix and work with a motorized flying fader.

Making the Most of Cubase's Mixing Tools

As I've discussed, Cubase offers multiple tools that ultimately provide the same end result. The reason the program has so many options is because there is no single perfect tool. I'm devoting this section to sorting through all the technical nonsense to show you why each tool is important and how you can achieve better results with each tool than you might already know.

First off, let's take a look at the VST mixer. This is where most people seem to go when starting a mix. After all, the VST mixer appears to be the centralized point at which all the audio signals come together in Cubase. It's a great way to work with multiple tracks at once, but because there can be so much going on in the VST mixer, most of the time you're going to end up seeing more than you need, which can be annoying or overwhelming at times. The VST mixer is designed so that you can hide elements when you don't need them; but the working environment can still appear to be cluttered with controls, and continuously changing views can become tedious.

The process of mixing is usually thought of as the last production stage of a project. I believe that mixing starts before the recording even starts and is a continuous process. By the time it comes down to a final mix, you should be concentrating on the overall balance of your audio in detail, but the basic balancing of the elements is always a factor. By keeping everything "mixed as you go," you'll find that the final stage of mixing is not so overwhelming and actually quite simple.

My advice is to work only with audio tracks if possible. Back in the early days, we used to keep MIDI tracks separate from audio tracks. This way we could save our audio tracks for instruments that couldn't be recorded via MIDI, and we could preserve the recording quality of the synths by not recording them to analog tape. These days, there's no real point to keeping the audio and MIDI separated because you have virtually *unlimited* audio tracks, and the digital recording quality sounds identical to that of the unrecorded synth. If you're using VST instruments or any sort of MIDI instrument, I feel that it's better to create an audio track for that instrument before mixing, as opposed to trying to blend in "live" audio from MIDI instruments with prerecorded tracks. I'm aware that sometimes recording live audio is the only option, but in most cases where you're creating a final mix, there's no need to utilize MIDI or VST instrument tracks. By having your synth's actual sound recorded as an audio track (as opposed to just the MIDI data), your synths will be easier to archive for future remixes as well.

Of course, you can use the VST mixer to help you get the right recording levels when creating these synth audio tracks, but this should all happen before the actual mixing session. During the final mix, you'll be able to concentrate on making volume changes to the synth's audio track as opposed to its VST instrument track or MIDI track. So, once again, before the final mix-down session, all your synths (as well as other instruments) should be on audio tracks, your MIDI tracks can be muted, and your synths should be disabled (to save you processing power). You can even go as far as to delete the MIDI tracks and instruments and resave the project under another name to clean up your mixing environment ahead of time.

The same way that creating audio tracks for your synths can help in making the final mix simple, you can also bounce other multiple audio tracks (such as the individual components of a drum kit or background vocal tracks) and effects (such as delays or reverb) to stereo audio tracks in order to simplify your mixing environment. By reducing your mix to fewer audio tracks before the final stage, you'll simplify the mixing process, eliminate the audio "mess" that the mixer can present, create parts that are easier to edit, and you'll be able to mix the majority of your project all within the project window.

Even though the VST mixer can be used to display EQ/effects and volume/pan settings during a mix, I find that it's simply easier to see and make adjustments to that channel by using the Audio Channel Settings display. This can be accessed by selecting the "e" from any audio track in the project window (as shown in Figure 4.1).

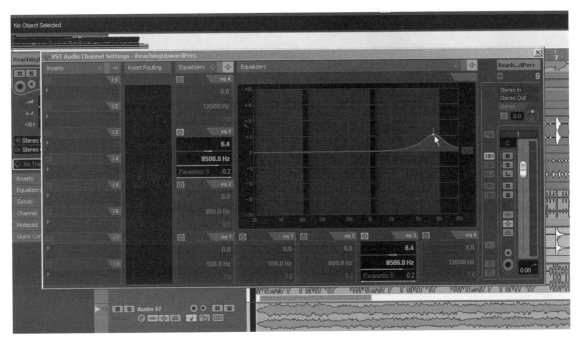

Figure 4.1 The Audio Channel Settings display.

Using the Audio Channel Settings display (instead of the VST mixer) makes sense when mixing in linear form from within the project window, as opposed to trying to record your faders with automation in the VST mixer, where it's not humanly possible to see what's happening because you can't visualize where your mix is going or coming from.

Here's an example of what I mean by mixing in *linear form*. Compare Figures 4.2 and 4.3. Figure 4.2 shows a mix in linear form within the project window. You can see what has happened in the mix, what is happening right now, and where the mix is going. The same mix is shown in Figure 4.3. Even though you can see multiple channels at once, you can't visualize where the mix is headed or coming from.

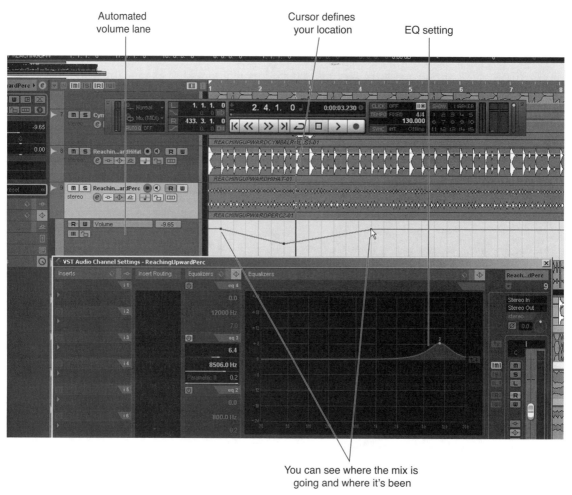

Figure 4.2 Mixing within the project window.

Figure 4.3   The same mix shown in the VST mixer.

Even though you can't see EQ or effects settings using the project window alone, each channel's Audio Channel Settings display shows everything else that you really need to see, which you can access at any time.

Automation Techniques in the Project Window

As I discussed before, there are multiple ways to automate a mix in Cubase. When most people think of automation, they think about flying faders and knobs. Some people also think that the ideal way to program automation is by turning a knob on a console, and then having it repeat that maneuver for them automatically. While the hands-on approach might seem appealing, it comes with a catch: It has to do with what happens when you want to change or correct the automation maneuver you performed. Because of the nature of hands-on automation programming, sometimes it can get messy when it's altered, and then you find yourself spending extra time correcting and repairing the automation data. Automation can be an indispensible tool when it comes to mixing. The key is in the *method* by which you program the automation.

Previously, I demonstrated how mixing in the project window makes more sense than mixing using the VST mixer due to the way the project window works in a linear fashion. This mainly concerns the automation. Technically, automation involves the Read and Write automation buttons in Cubase. The Write buttons, however, only need to be used when you are *physically* maneuvering a button, knob, or fader within Cubase in real time as the project is playing back.

Getting back to the basic idea that automation is strictly programming a mix, examine Figures 4.4 and 4.5.

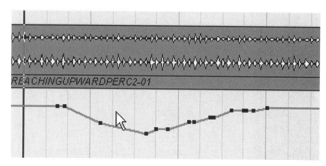

Figure 4.4 An automation performance from physically manipulating a fader using the VST mixer.

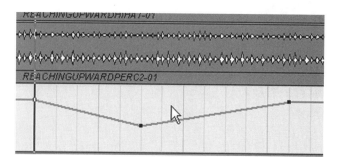

Figure 4.5 An automation performance "programmed" manually from within the project window.

For this example, I simply wanted to fade out a track at one point, and then bring it back up in the mix. I decided to perform this maneuver in several ways so that I could demonstrate the minor differences in the end result. In Figure 4.4, I used the Write automation button and moved the fader using the mouse in real time as I listened to the part. Notice how the movement created a lot of automation events; although it was a simple move, it appears to be complex and a bit messy (visually). In Figure 4.5, I created an automation lane for volume in the project window, and then simply drew in the mix I needed (using the Pencil and Line tools) for the track I needed it on. Notice how it looks pretty straightforward and not so messy. After I finished automating using both methods, I listened to each track, and they pretty much sounded the same.

Note: Cubase offers a variety of line tools for helping you create natural-sounding fades (adjustable from the toolbar). The important thing to know is that the more uniform (less messy) the automation line is, the less work the automation will create for your system.

When you factor in that 1) you can see the entire project in linear form within the project window without having to use the VST mixer, 2) you can easily create automation without the need to perform a maneuver perfectly, and 3) it sounds no different, then it makes more sense to use automation by drawing it in an automation lane in the project window than it does by moving a virtual fader while writing automation. It also saves you from having to flip back and forth between various windows. If you absolutely need to move a fader during automation, you can always use the fader in the Audio Channel Settings display and save yourself from having to utilize the VST mixer. Keep in mind that even when you draw automation in an automation lane, your fader will still move on playback as if it were physically moved during the writing process. Figure 4.6 shows even more examples of panning and effect automation that have been drawn in the project window.

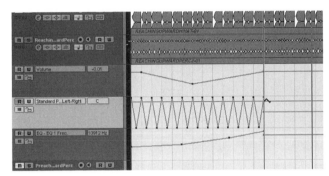

Figure 4.6   Multiple lanes of automation drawn in the project window.

When it comes to creating automation lanes, simply select the type of lane you need by changing the parameter in the type field of the newly added lane. By selecting More (in the default list of parameters located in the type field), you can view the entire list of available parameters for that channel (see Figure 4.7). If you have difficulty finding the particular lane you'd like to create, you can click the red Write button located on the control that you would like to automate (manually adjusting the virtual control that you're automating), and a lane will be created for it automatically under the audio track you are working with.

Not all automation events work as well as others. In fact, I find that basic volume and muting automations work best with some basic part editing in the project window. Here's how it works. Let's say you're creating a mix, and there's one lyric on a vocal track that's just a little softer than the other words on the same track. Using an automation lane for such a quick volume change is possible, but it's not the easiest or most focused method. The easiest way is to cut the audio event so the word that needs to be louder becomes its own isolated audio event (using the Split tool or another method); then adjust the volume of the isolated audio event by increasing the gain level of the event's envelope, as shown in Figure 4.8.

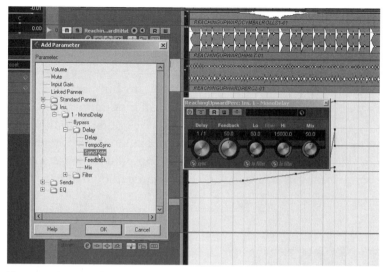

Figure 4.7 Creating a specific automation lane using the list of available parameters.

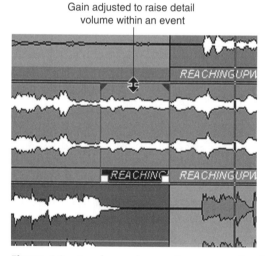

Figure 4.8 A volume change from some simple editing.

This same type of mixing can be applied on a broader scale as well and works even better when muting individual parts and sections in a mix. It's much easier to mute an audio event as opposed to recording mute automation. You can also fade in and out from audio event to audio event using the control located at the top right or left corner of the event. Figure 4.9 shows how I've created a mix similar to the one in Figure 4.5; it also shows how muting works in the track below it.

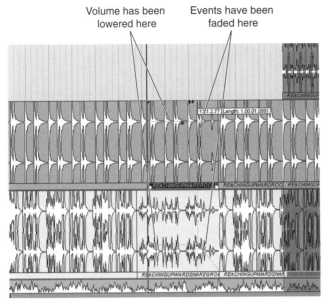

Figure 4.9 Broad volume changes and muting using some simple events editing.

When working with automation lanes, the new automation panel (shown in Figure 4.10) could become useful. The panel is accessed by pressing the Show Automation Panel located in the project window's toolbar, and it creates an easier way to quickly access read and write automation functions when programming automation in real time. It can also be used to hide, show, and disable automation lanes that you're working with, which can come in handy if you're working with a lot of automation lanes at once.

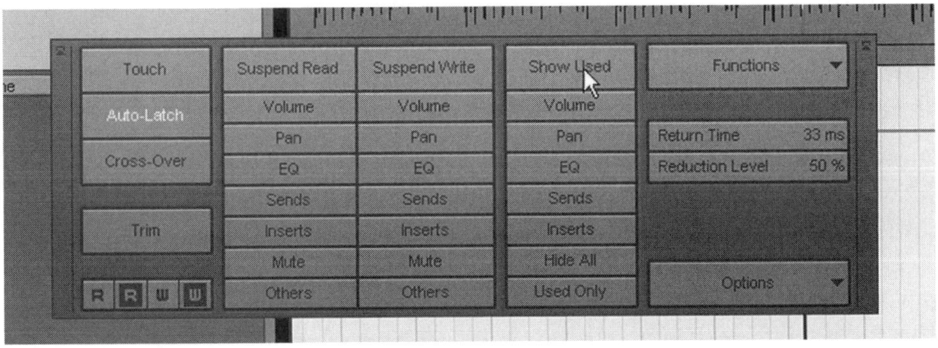

Figure 4.10 The new automation panel in Cubase 5.

Note: Remember that when it comes to mixing, not everything needs to be automated. In fact, your standard mix usually requires that the settings on several tracks remain the same throughout the final mix. This means that once you have your volumes, EQ, and effects set for some tracks, there's no need to automate some tracks.

Using Cubase's Effect Inserts and Sends

Before I discuss the VST plug-ins in Cubase, I believe there are still some working professionals who don't understand the difference between using a send and an insert on a track. An *insert* effect is inserted directly into the signal path of the track that it is activated on. This effect's sole purpose is to process that one particular audio track. When several insert effects are used on one individual track, the order in which they are inserted will make a big difference to the final result of the sound. A good comparison of an insert effect is sort of like using a "stomp box" with a guitar and amp. The guitar signal enters the stomp box before passing through to the amp. If you're using several pedals at once, the order of the pedals will affect your sound. It can be as subtle as, "Would you like *delay* on your distorted guitar or *distortion* on your delayed guitar?" But there is an audible difference. Because insert effects are dedicated to each particular track, using a lot of insert effects creates multiple instances of that effect, and each of these instances creates more of a burden on your computer's processor. When you're utilizing an insert effect, you control the mix of that effect (compared to the original direct signal) from the instance of the effect itself.

Using a *send* is the standard method of handling an effect when you need to use it on several tracks simultaneously. For instance, you might want to use the same reverb sound on several different drum or vocal tracks at once. The mix level of the effect on each track is determined by controlling how much signal (from each individual track utilizing the send) is sent to the effect. Effect sends can be used pre-fader or post-fader. Since each effect send acts like its own fader (by defining the level of signal sent), a pre-fader send means that the level of the fader on the audio channel of the audio track will not affect the level that's sent to a send destination (because the signal from the send is being sent from the audio channel *before* it reaches the channel fader in the path of the signal flow). A post-fader send means that the level of the signal from the channel's fader *will* affect the level of the signal sent to the effect send destination (because the signal is directed to the send *after* going through the channel fader).

When using an effect via a send, you need to determine whether you would like to use your effect's send as a pre-fader or post-fader send. The default method is to use the send in post-fader mode, but occasionally you might like to bypass the channel fader to send the signal directly to the effect. This type of routing is possible by selecting the Pre Fader button on the effect send (see Figure 4.11). Normally, when using multiple post-fader sends, since the signal is split, the order of each send effect on a track makes no difference in the final sound (as it does when using effects via inserts). When using a pre-fader send, you're going to end up hearing more of the affected sound than the original unaffected sound if the channel fader is at a lower level than your send's level.

Figure 4.11 The pre-fader send option viewed from within the Inspector.

Note: You can get very creative just by changing your effect's signal routing. Remember that sends are primarily used when working with multiple channels and utilizing the same effect. While EQ and dynamic plug-ins are commonly used as insert effects, any effect can be used with an insert, but the order of your effects as they're inserted will affect the sound of the overall combined effect on that track.

An Overview of Available Plug-In Effects

Cubase comes with a lot of plug-ins. In case you didn't know already, there's a full Cubase manual dedicated to the included effects. This can be found under the Help menu by selecting Documentations and then selecting Plug-In Reference. My aim in this section is to walk you through the massive group of effects and give you a "quick and dirty" reference guide from an outside perspective so you can jump in and start using them right away.

Delay Effects

When it comes to delays, Cubase 5 offers a variety of choices: the MonoDelay, StereoDelay, ModMachine, and PingPongDelay. While some delay types aren't included (multi-tap delay, sampling delay, tape delay, and so on), most of the time you should be able to get by with these four basic digital delays because they cover a wide range.

The **MonoDelay** is probably the most useful and can provide whatever standard echo effect or slap back effect is necessary. The **StereoDelay** is like two linked mono delays and is primarily to used on stereo recordings where you need slightly different delays on the left and right channels.

The **PingPongDelay** is similar to the MonoDelay but designed to feature only delays that are linked to a stereo panning effect. The main difference is the *spatial* control, which helps define the width of the panning. The **ModMachine** delay allows you to filter the feedback of the delay. This effect is normally used when you want something to sound weird or spacey, but it can also be used subtly.

The most important detail in all of these plug-in delays is the ability to sync to your project's tempo. Years ago, engineers had to break out their calculators to compute the tempo speed in milliseconds in order to get their delays to fall on the beat. Today, using Cubase, you just have to select the Sync button (as shown in Figure 4.12) and define the beat where you'd like the delay (1/4 notes, half notes, 1/8 notes, and so forth). All of the delays are VST3 effects except the stereo delay.

Figure 4.12 Syncing the delay to match the tempo of the project.

Distortion Effects

Distortion is usually what we're trying to avoid when recording, but it can also be used to give a "grungy" or "warming" effect on anything from guitar to vocal tracks. Cubase 5 comes with four different distortions; out of these, DaTube the only plug-in that isn't VST3.

If you're looking for a grungy distortion, your best bet is the **Amp Simulator** or the **Distortion** plug-in. The Amp Simulator effect offers the most control over the distortion and even provides a speaker cabinet emulator (like a guitar amp). While the intention is that you should be able to use these plug-ins to record guitar, the truth is that these included distortion plug-ins do not offer nearly as many capabilities as some third-party plug-ins (such as the Waves GTR3, Native Instruments Guitar Rig, iZotope Trash, IK Multimedia AmpliTube, or those by Line 6). If you're recording a lot of guitar, I highly recommend you explore other options because you'll be missing out on better possibilities. That being said, I have used the Cubase distortion effects on several other types of recordings, and they can definitely work in a pinch. **DaTube** is a software simulation of basic classic tube distortion (similar to that found on vintage mic pres) and is mostly used to give vocal tracks some extra warmth. The **SoftClipper** is similar to DaTube in that it's a subtle effect and isn't really meant to be noticed. It gives you the sound of clipping without actually clipping the signal (which is definitely something you don't want in your mix).

Dynamic Effects

When it comes to processing dynamics (loud/soft audio levels), Cubase has got it all. The following dynamic effects work in similar ways, but each has its own defined characteristics. With this much variety, possibly the only reason to use third-party plug-ins of this type would be to have an alternative.

Out of all of these, the **Compressor** and the **Limiter** cover the most basic features in their respective categories. Since they work so well together, I usually prefer to use **VSTDynamics**, which covers all the bases and also includes a noise gate (similar to the Gate effect mentioned a little later). The **Expander** is another type of processor specially designed to maximize loudness when working with audio that covers a wide dynamic range (very loud to very soft). The **Multiband-Compressor** is slightly different and enables you to compress a certain frequency range as opposed to the full range. This can greatly help in controlling the dynamics of certain frequencies without losing some of the frequency range. Multiband compression comes in very handy with audio tracks that contain a wide range of frequencies (such as a full mix used as a sample). **VintageCompressor** is simply an alternative to using the Compressor plug-in and simulates a more classic-sounding compression.

The **Gate** plug-in is simply a complex noise gate without any sort of compression or limiting. It is an automated muting type of effect, which responds according to the level of the audio signal of the track. **MIDI Gate** allows you to program the open and close of the gate via a MIDI track (as opposed to using the signal level) and acts independently from the signal (more like a programmable on/off switch). Both of these types of gate plug-ins could be used to create some interesting choppy effects to an audio track or simply to remove unwanted noise. The **DeEsser** was really designed with one purpose and that is to remove the sizzling sound that the letter "s" can sometimes bring to a vocal track. The **EnvelopeShaper** works similarly to a noise gate, except it can also boost the signal (as opposed to only cutting the signal). It also gives you more control over the attack and release of the affected signal. The **Maximizer** is a simple compressor/limiter specifically designed for getting a louder signal without running the risk of clipping. Be careful, though, because distortion can be added during this process. Overuse could lead to less clarity and definitely to a reduced dynamic range, which is not always a good solution for making a signal louder.

EQ Effects

The standard four-band parametric EQ that you get on every audio channel in Cubase is a lot better than the EQ you're going to get from most other hardware mixing consoles; but Cubase offers several alternatives if that's not enough.

If you're already familiar with the standard parametric EQ, you will find that the **StudioEQ** is very similar. One slight difference is that you can control the overall output level of the EQ. Keep in mind that by having the option of using the EQ as a plug-in, you can alter the sound of your effects chain within a group of inserts, which is something that you can't use with just the standard four-band channel EQ alone. The **GEQ-10** and **GEQ-30** are both graphic EQs (the number following GEQ reflects the number of EQ bands available). Graphic EQs allow you to get into more detail with multiple specific frequencies, as opposed to concentrating on only four frequencies when using the parametric EQ. Because of their nature, graphic EQs are often used on audio that covers a wide range of frequencies (such as a full music mix). All three EQ plug-ins are VST3.

Note: Even though effects can sometimes appear to be very similar, they often offer subtle differences in sound. You will discover that certain types of effects work better when working with certain types of audio. If one particular type isn't cutting it for you, try another.

Filter Effects

Filter effects generally consist of an automated EQ-based effect and are often used to create sweeping sounds in dance music. Cubase offers five filter effects, and they are all VST3. All of these filters can be a lot of fun to play around with, and they come with a variety of presets to give you a better idea of their capabilities. Out of these effects, DualFilter and Tone Booster are not automated, but they can be automated manually using an automation lane under the audio track.

DualFilter is a unique hi-pass/low-pass filter effect with a band booster to give it an extra kick if necessary. Using **Tone Booster** is a way to add a little harmonic distortion to a certain frequency range without clipping the signal (similar to an overdrive pedal for guitar). **StepFilter, Tonic,** and **WahWah** are sweeping filter effects that can be synced to match the tempo of the project. Out of the three, Tonic offers the most control for creating some interesting filtered textures. WahWah is similar to the guitar effect and can be controlled via a MIDI foot pedal, but it can also be used like an envelope filter without using a foot pedal at all.

Modulation Effects

The modulation effects in Cubase cover a lot of different ground. All of these modulation effects are VST3 plug-ins except for the RingModulator, Transformer, and Metalizer.

AutoPan works best on mono recordings to create an automated left/right panning effect. The **Rotary** is a similar panning effect but simulates the Doppler effect, such as a Leslie Cabinet on a Hammond B3 organ (which consisted of an amplified speaker spinning around at various speeds inside a cabinet). **Tremolo** is another classic effect where the amplitude of the signal increases and decreases quickly. A similar effect was used a lot on some famous recordings by The Doors. **Vibrato** can sometimes be confused with Tremolo, but Vibrato actually modulates pitch up and down quickly, as opposed to volume creating a slightly different effect (similar to the vocal tremolo effect). **Chorus**, StudioChorus, and Flanger are classic effects as well and are basically created by using varying degrees of delay with a little extra modulation. The main difference between Chorus and StudioChorus is that the **StudioChorus** effect is like using two choruses in one. Even though the **Cloner** might sound like a chorus, its effect actually works like a harmonizer by creating a double of the original pitch and slightly detuning the doubled pitches. The **RingModulator** is another classic effect that also duplicates the original signal, but then blends it with a sine wave to create yet another unique (almost metallic) quality. Both the **Metalizer** and **Tranceformer** effects are variations of the RingModulator, each with its own characteristics. And last but not least, the **Phaser** is another classic effect that can sometimes be confused with a Flanger. The Phaser actually utilizes an LFO (low-frequency oscillator), as opposed to using a delay, to alter the frequency spectrum that in turn gives you sort of a swooshing sound.

Note: When using some of the VST3 modulation, dynamic, filter, or delay plug-ins, it's possible to use *side-chain inputs* on the effects. A side-chain input lets you specify another signal to trigger the effect, in turn creating yet a different effect for the signal that's being processed. This can be a very useful mixing technique when blending or matching multiple tracks. For more info on side-chaining these effects, refer to Chapter 11 in the Cubase manual.

Miscellaneous Effects

Cubase 5 has grouped four miscellaneous effects into the "other" category. Technically, the Octaver and Tuner should probably be grouped into the pitch category, as they are both pitch-related. The **Octaver** works similarly to an octave foot pedal and simply creates a duplicate pitch two octaves below the original pitch. It also gives you control over the volume of each of the two octaves. The **Tuner** is just like a guitar tuner. It's simply a tool that analyzes the tuning of an instrument and is best used on an input channel as an insert. It has no real affect on the instrument. The Bitcrusher and Chopper are both similar to filter effects in their end results. The **Bitcrusher** is designed to distort the signal by simulating a lower bit rate and is primarily used to achieve a low-fi sound. The **Chopper** sounds more like a noise gate or tremolo that syncs with the project tempo and "chops" up the signal in time. It can also be used like the AutoPan to create a harsh panning-type effect.

The **Grungelizer** has been grouped to its own category of "restoration," which really doesn't make much sense either, as it adds characteristics that take away from actual recording quality. The Grungelizer simply adds noises that are commonly found in older recordings (such as AC hum, vinyl, and tape hiss) to give the processed signal more of a vintage sound.

Pitch Shift Effects

PitchCorrect is a real-time plug-in effect that allows you to specify a scale and a degree to which the note should be "pulled" to the correct pitch. It is very easy to use, but offers a different result than that of VariAudio. Whereas VariAudio is a pitch editor that utilizes the AudioWarp technology to correct pitches, the PitchCorrect plug-in uses a technology similar to that of Antares' Auto-Tune. While I prefer the more "natural" result of pitch correction using VariAudio over PitchCorrect as a plug-in, I can say that all of the pitch "bases" are pretty well covered between these two pitch correction tools in Cubase. This plug-in is brand new for Cubase 5 and is VST3. Now that we have PitchCorrect, there's not as much need for using Auto-Tune when working with Cubase as there was in the past.

Reverb Effects

Cubase 5 has finally made leaps and bounds in the basic reverb department. With these combined reverb processors, you're going to find that there are fewer reasons to use a third-party reverb plug-in. My only complaint is that it would be nice to have some simulated "spring reverb" effects, as well as some other classic reverb sounds. Sometimes the new technology sounds *too* good!

REVerence is a high-quality convolution reverb effect that truly delivers incredible results. Convolution reverbs are the latest and greatest in reverb technology (using impulse response modeling). **Roomworks** is another fantastic digital reverb. (**Roomworks SE** is similar but with fewer parameters and is less CPU-consuming).

Spatial Effects

The spatial effects included in Cubase offer a fairly basic way to modify the general field of sound of a particular audio track. The **MonoToStereo** effect uses a delay to spread a mono signal across the stereo field. **StereoEnhancer** is a basic stereo widener that can be used to spread out the image of the sound across the stereo field. Although popular, this effect shouldn't be overused on parts that are prominent in the mix (due to the coloration effect on the sound). The surround plug-ins include the **Mix6to2 mixer** (which is simply a submixer that converts surround mixes back into a stereo mix) and **Surround Panner** (which is a necessity when it comes to creating a mix outside of your normal L/R stereo field).

Tools

The last group of VST plug-ins aren't effects at all, but extra tools that can help you analyze audio as well as work with other equipment. The **MultiScope** tool covers three basic audio analysis tools, including an oscilloscope, a phase correlator, and a frequency spectrum analyzer; they can all come in very handy and enable you to take a closer look at your audio in real time. The SMPTE Generator and Test Generator are great, particularly if you're working with some analog tape recorders in addition to Cubase. The **SMPTE Generator** can output timecode to a tape track, which can then be redirected to Cubase in order for Cubase to "chase" and lock to the tape machine. The **Test Generator** can create test tones that can help calibrate recording meters (basic alignment), as well as serve other testing purposes.

To summarize, the bang for the buck that you get with Cubase 5 in terms of plug-ins is phenomenal, especially when you consider that most third-party plug-ins can cost as much or more than Cubase. Even with all the third-party plug-ins available, I still find myself using the Cubase plug-ins because most of the time, they're as good as the rest and sometimes even better.

Interfacing External Hardware Effects Processors

As just discussed, Cubase is chock-full of plug-ins that can meet the demands of most users. However, as wonderful as it would be to have *everything* in one box, it's simply impossible. If there's a sound you're looking for that's "outside the box" (or not available as a plug-in), then you're just going to have approach routing the effect a little differently. I don't think there's a single new processor that can't be duplicated by a plug-in. But on the other hand, there are a lot of vintage processors that people often have a soft spot for. This section will discuss how to interface an older analog external classic processor with Cubase.

Note: Most of the time, the only reason to use an external digital processor (such as that included with the MR816) would be to reserve some of your processing power (because most digital processors can be better simulated with similar plug-ins).

Interfacing with an external processor is similar to setting up to record an external instrument. An interface point must first be created under VST Connections. This time, however, you'll need to designate at least one specific output from your audio interface as the effects send and at least one specific input from your audio interface as the effects return.

Note: Even though a lot of vintage processors have stereo outputs, they are often not *true* stereo (dual channel) effects. So instead of using two outputs on your audio interface, you can probably only run a single output from your interface into the mono input of the external processor, and then run the stereo signal from the effect processor back into two separate inputs on your audio interface. This way you can still capture the pseudo-stereo effect from the processor.

For this example, I'm going to run a mono signal out to a classic Roland delay's input, then return the processed signal from the Roland's output to Cubase. First, open the VST Connections window. Select the External FX tab, and then select Add External Effect. Next, enter the info as needed into the Add External FX dialog (as shown in Figure 4.13).

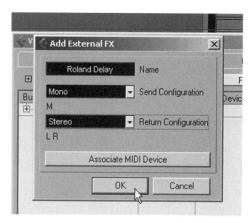

Figure 4.13 Setting up a connection to an external processor.

You can take the time to create a MIDI device (if your vintage gear actually responds to MIDI), but it is not necessary if you're simply looking to process the signal and manually make adjustments on the processor itself. Once you have entered the required info, you just need to designate the ins and outs of your audio interface, as shown in Figure 4.14.

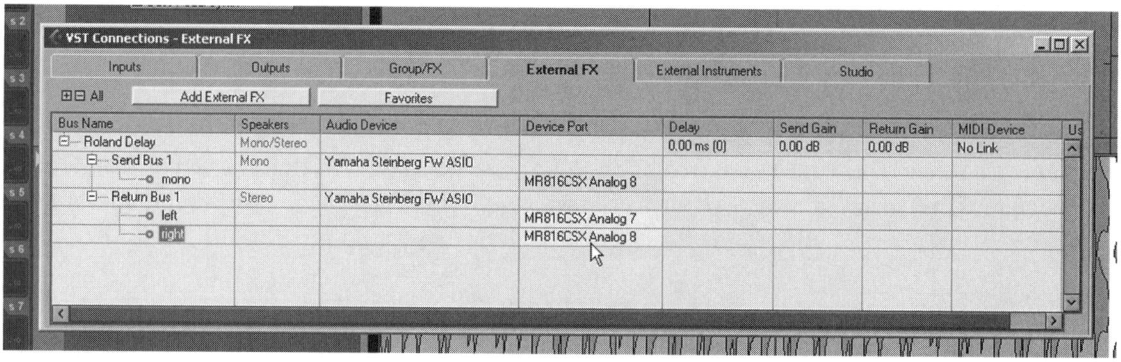

Bus Name	Speakers	Audio Device	Device Port	Delay	Send Gain	Return Gain	MIDI Device	Us
⊟ Roland Delay	Mono/Stereo			0.00 ms (0)	0.00 dB	0.00 dB	No Link	
⊟ Send Bus 1	Mono	Yamaha Steinberg FW ASIO						
—o mono			MR816CSX Analog 8					
⊟ Return Bus 1	Stereo	Yamaha Steinberg FW ASIO						
—o left			MR816CSX Analog 7					
—o right			MR816CSX Analog 8					

Figure 4.14 Designating the effects send and returns ins and outs.

In this example, I have specified output 8 on my MR816 as the mono send for my Roland delay and specified inputs 7 and 8 on the MR816 as the stereo returns. There are other options in this same window for adjusting the input and output gain. Adjusting the delay compensation here may also be necessary, depending on the gear you're using and the way you're monitoring in Cubase (so that you aren't hearing more delay than you intend).

When you're finished making your settings, you should be able to open the effect as an insert, or create a send for the effect and it will appear under the External Effects heading in your list of plug-ins. Once your effect is active on an audio track, you will also be able to select the input/

output level and delay compensation controls as well by selecting "e" from the active effect (as shown in Figure 4.15).

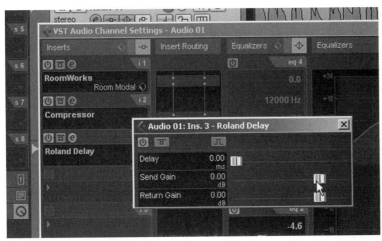

Figure 4.15 Now the external effect can be treated similarly to an internal effect plug-in.

Of course, when using any external hardware, you still have to deal with ground loops and noise along with all the other regular issues, as if you were recording the old-school analog way, but that's a small price to pay in order to get "the sound."

Mixing with the CC121

If you absolutely have to get your hands on a fader during the mixing process in Cubase, there's no easier way than using the CC121. What's great about the CC121 is that there's no reason to assign faders to certain tracks or channels. You start by selecting an audio track that you want to mix (by using the channel select buttons on the CC121 to quickly change from channel to channel), then you select the red W button on the track by using the same buttons located on the CC121 before performing your mix (see Figure 4.16). You can go back and add moves (such as muting, EQ, or panning), and the automation will be created without affecting the other automation type. Keep in mind that in order to hear (and see) the automation that you performed previously, you also need to have the green R button selected (read automation).

The fader itself is motorized and should move exactly as you programmed it during the write automation process. The Mute buttons will light up as a channel is muted, but the knobs (pan, EQ) remain stationary. You repeat this process for each individual track, making adjustments to only one track at a time (which is recommended when it comes to writing automation anyway). Your single flying fader will display the motions of whichever track is selected during the playback of your project.

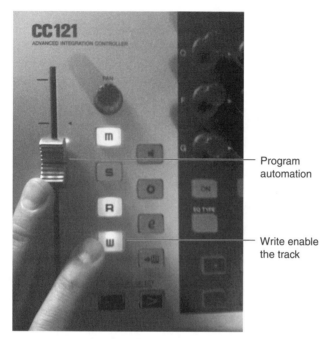

Figure 4.16 Preparing to record hands-on automation with the CC121.

Even though I own the CC121 and I *still* prefer to program automation by drawing it in, I think that there is something appealing about having the flashy lights and moving fader in the studio. It makes working a little more fun, it's quick to program, and it's a great conversation piece for other artists or producers who might be working with you.

Creating the Final Output: Exporting Audio

If you've gotten this far, chances are you've already exported an audio mix in Cubase. I'd like to discuss a few details concerning available features that you might not already be aware of, as well as some recommended settings for getting the best possible results during an export. You start every audio mix-down export by selecting Export Audio Mixdown from the Export menu located in the File menu. Upon selection, the Export Audio Mixdown dialog will appear, as shown in Figure 4.17.

There are multiple ways to export using Cubase 5. The most common is a standard stereo mix export. By default, the format that most Mac users will mix down to is AIFF, and the format that Windows users will default to is WAV. While Cubase does offer other formats, if you're creating a stereo mix for broadcast, I highly recommend that you stick with either an AIFF or WAV file. The reason being is that most of the other file formats are compressed. The difference in file type can greatly affect the quality of the recording.

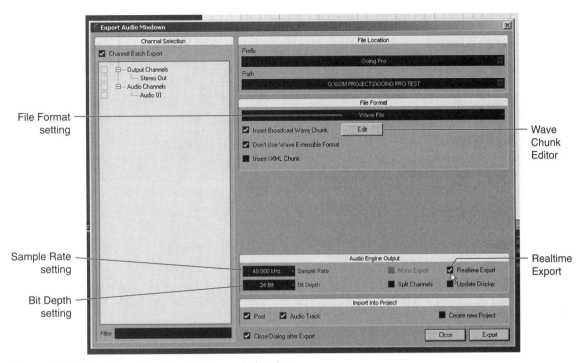

Figure 4.17 The Export Audio Mixdown dialog box.

There are folks who will debate me, but for the best quality with the least amount of loss, you should export at 96 KHz and utilize 32-bit (float). This is the best way to go even if, for instance, your project was recorded in 16-bit and at 44.1 KHz. The file size for the mix will be larger, but when it's your final mix, you should always use the best possible settings. You can always dither down and change the resolution after you have created a file within a wave editor, such as Wave-Lab or even in Cubase. Here's why it's important to use those settings (in my layman's terms). Cubase uses 32-bit (float) internally in its processing. This means that any signal processing that occurs (VST plug-ins) will be crammed into a smaller bit depth if the output settings are less. When extra data is crammed into a tighter space, some of that data either gets lost or distorted. Dithering down is an important step that will affect the final sound. To *dither* is to add "noise" to the process while stepping down to the next smaller bit depth. Adding noise might sound like a bad thing, but in theory, this noise ends up getting (mostly) lost, and the important audio (which might normally be affected by the bit conversion) is kept. Even if your sound card is 24-bit, this export process will make no difference because it is an *internal* process. You can hear the difference between an export that's done at 16-bit and an export that's done in 32-bit. It's more difficult to distinguish the difference from a 24-bit mix and a 32-bit (float) mix. Remember that you can dither down to a lower bit depth without much loss, but dithering up to a higher bit depth later will not make your mix sound any better—so opt for the higher bit depth when exporting.

Without getting too technical, 32-bit (float) is 24-bit with an 8-bit "cushion" for processing. A 32-bit (float) has been the standard in processing for some time, but now that operating systems are capable of running at 64-bit, we might be seeing changes within the next couple of years. It can be very taxing to stay current with the changes, but in the future you should know that if your processing is handled at 64-bit, then you'd want to export in 64-bit as well. Cubase is capable of exporting in Waves64 format (64-bit), but since most processing is handled in 32-bit (float), there's no real benefit to using this format in Cubase at this time (except that you can export a file as large as 4 GB as opposed to the 2 GB limit for WAV files).

Broadcast Wave files allow you to record data as well as audio. This is similar to tagging MP3s, except there isn't much room for data. The catch is that the data can only be accessed from programs or CD players that can read Broadcast Wave files; and even though there are many people who use them, there are many who have no idea how to access the data. What this boils down to is that the info you can put into a Broadcast Wave file is only good if it's accessible. For general mixing and file handling, just keeping your file name correct is good enough without having to worry about tagging a Broadcast Wave. For cases where it's necessary, you can add up to three lines, include a timecode reference, and include the date and time (as shown in Figure 4.18).

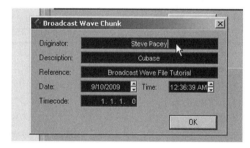

Figure 4.18   Creating a Broadcast Wave chunk for your export.

Creating a Broadcast Wave file is as easy as exporting a WAV file; just check the box that is labeled Insert Broadcast Wave Chunk and select the Edit button to enter the appropriate data. Once you have exported the file, the data can be viewed in other programs, such as WaveLab from within its Wave Attributes dialog box (shown in Figure 4.19).

There are a couple of other check boxes on the Export Audio Mixdown dialog box that need to be addressed: Don't Use Wave Extensible Format and Insert iXML Chunk. For the most part, unless you're creating surround sound mixes, there's no good reason to use Wave Extensible Format, and you're better off leaving it unchecked for a standard stereo mix. Wave Extensible Format was created by Microsoft for managing multi-channel files, such as 5.1 surround sound. In regard to inserting iXML chunks, even though Cubase allows you to export the data, it doesn't really let you alter or even *see* the data that you're exporting. For this reason alone, I don't think it's necessary to ever check this box. Maybe in the future, Cubase will allow you to

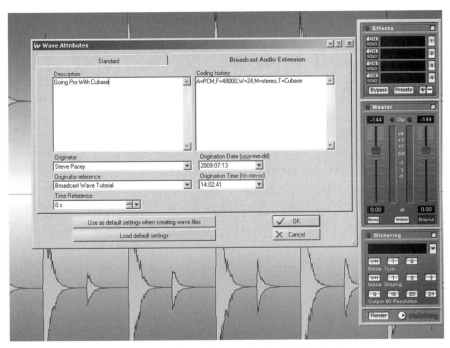

Figure 4.19 Viewing the Broadcast Wave chunk in WaveLab.

view and edit the information before writing it to the file, which will help when it comes to remixing or archiving a project or using it along with video in a way that makes sense.

Using Realtime Export vs. a Standard Export

Despite what several believe, there is usually no significant benefit to exporting via real time as opposed to doing a standard export. Sometimes though, a real-time export is a *must* due to CPU clipping that can occur during a standard export when using certain plug-ins. Unfortunately, when you're listening in real time, you can't hear whether or not your CPU will clip during export. However, if you're using a lot of processor plug-ins (and particularly third-party plug-ins), you run a greater risk of clipping during a standard export.

I normally utilize the standard export. I also *always* listen to the export from beginning to end to make sure there aren't any problems with the final output. If there is noticeable clipping, I redo the export using a real-time export, and when I'm finished, I check my work again to make sure there isn't any audible clipping during the processing. It might sound redundant, but double-checking is the only way to guarantee accurate results.

It's pretty standard for me to use Import into Project after exporting audio so that I can listen to the finished result. I usually do that by selecting Audio Track at the bottom of the Export Audio Mixdown dialog so that the export is brought right back into the project that it came from. The important thing to remember when importing a final mix back into the project is that you need to solo the export on its track (so that you aren't monitoring files from the original mix); you also have to make sure to bypass any effects that you might have on your master bus.

Once you have played back your mix and determined that you need to do a real-time export, you can check the Realtime Export box from the Export Audio Mixdown dialog (refer to Figure 4.17). When you export your audio using the Realtime Export option (as opposed to the standard export), Cubase will play the project in real time from the left locator to the right locator and create a file during the entire process. While this real-time export is happening, you can't make any changes and shouldn't even touch your computer until the process is complete. If you would like to watch your meters for clipping during the process, you need to select Update Display from the Export Audio Mixdown dialog, and then position all of the meters that you intend to watch before actually clicking the Export button. Be careful, though—sometimes the extra effort of updating your display can push your CPU right into the "clip zone," which is exactly what you're trying to avoid.

If you still run into problems with your processing, I suggest going back into your mix and applying the processing directly to the track (bouncing) to save on processing power before attempting the mix again. Once your track has been bounced, then deactivate the original "problem" plug-in before attempting another mix-down export.

5   Interfacing Cubase 5 with the Rest of the World

Even though you really *can* do almost everything in Steinberg's little world, there are times when you just can't avoid working with other platforms. Cubase covers almost every angle, but Steinberg has always left the door open for outside possibilities. In this chapter, I'll go over interfacing Cubase with some other popular platforms (such as Pro Tools, Nuendo, and Reason), as well as working with video.

Working with a Cubase Project in Nuendo

For those who aren't familiar, Nuendo is Steinberg's top of the line DAW and is used in professional studios all over the world. Nuendo and Cubase are very similar. In fact, if you know Cubase, you can easily go from working in Cubase to working in Nuendo and hardly realize the differences. Nuendo has become slightly more common in professional studios mostly due to its design for working in a post-production (video-related) environment. Does this make it a DAW that's more pro? Not really. The tools used to create music in Cubase slightly outshine Nuendo, which could possibly make Cubase a better DAW for anyone specifically working with music production. As a pro, there may be times in your career when you need to take your project to another studio. If that studio has Nuendo (or Cubase), transferring your project into their system will be much easier than if their system were any other DAW (such as Pro Tools or MOTU).

Nuendo recognizes and opens Cubase project files. Because of this, all you need to bring to the other studio is the folder that contains all of your Cubase project and audio files. If you've followed the backup procedures as I discussed in Chapter 1 and your files are organized properly within the project folder, you shouldn't have an issue loading your project into Nuendo.

However, there are a few catches to making this transfer. The first is that, in order to make a smooth transition from Cubase to Nuendo, the software version of Nuendo you're transferring to should be as current as (or newer than) the version of Cubase you're using in your project. So if your own software version is newer than the studio you're going to, there could be compatibility issues. Check with the other studio first to make sure that this is not the case. Steinberg provides a compatibility chart on its site (www.steinberg.net) in case you have questions. If there appears to be a version compatibility issue, I recommend following the instructions in the next section regarding using Cubase with any other DAWs to ensure compatibility.

There's also an issue regarding plug-in compatibility. If you're taking a Cubase 5 project into a studio with Nuendo (or Cubase) and they don't have, for example, a certain distortion, VST instrument, or reverb that you've used in your project, then that plug-in will show as missing on the other studio's system. So you will not be able to use that plug-in on their system. If you can make certain that the studio you're transferring your project to has the same plug-ins that you've used in your project, you should be okay. If for some reason they have some but not all of your plug-ins, you should bounce the effect(s) that they don't have to an audio track in your project so that you can still re-create the effect on their system. Once you've bounced the effect, remove the plug-in from your project and resave the project under a new name so that the plug-in doesn't appear as missing on the other system during the transfer.

As with plug-in compatibility, you also have to make sure that you're not using any ReWire instruments or video players (such as QuickTime) in your project if that software will not be available on the system you're transferring to. If the programs *are* available, the software versions of those programs on the other system should also be the same versions or newer than the ones on your own system.

There's one more slight catch that has to do with some data that is only available in Cubase and that Nuendo isn't capable of editing. This issue is not a big deal, but if you're regularly working between the two platforms you should consider downloading and installing the Nuendo Expansion Kit (NEK) from Steinberg's website, which provides a few more editing tools and VST instruments that are missing between the two platforms. This expansion is for Nuendo 4 and at this point it has not been determined if an expansion will be necessary when Nuendo 5 is released.

Note: There shouldn't be any issues when transferring Cubase or Nuendo projects between Windows or Mac platforms because Cubase and Nuendo run on both platforms.

When it comes to transferring files from your system to the media (another hard drive, CD-R, DVD-R, and so forth) that will be used to load the project into the other studio's system, remember that you need to transfer the entire project *folder*, which contains not only the project files, but *all* of the files associated with the project. To do this, I recommend using the Backup Project feature (located under the File menu) to duplicate to a new folder everything that's necessary to run your Cubase project. Once the new folder is created, label it something like "Nuendo Project," and then copy it to your new disk. I recommend testing (by loading) the transferred project in your own Cubase system from the same media before trusting that everything was transferred successfully and heading out to the other studio.

To open the transferred Cubase project in the Nuendo system, select Open Cubase Project from the File menu, and then select the project you would like to open from the project folder located on your transferred media.

Transferring to Pro Tools or Another DAW

Working between two different studios has always come with compatibility issues. Even though you can run into problems when working between multiple DAWs, it's a lot easier than it used to be. For example, in the "old" days, we had to think about whether the project was on 16-track 1/2" or 24-track 2", whether the studio was using ADAT or DA-88, Dolby or DBX, and so on. You actually used to have to *log* everything! Yuck!

Even though there are many different types of DAWs out there (Pro Tools, Digital Performer, Sonar, Logic, and so on), they all pretty much do the same thing. If you need to work in another program, transferring your Cubase project to them isn't very difficult if you follow the instructions in this tutorial.

Using OMF Files Between DAWs

Utilizing OMFI files during a transfer can be a useful way to work between two different DAW programs. OMFI stands for Open Media Framework Interchange, and this file format has been developed as sort of a basic "translator" when working between multiple DAW platforms. There are currently two versions of OMFI files (the extension is abbreviated as .omf). If you'll be transferring your project to new versions of DAW software, you'll want to use the OMF 2.0 format. You should verify with the studio which format their system needs, as some older software versions may only recognize OMF 1.0 files.

OMF 2.0 only utilizes very limited data from your Cubase project. When you create an OMF file, it does *not* translate the project tempo, pan settings, EQ settings, or effects settings. It covers only the volume settings made within the parts of the mix (not automation), and it ignores muted tracks, treating them as though they are part of the mix. This means that any real mixing prior to the transfer will be lost in the standard creation of an OMF file. Of course, the usual reason a project is transferred is for mixing or remixing, so in some circumstances this might be a reasonable loss.

Another thing that you should know when transferring your project via OMF is that its standards require that every audio file be in stereo format and at 16-bit or 24-bit. If you're working with mono files, they will be converted to stereo files in the process of exporting the OMF. Also, if you're working in 32-bit (float), your project will have to be truncated to 24-bit (or 16-bit) resolution before creating the OMF, or else the file will automatically be truncated to the output settings during the OMF export.

So depending on what you need out of the mix, there are multiple steps you can take in order to make sure that your Cubase project opens correctly on another DAW. If you would like to preserve your EQ and automation settings (your mix), the easy way would be to export new audio files with those particular EQ settings within the audio file itself (in other words, bounce the mix). If you're unsure whether you want to keep those EQ/automation settings, you can always make a duplicate of the track in Cubase and remove the EQ, effects, and automation from the duplicated track. This way you will have both an *unmixed* and a *mixed* track to A/B when you're

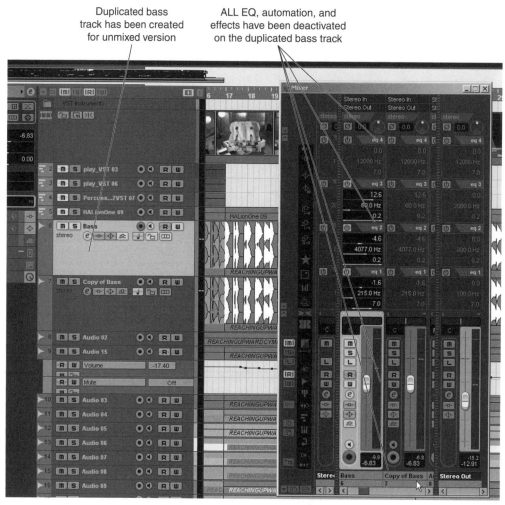

Duplicated bass track has been created for unmixed version

ALL EQ, automation, and effects have been deactivated on the duplicated bass track

Figure 5.1 Duplicating mixed and unmixed tracks before export.

at the other studio (as shown in Figure 5.1). Do *not* mute the duplicate track as it will need to be unmuted during the Export Audio Mixdown process.

Using Channel Batch Export in Cubase

A sure fire way to ensure that all of your tracks stay in time is to set your left locator to the very start of the project (even if your audio starts a few measures from the first bar) and set your right locator a few bars after the last audio track ends. By doing so, you'll be creating new audio parts (disregarding all of your previous edits) that all start at absolute zero. When all the audio files start at the exact same point, there's no chance of sync issues between the tracks after import. You should make notes regarding the project sample rate and tempo so that you can make the appropriate settings on import into the new DAW.

Note: If you haven't named your tracks yet, there's no better time than now (before the export). Naming your tracks will make it much easier to set up your mix on the new DAW system.

As I mentioned before, OMF files can only be exported in 24-bit or 16-bit. If you're working in 32-bit (float) and you want to use the OMF format, you'll need to export your mix in 24-bit. In this truncating process, it's probably best *not* to dither—it's better to save the dithering process for later when you're creating a final stereo mix (or even later if you're having your final track professionally mastered). During the export process, you will be creating duplicate files that will all be the same sample rate and bit depth, which is something you can verify again after the export process.

Once your mixed and unmixed tracks are set up and your left and right locators are set, the last settings are to be made within the Export Audio Mixdown dialog (accessed from the File menu). Before moving to this step, it's always a good idea to save your project under a new name (such as "Joe's Mix Export to Pro Tools-1"). In the Export Audio Mixdown dialog, adjust your Bit Depth setting to either 16 Bit or 24 Bit, and set Sample Rate to the desired setting (this can be up to 96 KHz) from within the Audio Engine Output section. Since you're going to be creating duplicate audio files for every track in this Cubase project, check the Channel Batch Export box in the upper-left corner; then select Audio Channels in the panel below it (as shown in Figure 5.2).

It's possible that you can also export your audio from VST instruments or effects as an audio track (if you haven't yet taken the steps to do so) by also selecting them for export along with the Audio Channels. Now create a name (usually the project name) that will be associated with all the tracks, a location to store these new audio files (path), and the file type (either Wave or AIFF). Next, check the Create New Project box under the Import into Project section (as shown in Figure 5.3). And finally, check the Close Dialog After Export box. Once you're finished, click Export.

After exporting, a new project will be created with all new audio files (tracks). The original tracks have been bounced, and the bounced files (represented in the new project) now contain all the processing that was active in the original project. Since this is a new project, there are no active plug-ins or EQ, and there is no automation being used. Also, all of these new tracks should appear as one "block" of audio tracks (as opposed to many various lengths) because the left and right locators were set and all the tracks were exported at once. Lastly, you'll notice that all the track names are similar, with the addition of the name that you created during export (see Figure 5.4).

At this point, your tempo is also reset to the standard 120 bpm, but you should be able to reset the tempo to your old settings to get things somewhat back to normal. If you were working with a tempo map (with tempo changes), unfortunately you will have to re-create that tempo map on the new system. With this new project, you should listen to your mix to verify that all the data has transferred without problems. During this listening process, you'll need to temporarily mute any duplicated unmixed tracks that you also created during the export process. If there are any

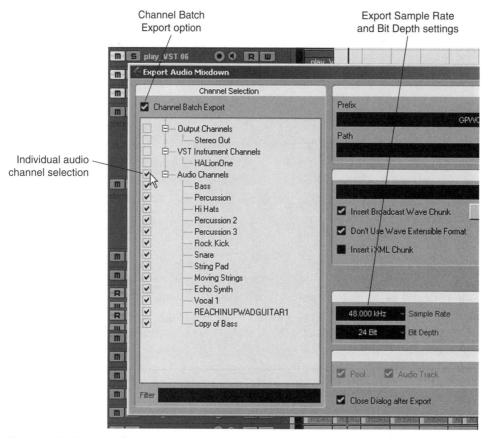

Figure 5.2   Settings for the Channel Batch Export option.

problems with your mix at this point, you'll need to go back into the original project, adjust your settings, and redo the export until you get back to this point again and everything sounds the way it should.

Creating an OMF

Once your mix has been verified, you're ready to create an OMF file for export. If you've muted tracks or changed volumes, you should un-mute the tracks once again before proceeding. There are a couple of different ways to create an OMF 2.0 file. Since it's not difficult to make the OMFs at this point, I recommend creating both of them to take with you in the transfer process. The first way is to include the audio within the OMF itself and the next is to create an OMF that references audio files within a folder. To create the OMF files for your newly bounced project, select Export from the File menu, and then select OMF. The OMF Export Options dialog will appear, as shown in Figure 5.5.

Use the Select All button to check all the tracks that are to be converted to the OMF file. If necessary, you can deselect certain tracks on the left. Check the boxes From Left to Right

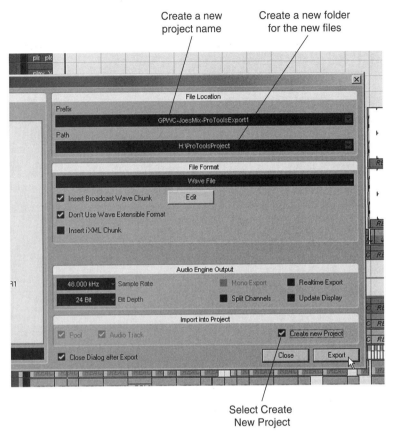

Create a new
project name

Create a new folder
for the new files

Select Create
New Project

Figure 5.3 Making the final export settings.

Locator and Copy Media. It's important that the left and right locators are set as they were when you originally bounced the material. Duplicate audio files will once again be created during this process. Select the OMF 2.0 File option (or OMF 1.0 File, if necessary), as well as Export All to One File. Check the Export Clip Names box, and set Export Sample Size to Same as Project. (Since you've already converted to 24-bit or 16-bit, your project should be ready.)

Note: If you want to include the event's volume envelope and fades, you can do so by checking the Export Clip Based Volume and Use Fade Curves options. Note that these options will only work if you are exporting an OMF 2.0 file. Keep in mind that this only relates to mixing that might be included from editing within the event and doesn't include automation lane data. These options would be more beneficial if you had bypassed bouncing the mix, as was done in the previous step (which, again, is *not* recommended if you need to retain EQ and effects settings).

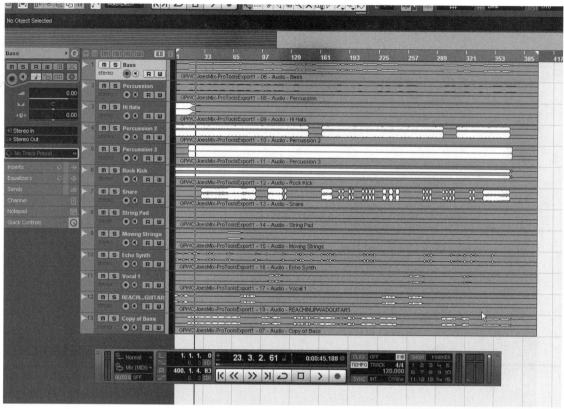

Figure 5.4 The newly created "transfer" project.

The final step in creating the OMF is to define a destination folder for the OMF files, and then naming the OMF file itself. When setting the Media Destination Path in the Export Options dialog, I recommend creating a new folder with the project's name and with OMF in the title somewhere. Once you've created the folder, click OK, and then create a name for the OMF. Again, I recommend using the project name, though this time with something that specifies that this is the all-in-one file (as you will be creating two types). Once you have your name in place, save the OMF. You will see the export process occur as it normally does when exporting batch files. Once the process is complete, repeat all the steps again, but this time select the Export Media File References option. Create a new destination folder, and name the OMF something to signify that it's the "reference" OMF. Once this process is complete, you should have two separate folders containing two separate batches of files for your Cubase project (as shown in Figure 5.6). These folders can then be copied to any hard drive, CD, or DVD, and then transferred to the new DAW by using that DAW's Import OMF option.

For testing purposes, I recommend attempting to reload the OMF files into Cubase from scratch before you leave your studio. To do so, simply select Import from the File menu, and then select

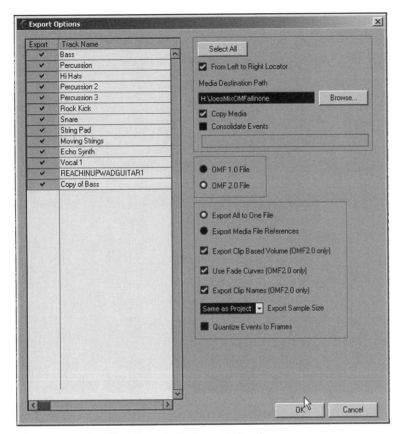

Figure 5.5   The OMF Export Options dialog box.

the OMF file from your newly created OMF folder. Then click the Select All button again, and create a new project on import. You should see something very similar to your original bounced Cubase project. On listening, it should sound identical to your original bounced Cubase project, as well. Remember that when you load the OMF, you'll need to mute either duplicate mixed or unmixed tracks before listening and mixing if they were originally created before bouncing.

Note: Keep in mind that you can also create an OMF without bouncing to add to your collection of OMFs. My thoughts when transferring to another DAW is that the more options you can provide, the better off you're going to be. In a worst-case scenario—if necessary, you should also be able to import each track (audio file) individually from the OMF file, and then manually sync them by setting them all at absolute zero and adjusting the tempo of the new DAW.

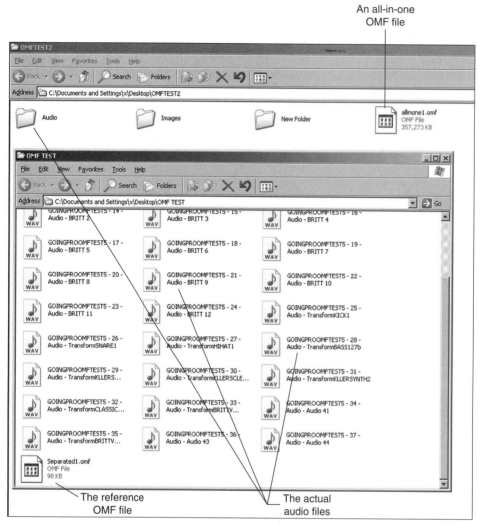

Figure 5.6 A close-up look at a folder containing OMF files.

Working with Video Files in Cubase

If you think dealing with multiple audio file formats is a headache, then you're really going to hate dealing with multiple video file formats. But if you regularly work with video productions (like me), it's inevitable that you're going to have to deal with multiple formats. Video files can come in many formats, not to mention they can have different video codecs, frame rates, and audio sampling rates. Working with these files can literally become a nightmare, and sometimes makes me wish for the days of VHS or Beta. That being said, I'll never go back to syncing externally to a video deck because video files sync a lot better than using an external video source; most computers are now capable of handling video and audio without major headaches.

The key to working with video files is to determine the exact video file type that works best with your system and limit yourself to using only that particular file type. I'd love to tell you that all you have to do is request the proper file format from the video producers you're working with. But the truth of the matter is you'll often run into video editors and producers who end up giving you the wrong format, no matter how well you communicate the exact specs you're going to need. Because of this, I recommend owning some video editing software as well. Basic software (such as Sony Vegas, Adobe Premiere, or Apple Final Cut Pro) can really help speed up the process, and it also comes in very handy when you're troubleshooting your system. There are plenty of video conversion tools available online as well, but I prefer working with a video editor platform because it allows me to manipulate the video (if necessary) in ways that can help streamline the Cubase working experience. By manipulating the video, I'm referring to only cutting out parts that need to be scored or changing the file format. You might be surprised to know that most video editing tools are similar to the tools you work with in Cubase. The transition from working in audio to video is not as difficult as you might think.

When it comes to playing video files in Cubase on a Windows platform, there are three video playback engines you can choose from: DirectShow Video, Video for Windows, and QuickTime. Mac users only have QuickTime to work with. But as I mentioned before, having many options is not the key—the key is in having the one option that works. When it comes to basic video monitoring, there are really only two important factors: *sync* and *compatibility*. If you absolutely have to see your picture in HD quality on a 60" Plasma TV, you either need to invest some money into your system or wait a few years. Because Cubase requires so much of your computer's resources, some users will be lucky to monitor video even in a small 2" window on their computer. If you're lucky enough to own a multi-display video card, you can also use this to expand the picture over a whole monitor. If the video is not properly in sync, your work will not sync to the final video as it should. If the video is not fully compatible, not only will you most likely have sync issues, but it might cause your system to crash often, have audio glitches, or not work at all.

There are three main factors that can affect the performance of the video file from within Cubase: the codec (which deals with video compression), the actual size of the video file, and most important, the video file format. The more compressed a video file is, the more work it is for your processor. The larger a video file is, the more of a workload it is on your hard drive. A lot of video editors I work with are using Final Cut Pro, so files are often transferred over the Internet, and I usually end up receiving a highly compressed QuickTime H.264 MP4 file format. The compression of the H.264 format delivers high quality in a remarkably small file size, but to view the file requires a great deal of processing power (compared to some other formats), which can conflict with the audio engine in Cubase.

As I mentioned before, Windows users have three choices, but the most desirable option for most users (due to the ability to custom size the video) is the QuickTime format (which is, again, the only choice for Mac users). This being said, QuickTime is the most taxing video playback engine to use on a Windows system because it has to be loaded and run in the background while Cubase is running. This also creates an environment that's more likely to have conflicts. Nonetheless, the Video for Windows option is pretty outdated for most users and DirectShow Video offers much less in terms of viewing options.

When working with video and Cubase, there are a lot of conflicting possibilities. If you find that you're having issues, it's important to be aware of the possibilities so that you can pinpoint exactly where the issue is and eliminate the problem. Sometimes QuickTime will work correctly by itself, and Cubase will work correctly by itself, but when you're using the two applications together, the system crashes. Here's a partial list of what could be causing such crashes (or performance issues) in a priority-based order. These options assume that you have a fairly updated computer (approximately one to two years old).

1. **Software version conflicts:** Make sure you have downloaded and installed the latest software versions of both QuickTime and Cubase. Steinberg is usually good at keeping up with changes in QuickTime versions, but occasionally they're a little behind; so don't upgrade your QuickTime software if you're in the middle of a project and everything is working as it should.

2. **Video card settings:** Sometimes video cards have "acceleration" settings or other settings that can cause issues. Try adjusting these or deactivating/activating the video card features. Also, make sure your video card's driver is up to date.

3. **The codec (video compression):** As I mentioned before, the smaller a video file, usually the more compressed it is and the bigger workload it puts on the processor. Try converting the video to an uncompressed format or a video format that uses less compression, such as a QuickTime Movie file using a Photo JPEG codec. If you're getting a blank screen or an info message that includes zeros, most likely you're trying to use a codec that isn't available on your system (and that would be *another* reason to convert to another codec/file type).

4. **The hard drive:** Large video files conflict with audio files when working. I highly recommend using an additional external hard drive for handling your video files.

5. **The video card:** Last, but not least, you might need a new video card. Sometimes working in Cubase and QuickTime together (with the specific audio interface and video card combination) is a toxic combination, and there's nothing you can do but change the one component that is the least of your priorities, which is the video card (and driver) itself. I believe this issue is a little less likely to happen when using a Mac because the Mac platform is a little more controlled and limited in video card selection than Windows.

There are a couple more specific settings that need to be made in order to utilize QuickTime in Cubase on a Windows computer. First off, in order to run QuickTime at all, Cubase needs to boot up QuickTime during its own boot up process. To make sure that QuickTime loads

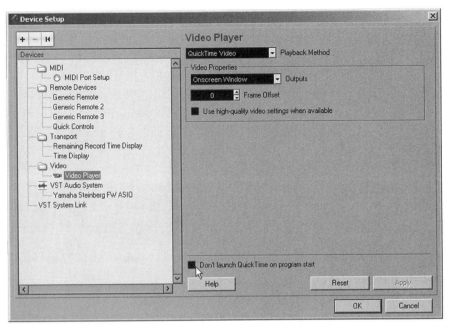

Figure 5.7   Making sure QuickTime is launched and available in Cubase on a Windows system.

correctly, you need to make sure that the Don't Launch QuickTime on Program Start box is unchecked in the Device Setup Video Player settings (see Figure 5.7). If you decide *not* to use QuickTime, make sure this box is checked—it will save your processor some work and help avoid system conflicts.

Once QuickTime has been launched in Cubase, the QuickTime settings can be accessed. If you're using highly compressed QuickTime files and you're having system issues, make sure that the Use High-Quality Video Settings When Available box is unchecked (see Figure 5.8). This will free up some of the processing power for the audio (but your video quality will be compromised in the process).

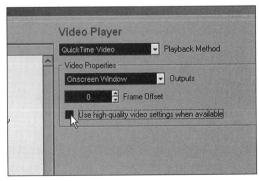

Figure 5.8   Lowering the video quality on compressed QuickTime files to save on processing.

When importing video files to a video track, you have the option of importing audio as well as creating thumbnails for your video file. In most cases, you'll want to utilize both the audio import and create thumbnails features. When importing audio with video, an audio track containing the audio from the video is automatically created in the project window. If there is no audio present on the video, a blank audio track will be created. You can delete and edit this audio track like any other audio track, and it will not affect the video file. There have been cases where importing thumbnails has created technical issues, so if you run into problems, you might want to try importing without thumbnails. By checking the boxes located at the bottom of the import screen, you can activate or deactivate the process (see Figure 5.9).

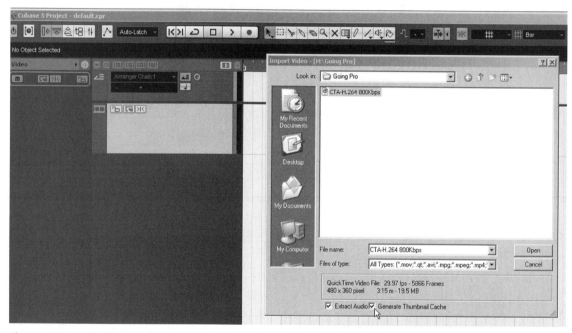

Figure 5.9 Activating or deactivating the audio track or thumbnail cache creation during import.

Note: The sample rate of the audio from the video needs to match the sample rate of the project. Make sure that the audio file is converted during the import process because conflicting sample rates can cause major sync issues and system crashes during playback.

If you're working with video from an external source (such as syncing from a video tape), you can adjust the frame rate to match the video from within the Project Setup dialog. When dealing with video from an external source, this frame rate setting is important. If the frame rate in the Project Setup dialog does not match the frame rate of the video, your audio sync will not match the video. So when syncing to video tapes, make sure to verify the frame rate with the video editor. If you're using video files, this setting within Project Setup is irrelevant because the frame rate is embedded in the file. You can, however, use the frame rate in the file (for visual cues) by activating the Show Frame Numbers option available on a video track.

Connecting Reason to Cubase Using ReWire

Without a doubt, Reason has become one of the most popular audio applications of this generation. If you're already familiar with Reason, you know that you can record and easily edit MIDI in the program; but you can't record any *audio* except in the form of a final stereo export mix. The solution to this issue is to use the audio engine of a DAW, such as Cubase. Steinberg and Propellerhead Software have been working together for years, and ReWire was developed as a way to "piggyback" onto another DAW from an external audio source; it has been available since ReBirth (which was Reason's predecessor). ReWire isn't limited to just working with Reason. It can be used with a lot of other programs that also require an audio engine.

Note: If you don't own Reason and would like to try it out (along with ReWire and Cubase), visit the Propellerhead website at www.propellerheads.se and select Downloads to get the Reason 4 demo for a free test spin. This demo is fully functional and will work completely (for 20 minutes at a time) with ReWire and Cubase.

Reason *does* have its own standalone audio engine, but when it's working with Cubase it bypasses its own audio engine and uses Cubase's engine instead. If you're a Cubase/Reason user like me, you'll probably notice a dramatic change in the way that Reason sounds when it's being used through Cubase's ReWire as opposed to its own audio engine (although Reason 4's sound engine has dramatically improved as well).

When using ReWire, Cubase is considered to be the host (master) application and Reason (or any device using ReWire) is the slave. This means that Reason's Transport will be controlled by Cubase's Transport. This is a standard procedure when it comes to syncing anything, but it's very easy to do when using Reason and ReWire. Because Cubase is the host application, it must be opened before opening Reason. When Reason opens it should automatically be set to ReWire slave mode (see Figure 5.10). If you have not set up a keyboard control surface, a message might appear stating that Reason cannot set up control surfaces properly; but you can just bypass this warning if you aren't using a control surface and set up the control surface later if you so desire.

Note: Under VST Audio System in Cubase, you need to make sure that the Release Driver When Application Is in Background box is unchecked before opening Reason to avoid a battle over the ASIO driver between Cubase and Reason. This should further prevent Cubase from mistakenly releasing the driver to Reason when Reason is not in the background during the boot-up sequence.

Figure 5.10   Reason enters ReWire Slave Mode on boot-up when Cubase is already open and running.

The next step is to activate the ReWire channels so that you can actually hear Reason. To do so, select the Reason ReWire option under the Devices menu in Cubase. By selecting and activating the stereo channel (left/right), a special ReWire track will also be created in the Cubase project (as shown in Figure 5.11). The ReWire connections panel for Reason 4 has 64 inputs. This means you can output 64 individual channels of audio from Reason into Cubase by patching instruments to the output and activating their respective inputs in Cubase, as shown in Figure 5.12.

Note: ReWire channels (besides the master outs) are mono, but the Cubase default is to treat them as a stereo file with a mono signal. You can change the setting on each individual ReWire track in Cubase to specify which signal the track is (left or right) if you're using two individual ReWire inputs as a stereo pair.

Once everything is routed the way you like, you can then export the ReWire tracks as audio tracks if necessary by using the Channel Batch Export option (as demonstrated in the previous

Figure 5.11   Creating a ReWire track in the project window.

section "Using Channel Batch Export in Cubase." Instead of creating another project with the export audio (as in the previous example), you can instead re-import the audio files into the same project as the audio files (as shown in Figures 5.13 and 5.14).

The end result is similar to using the VST instruments in Cubase. As I mentioned before, ReWire can be used with other instruments or software programs that utilize the ReWire technology; and ReWire is available on other DAWs as well. If we could just get all the DAWs to work together like this, the audio world would be a happier place!

Figure 5.12 Patching instruments to individual ReWire channels in Cubase.

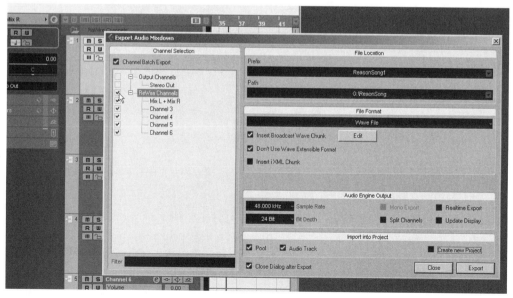

Figure 5.13 Creating multiple audio tracks from Reason using Channel Batch Export in Cubase.

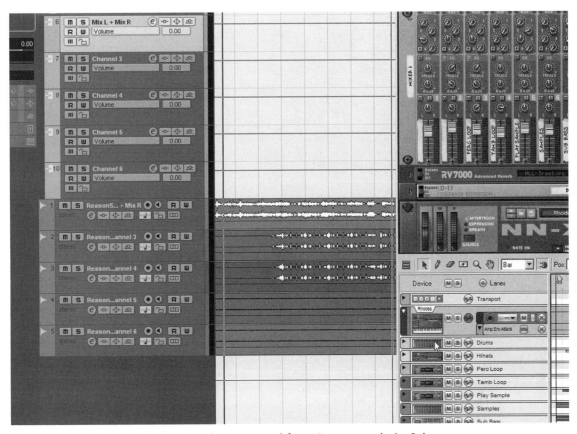

Figure 5.14   Audio tracks that have been created from Reason tracks in Cubase.

Index

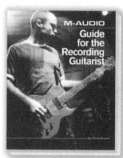